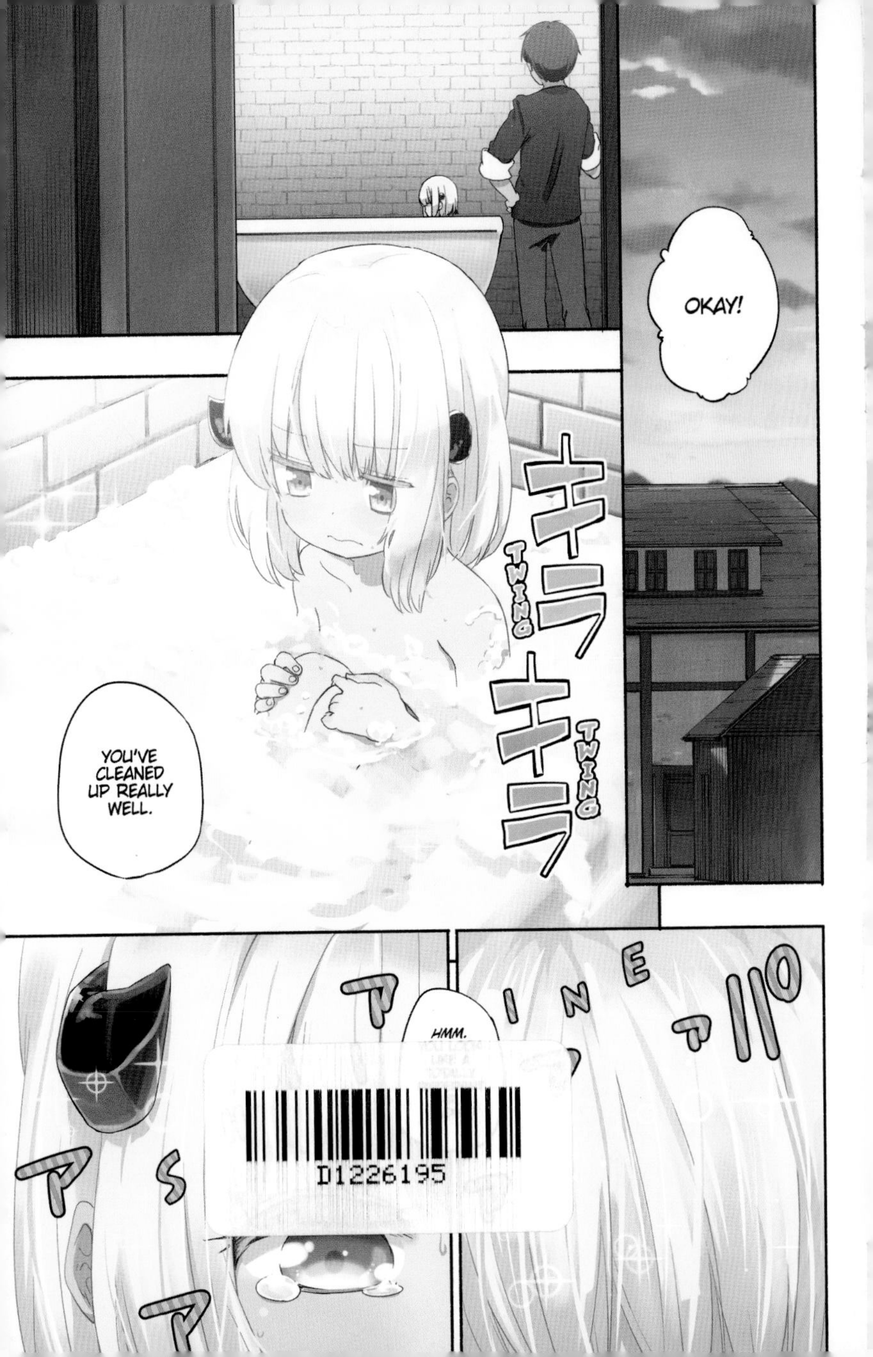
OKAY!
キラ キラ
TWING TWING
YOU'VE CLEANED UP REALLY WELL.
HMM.

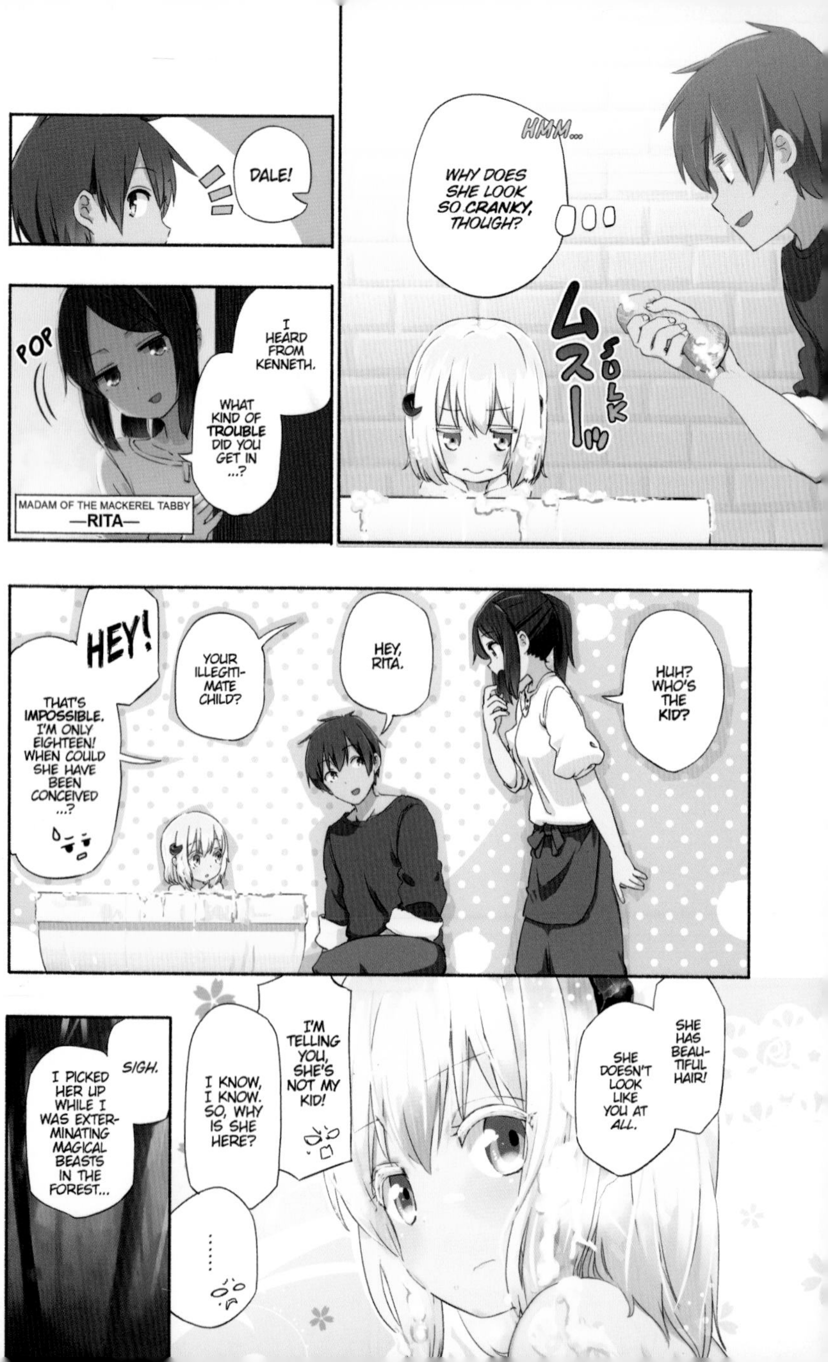
HMM...
WHY DOES SHE LOOK SO CRANKY, THOUGH?
ムスーッ
SULK
DALE!
POP
I HEARD FROM KENNETH.
WHAT KIND OF TROUBLE DID YOU GET IN ...?
MADAM OF THE MACKEREL TABBY
—RITA—
HUH? WHO'S THE KID?
HEY, RITA.
YOUR ILLEGITIMATE CHILD?
HEY!
THAT'S IMPOSSIBLE. I'M ONLY EIGHTEEN! WHEN COULD SHE HAVE BEEN CONCEIVED ...?
SHE HAS BEAUTIFUL HAIR!
SHE DOESN'T LOOK LIKE YOU AT ALL.
I'M TELLING YOU, SHE'S NOT MY KID!
I KNOW, I KNOW. SO, WHY IS SHE HERE?
......
SIGH.
I PICKED HER UP WHILE I WAS EXTERMINATING MAGICAL BEASTS IN THE FOREST...

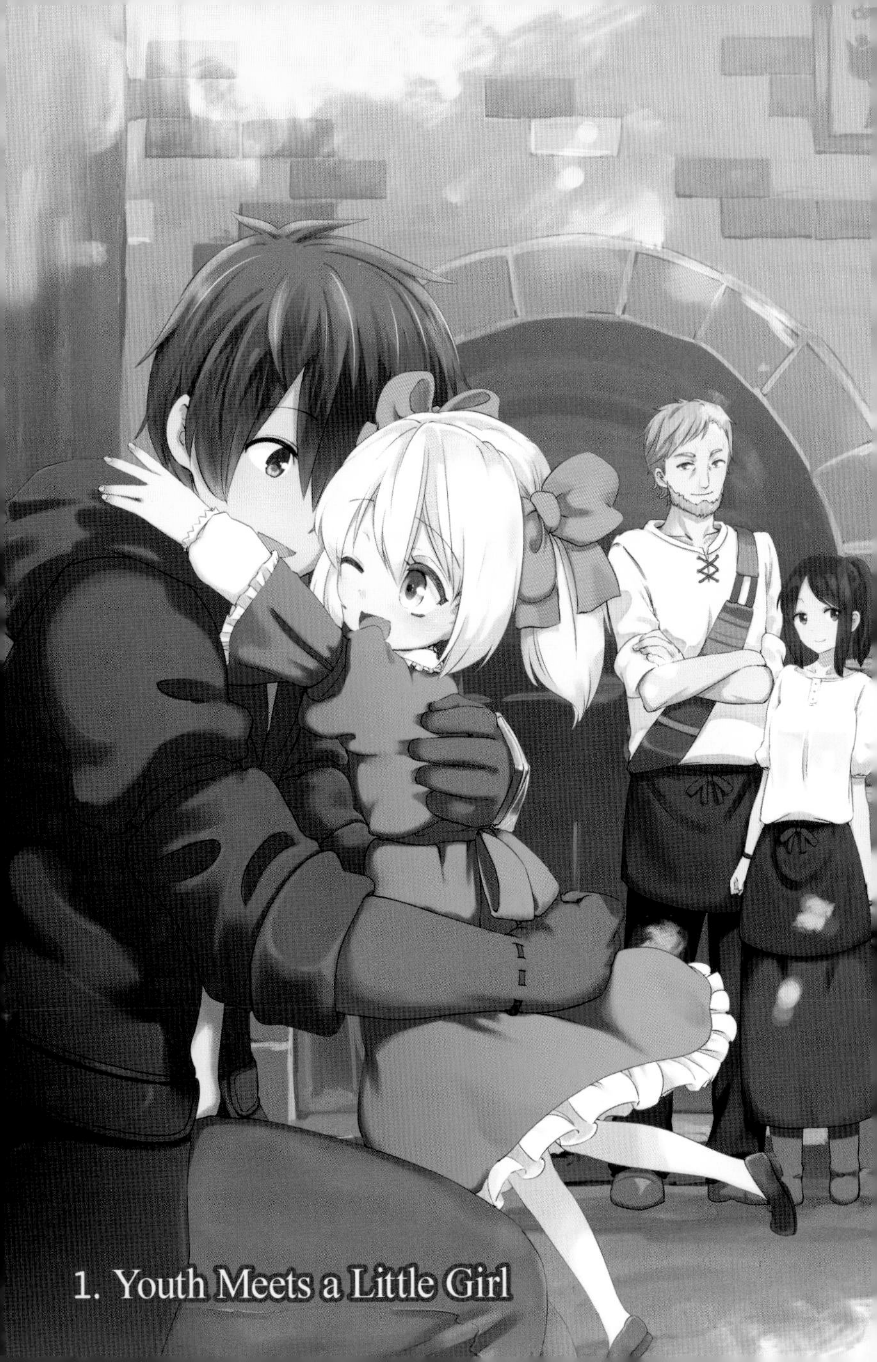

1. Youth Meets a Little Girl

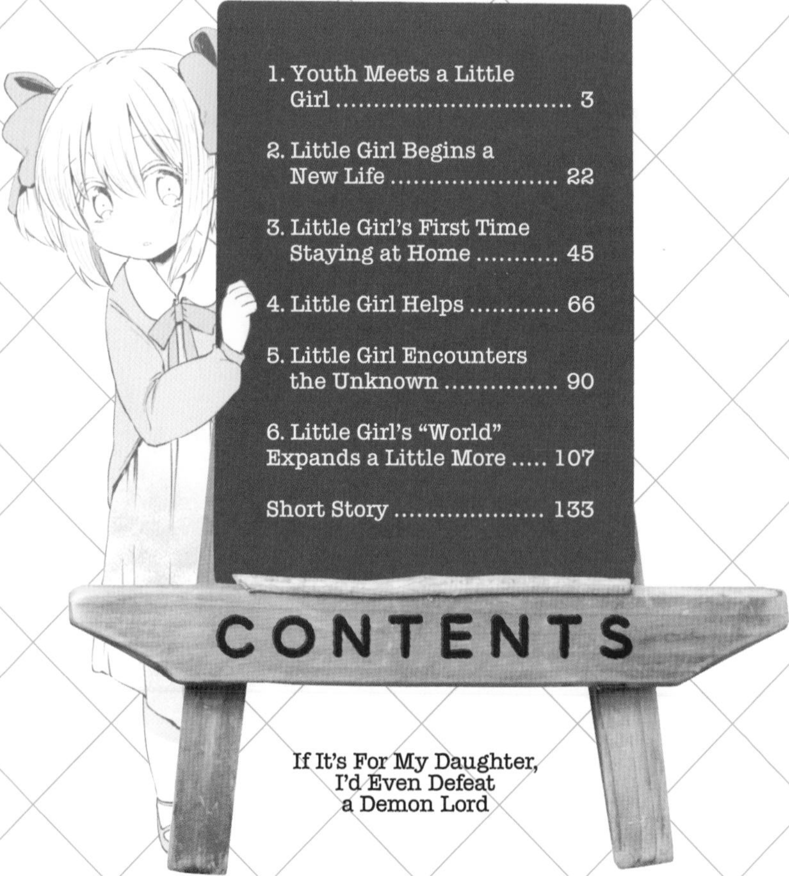

CONTENTS

If It's For My Daughter, I'd Even Defeat a Demon Lord

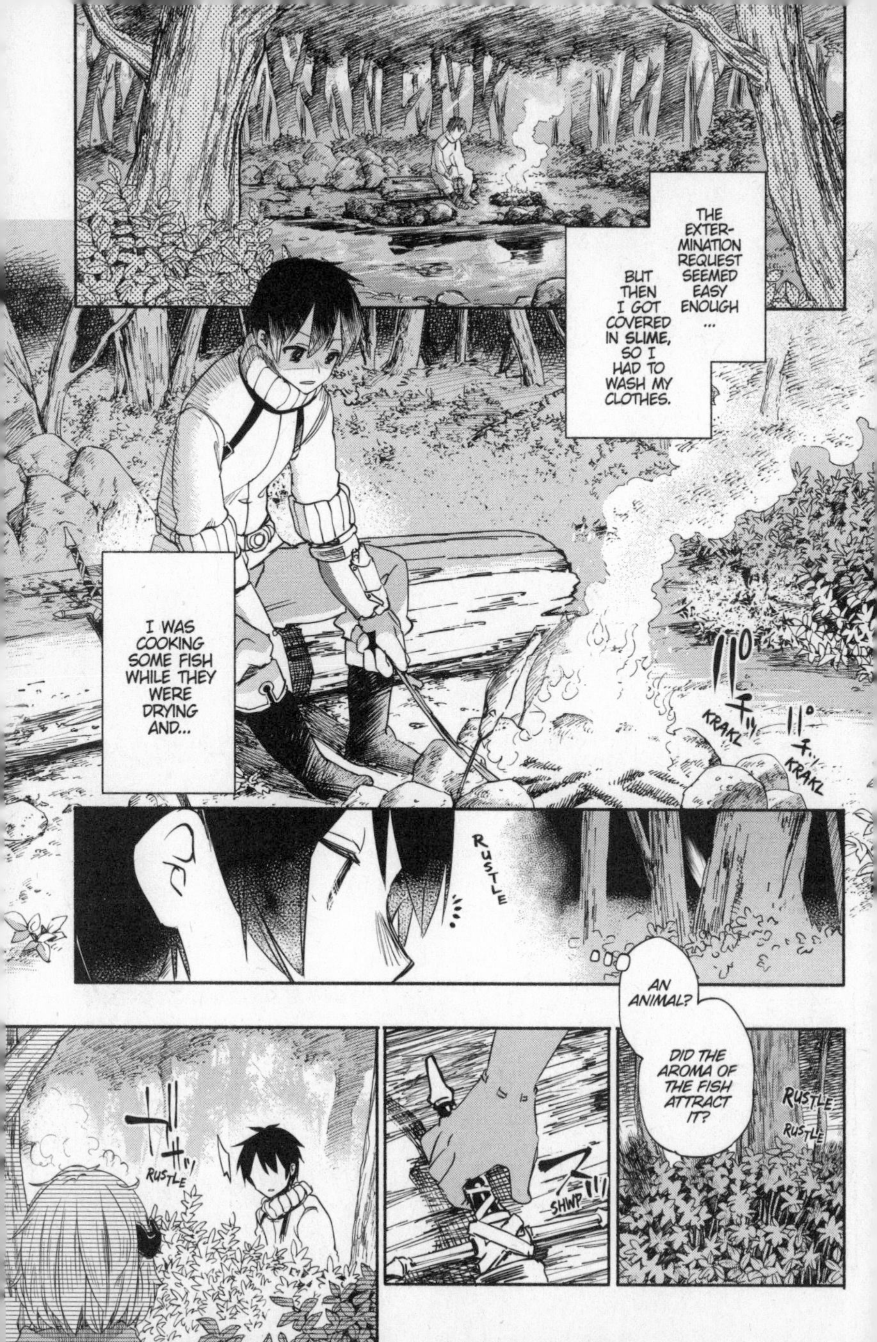
THE EXTER-MINATION REQUEST SEEMED EASY ENOUGH ...
BUT THEN I GOT COVERED IN SLIME, SO I HAD TO WASH MY CLOTHES.
I WAS COOKING SOME FISH WHILE THEY WERE DRYING AND...
KRAKL
KRAKL
RUSTLE
AN ANIMAL?
DID THE AROMA OF THE FISH ATTRACT IT?
RUSTLE
RUSTLE
SHWP
RUSTLE

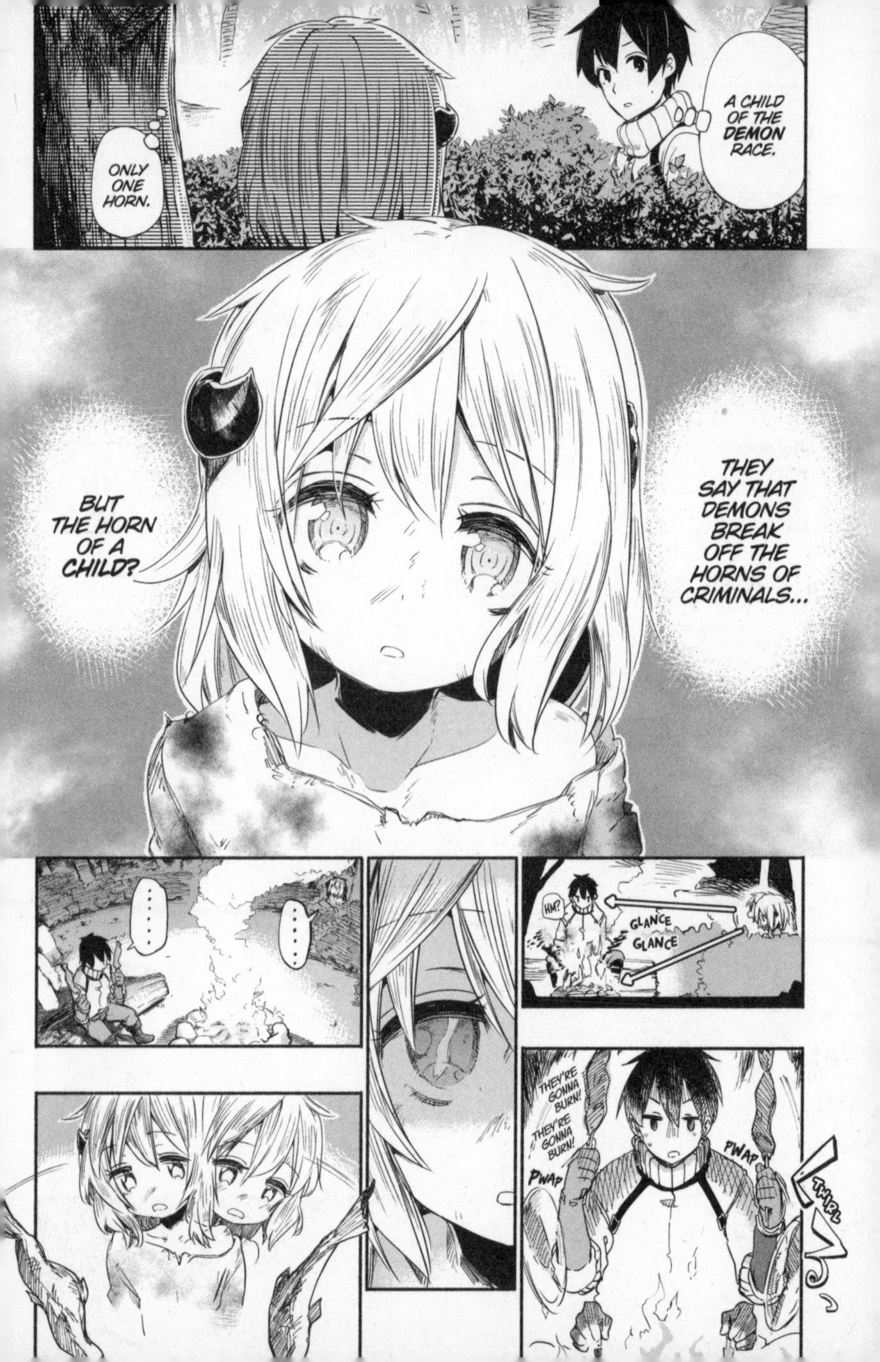
A CHILD OF THE DEMON RACE.
ONLY ONE HORN.
THEY SAY THAT DEMONS BREAK OFF THE HORNS OF CRIMINALS...
BUT THE HORN OF A CHILD?
HM?
GLANCE
GLANCE
THEY'RE GONNA BURN!
THEY'RE GONNA BURN!
TWIRL
PWAP
PWAP
......
......

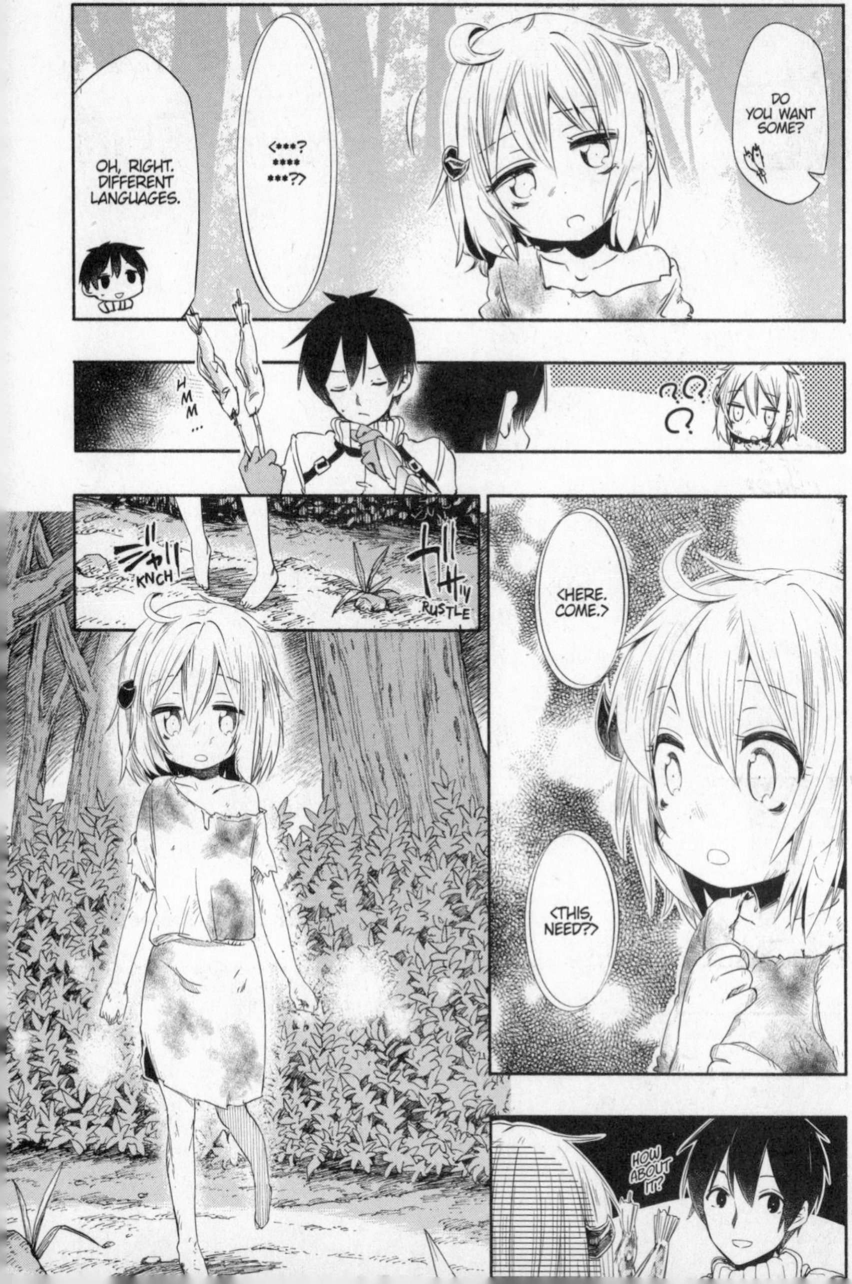
DO YOU WANT SOME?
<***? **** ***?>
OH, RIGHT. DIFFERENT LANGUAGES.
HMM...
<HERE. COME.>
<THIS, NEED?>
HOW ABOUT IT?
RUSTLE
KNCH

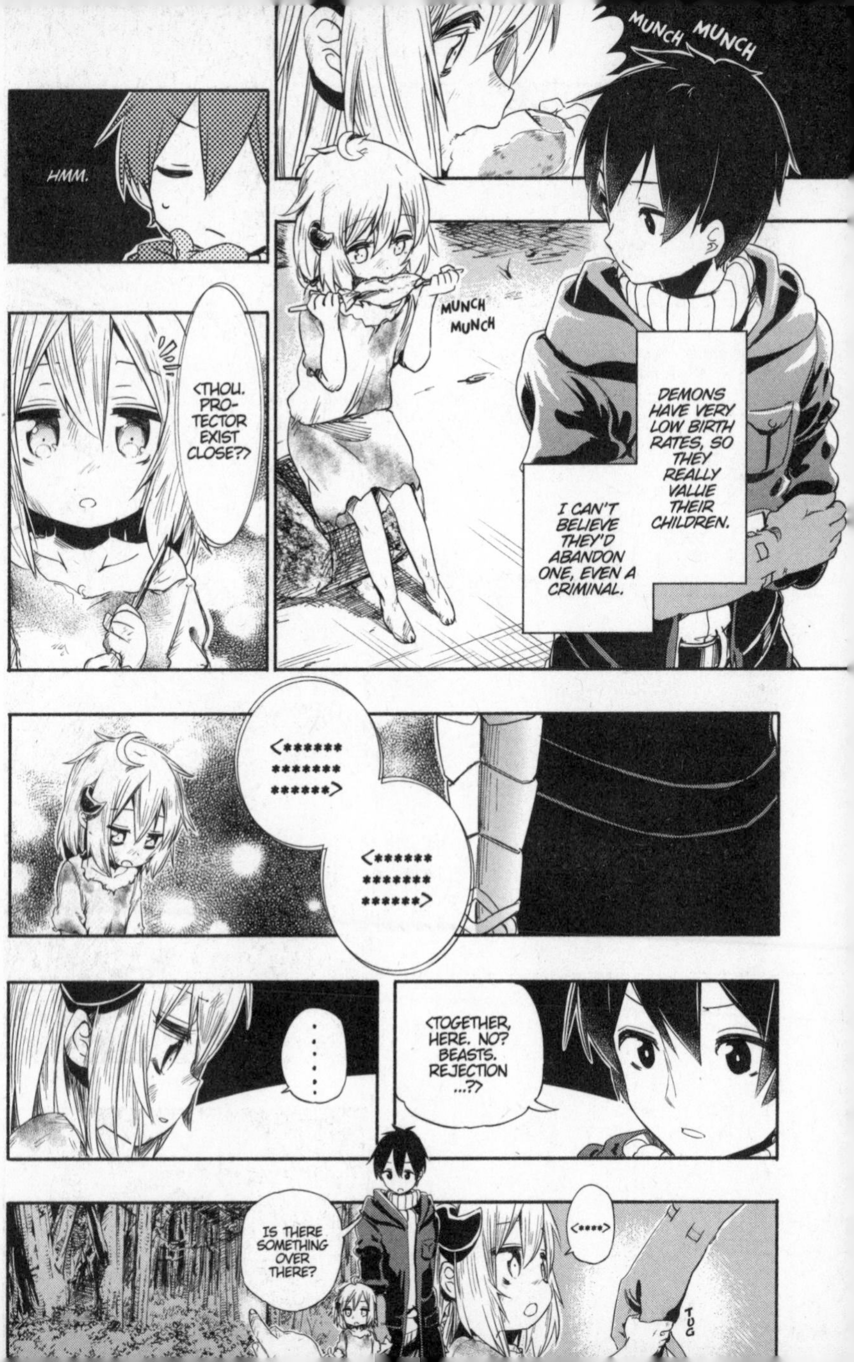
MUNCH MUNCH
HMM.
DEMONS HAVE VERY LOW BIRTH RATES, SO THEY REALLY VALUE THEIR CHILDREN.
I CAN'T BELIEVE THEY'D ABANDON ONE, EVEN A CRIMINAL.
MUNCH MUNCH
<THOU. PRO-TECTOR EXIST CLOSE?>
<********************>
<********************>
<TOGETHER, HERE. NO? BEASTS. REJECTION ...?>
......
<****>
IS THERE SOMETHING OVER THERE?
TUG

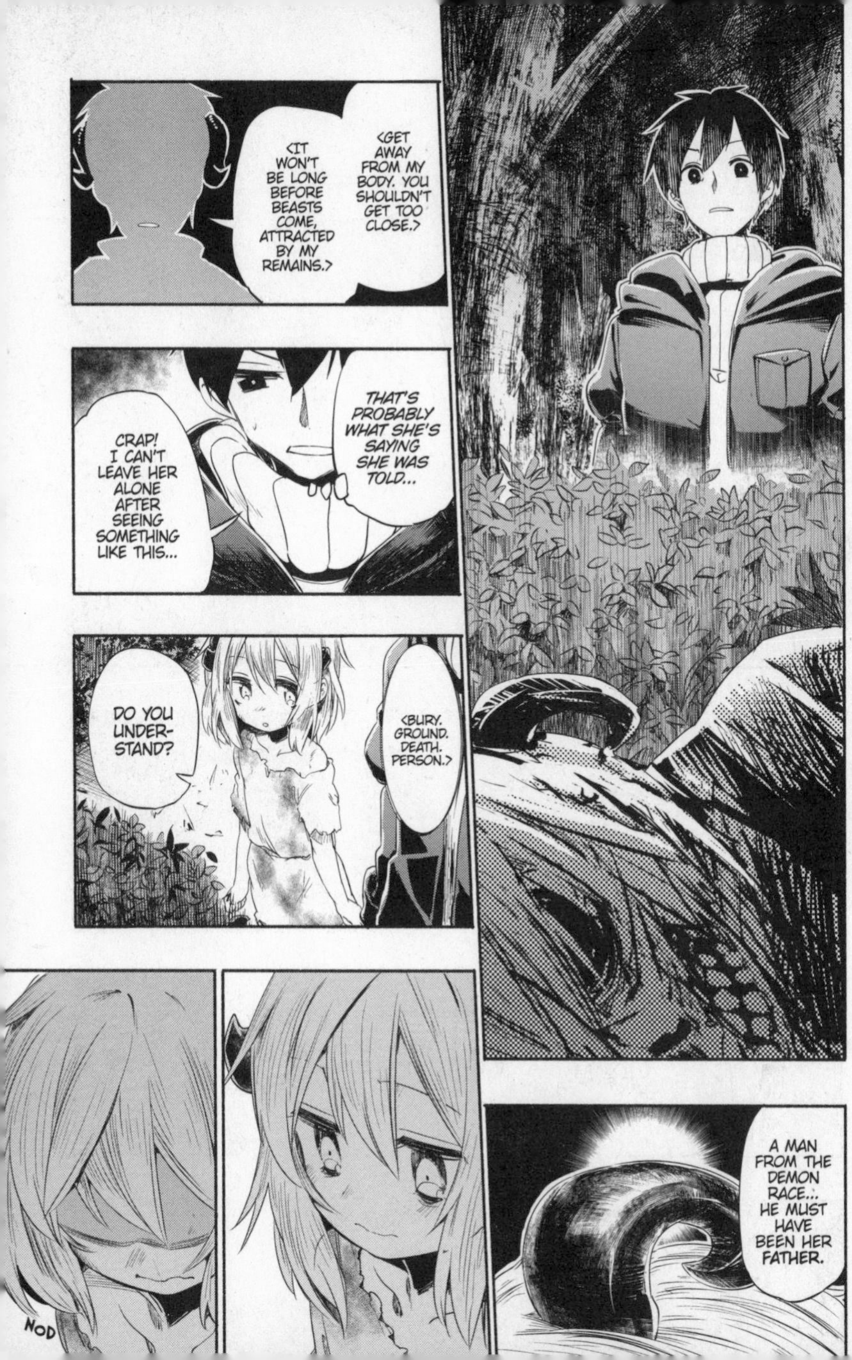
<GET AWAY FROM MY BODY. YOU SHOULDN'T GET TOO CLOSE.>
<IT WON'T BE LONG BEFORE BEASTS COME, ATTRACTED BY MY REMAINS.>
THAT'S PROBABLY WHAT SHE'S SAYING SHE WAS TOLD...
CRAP! I CAN'T LEAVE HER ALONE AFTER SEEING SOMETHING LIKE THIS...
<BURY. GROUND. DEATH. PERSON.>
DO YOU UNDER-STAND?
A MAN FROM THE DEMON RACE... HE MUST HAVE BEEN HER FATHER.
NOD

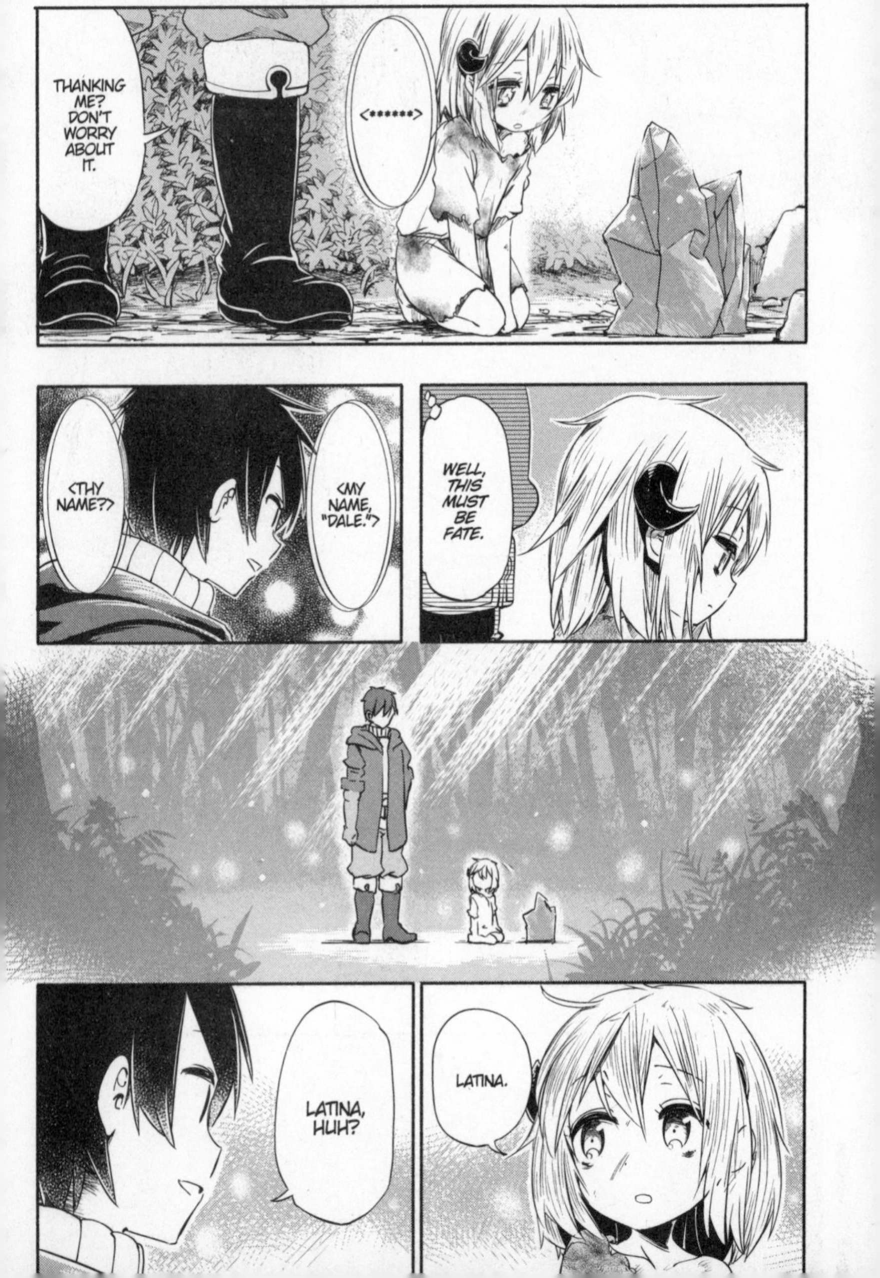
<******>
THANKING ME? DON'T WORRY ABOUT IT.
WELL, THIS MUST BE FATE.
<MY NAME, "DALE.">
<THY NAME?>
LATINA.
LATINA, HUH?

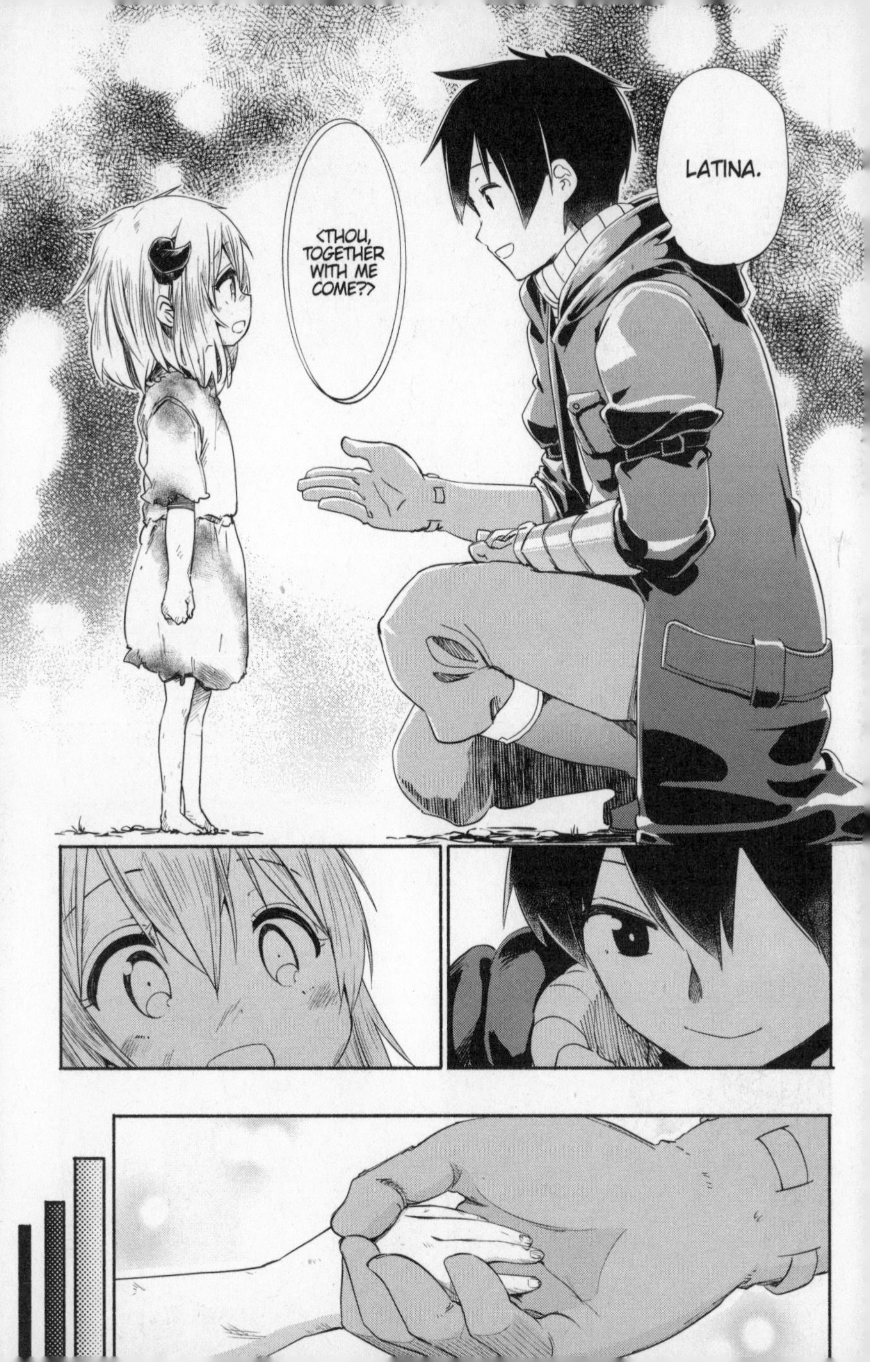
LATINA.
<THOU, TOGETHER WITH ME COME?>

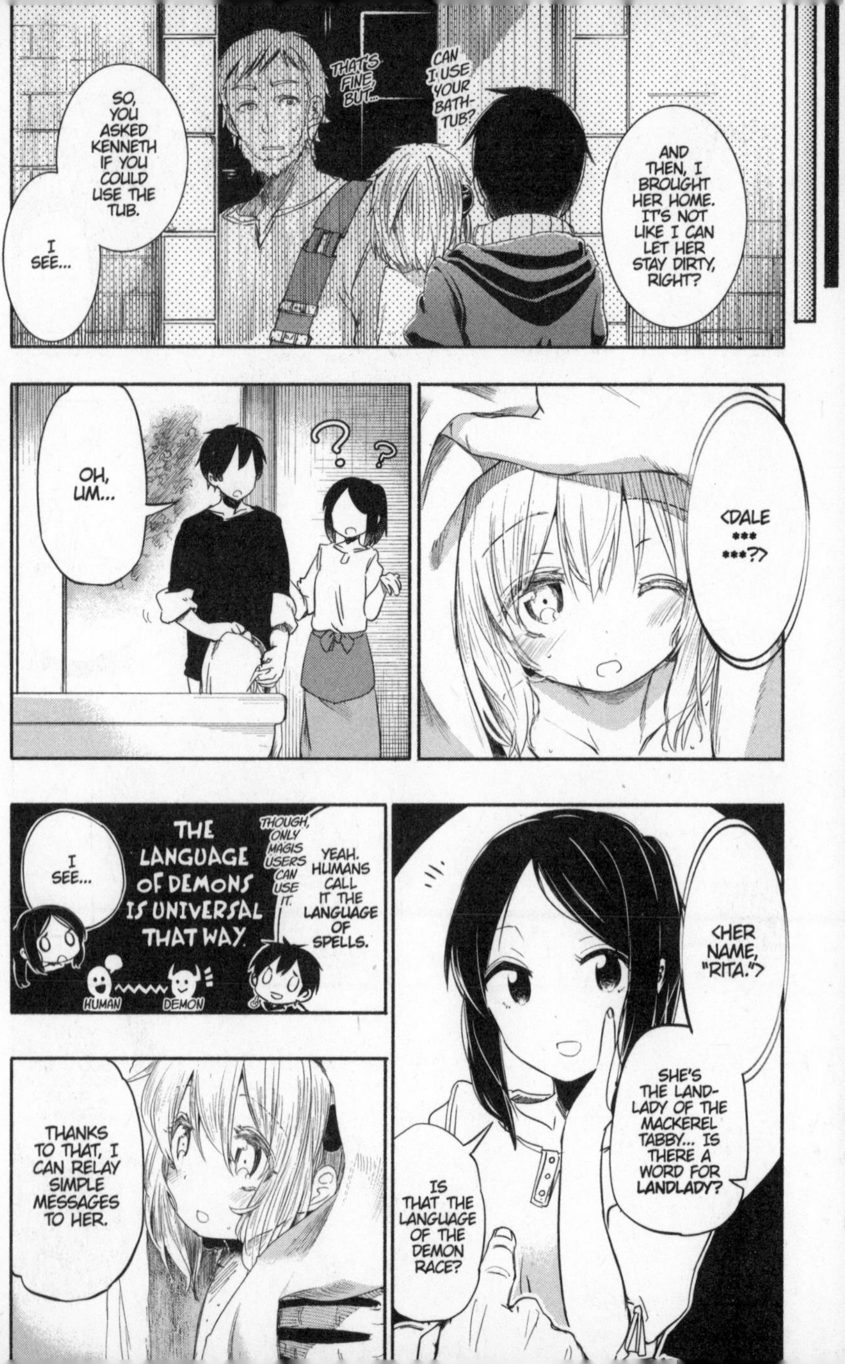
AND THEN, I BROUGHT HER HOME. IT'S NOT LIKE I CAN LET HER STAY DIRTY, RIGHT?
CAN I USE YOUR BATH-TUB?
THAT'S FINE, BUT...
SO, YOU ASKED KENNETH IF YOU COULD USE THE TUB.
I SEE...
<DALE *** ***?>
OH, UM...
<HER NAME, "RITA.">
YEAH. HUMANS CALL IT THE LANGUAGE OF SPELLS.
THOUGH, ONLY MAGIS USERS CAN USE IT.
THE LANGUAGE OF DEMONS IS UNIVERSAL THAT WAY.
I SEE...
HUMAN
DEMON
SHE'S THE LAND-LADY OF THE MACKEREL TABBY... IS THERE A WORD FOR LANDLADY?
IS THAT THE LANGUAGE OF THE DEMON RACE?
THANKS TO THAT, I CAN RELAY SIMPLE MESSAGES TO HER.

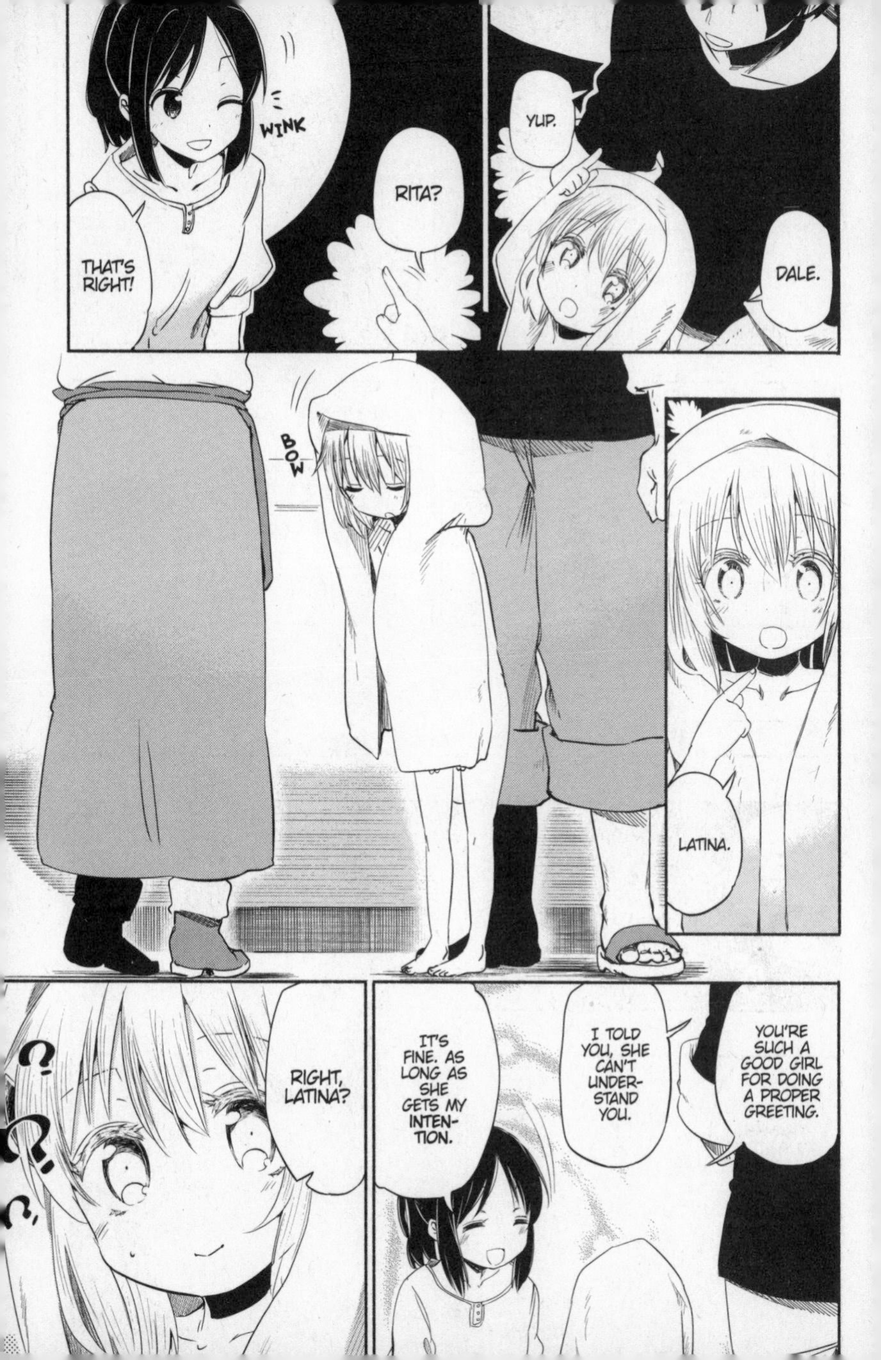
DALE.
YUP.
RITA?
WINK
THAT'S RIGHT!
LATINA.
BOW
YOU'RE SUCH A GOOD GIRL FOR DOING A PROPER GREETING.
I TOLD YOU, SHE CAN'T UNDER-STAND YOU.
IT'S FINE. AS LONG AS SHE GETS MY INTEN-TION.
RIGHT, LATINA?

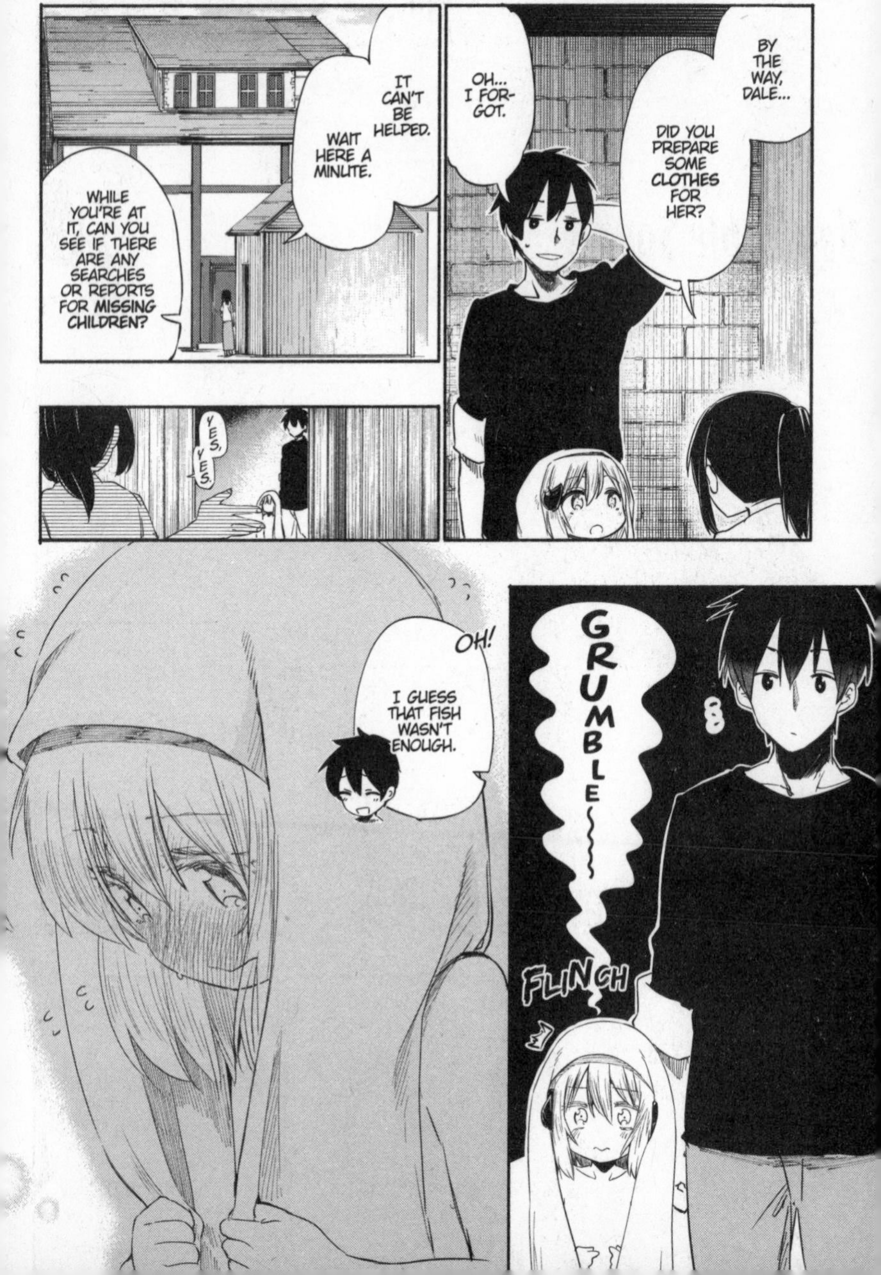
BY THE WAY, DALE...
DID YOU PREPARE SOME CLOTHES FOR HER?
OH... I FOR-GOT.
IT CAN'T BE HELPED.
WAIT HERE A MINUTE.
WHILE YOU'RE AT IT, CAN YOU SEE IF THERE ARE ANY SEARCHES OR REPORTS FOR MISSING CHILDREN?
YES, YES.
GRUMBLE
FLINCH
OH!
I GUESS THAT FISH WASN'T ENOUGH.

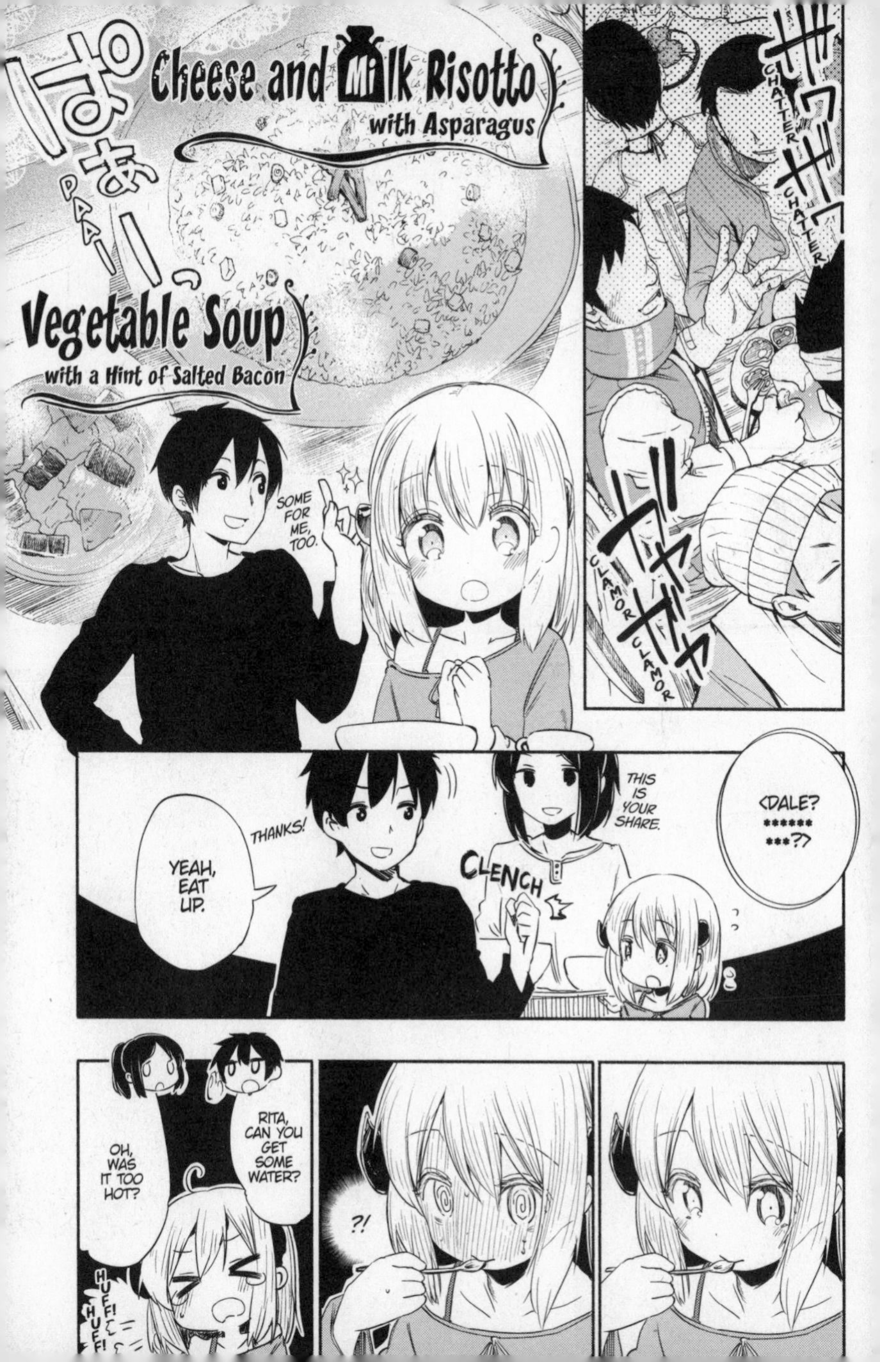
ザワザワ
CHATTER CHATTER
ガヤガヤ
CLAMOR CLAMOR
ぱぁ〜っ
PAAA
Cheese and Milk Risotto with Asparagus
Vegetable Soup with a Hint of Salted Bacon
SOME FOR ME, TOO.
<DALE? ****** ***?>
THIS IS YOUR SHARE.
CLENCH
THANKS!
YEAH, EAT UP.
?!
RITA, CAN YOU GET SOME WATER?
OH, WAS IT TOO HOT?
HUFF! HUFF!

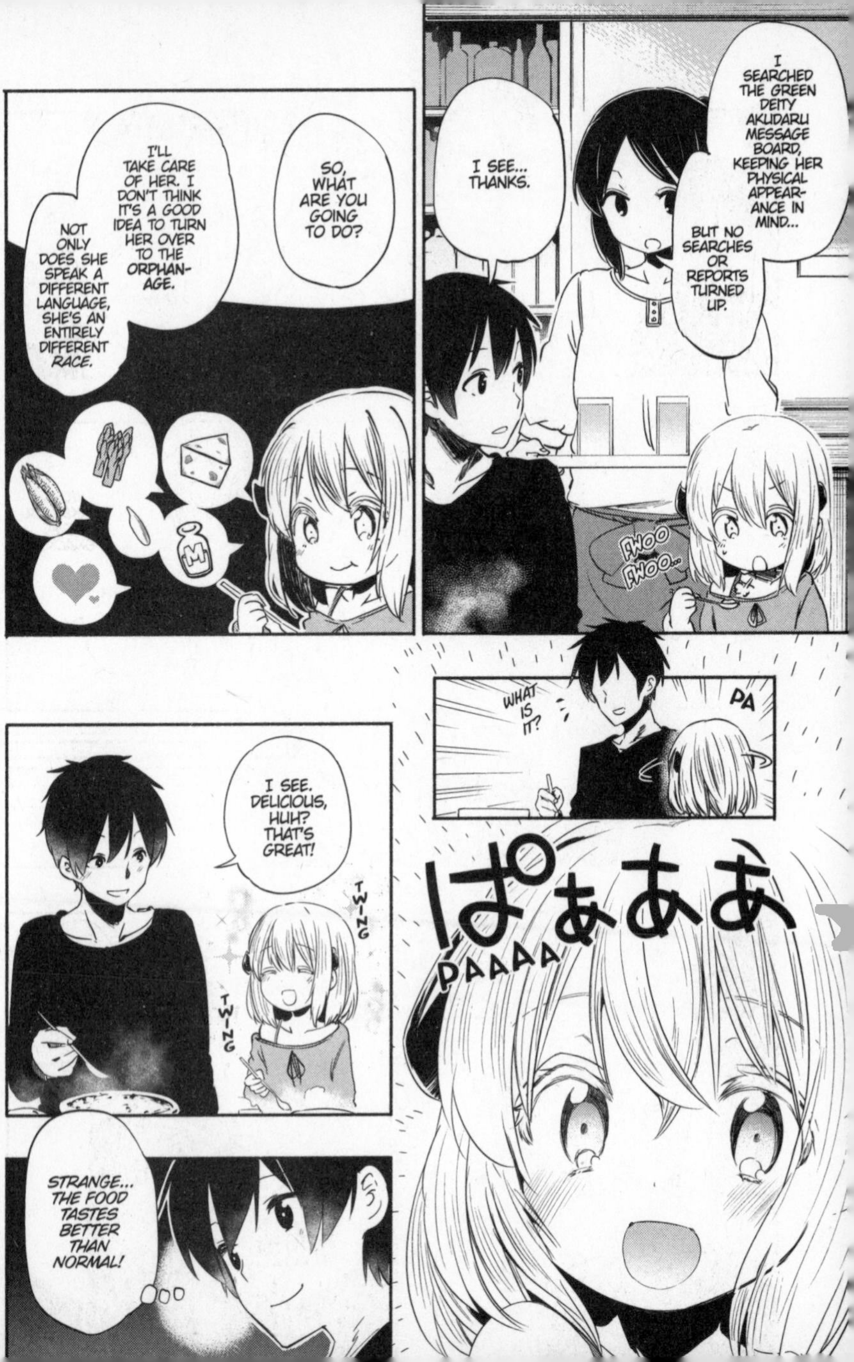
I SEARCHED THE GREEN DEITY AKUDARU MESSAGE BOARD, KEEPING HER PHYSICAL APPEARANCE IN MIND...
BUT NO SEARCHES OR REPORTS TURNED UP.
I SEE... THANKS.
FWOO FWOO...
SO, WHAT ARE YOU GOING TO DO?
I'LL TAKE CARE OF HER. I DON'T THINK IT'S A GOOD IDEA TO TURN HER OVER TO THE ORPHANAGE.
NOT ONLY DOES SHE SPEAK A DIFFERENT LANGUAGE, SHE'S AN ENTIRELY DIFFERENT RACE.
M
PA
WHAT IS IT?
ぱぁああ
PAAAA
I SEE. DELICIOUS, HUH? THAT'S GREAT!
TWING
TWING
STRANGE... THE FOOD TASTES BETTER THAN NORMAL!

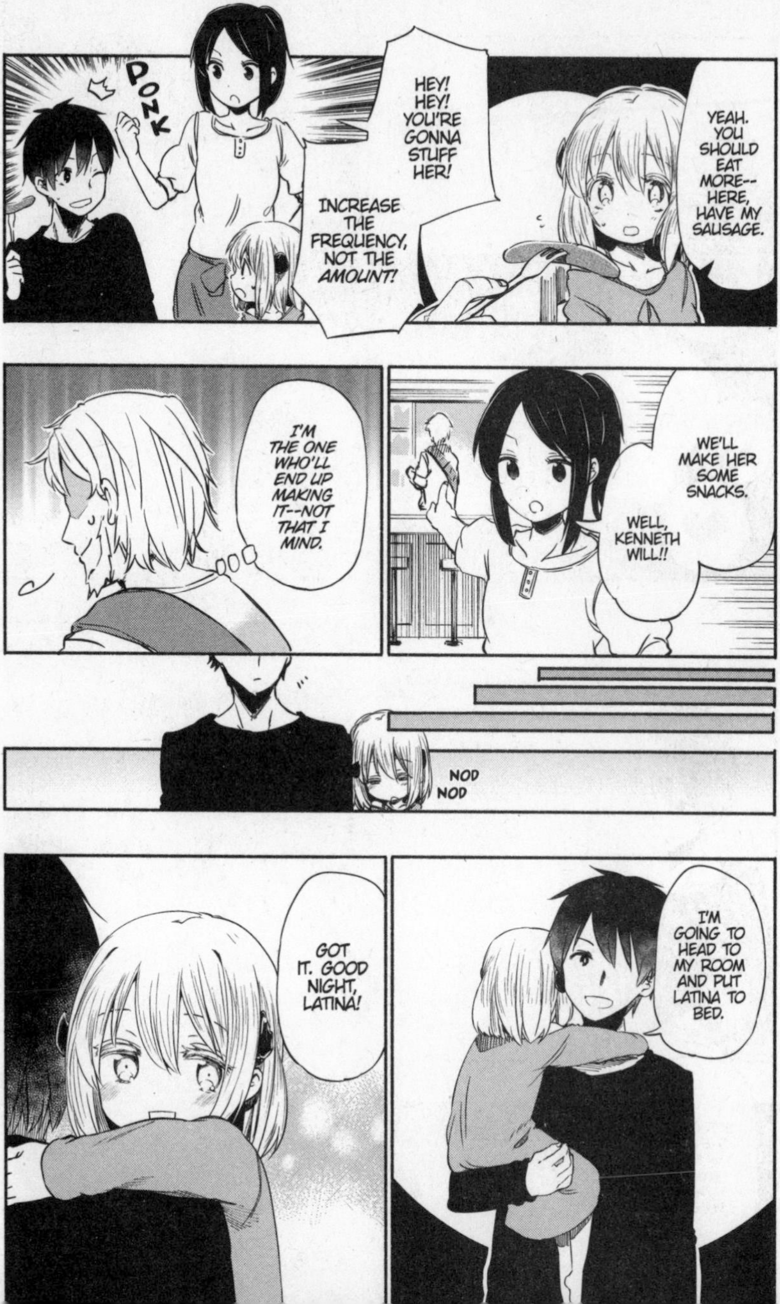
YEAH. YOU SHOULD EAT MORE--HERE, HAVE MY SAUSAGE.
HEY! HEY! YOU'RE GONNA STUFF HER!
INCREASE THE FREQUENCY, NOT THE *AMOUNT!*
DONK
WE'LL MAKE HER SOME SNACKS.
WELL, KENNETH WILL!!
I'M THE ONE WHO'LL END UP MAKING IT--NOT THAT I MIND.
NOD NOD
I'M GOING TO HEAD TO MY ROOM AND PUT LATINA TO BED.
GOT IT. GOOD NIGHT, LATINA!

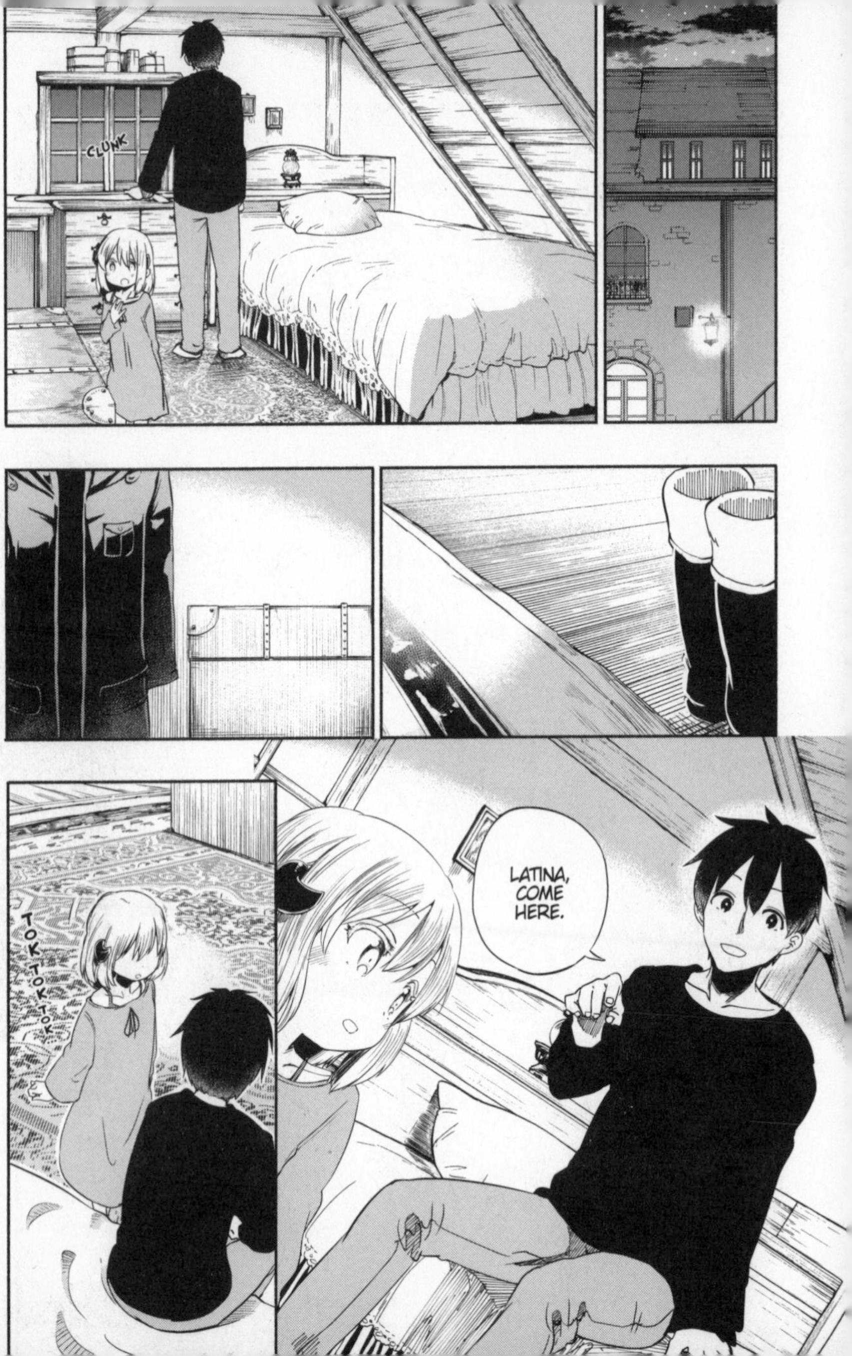
CLUNK
LATINA, COME HERE.
TOK TOK TOK

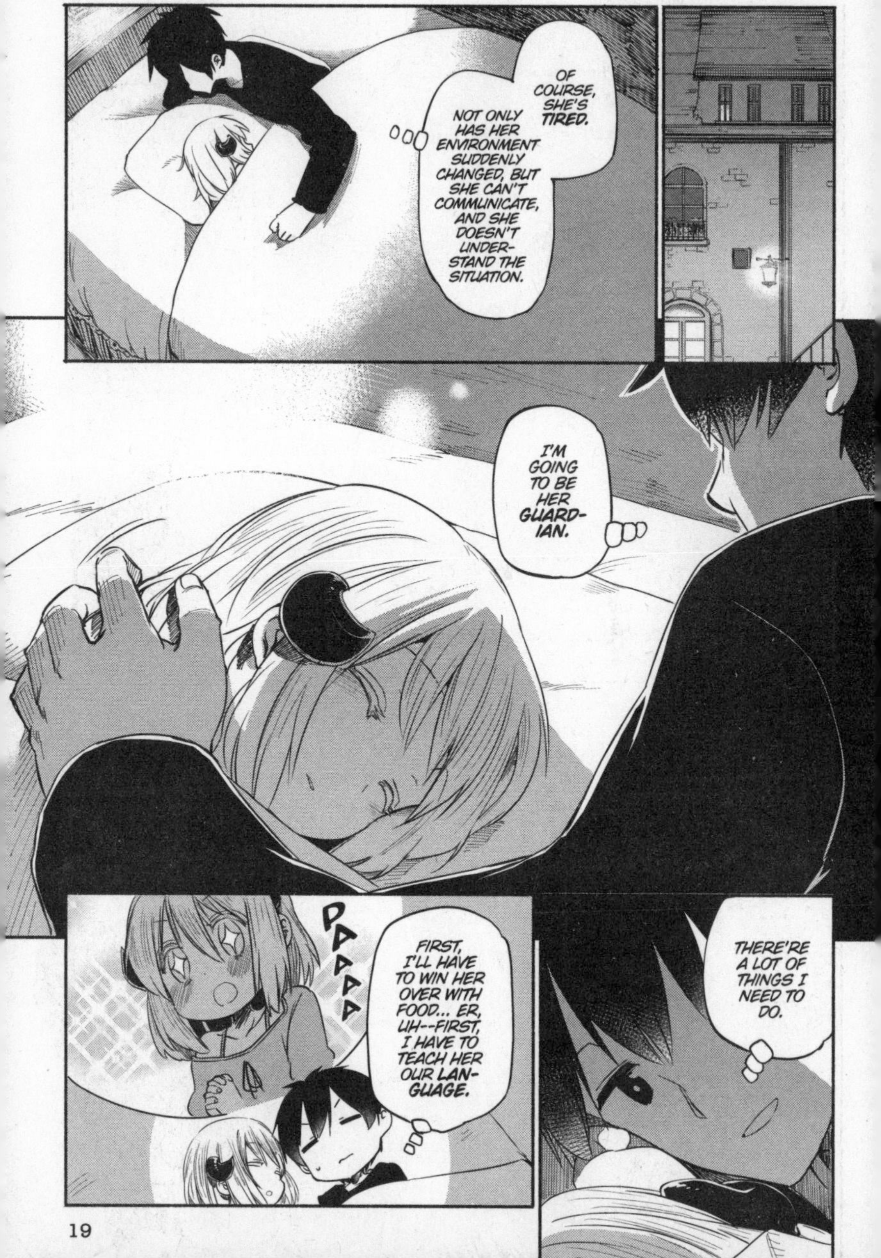
OF COURSE, SHE'S TIRED.
NOT ONLY HAS HER ENVIRONMENT SUDDENLY CHANGED, BUT SHE CAN'T COMMUNICATE, AND SHE DOESN'T UNDER-STAND THE SITUATION.
I'M GOING TO BE HER GUARD-IAN.
THERE'RE A LOT OF THINGS I NEED TO DO.
FIRST, I'LL HAVE TO WIN HER OVER WITH FOOD... ER, UH--FIRST, I HAVE TO TEACH HER OUR LAN-GUAGE.

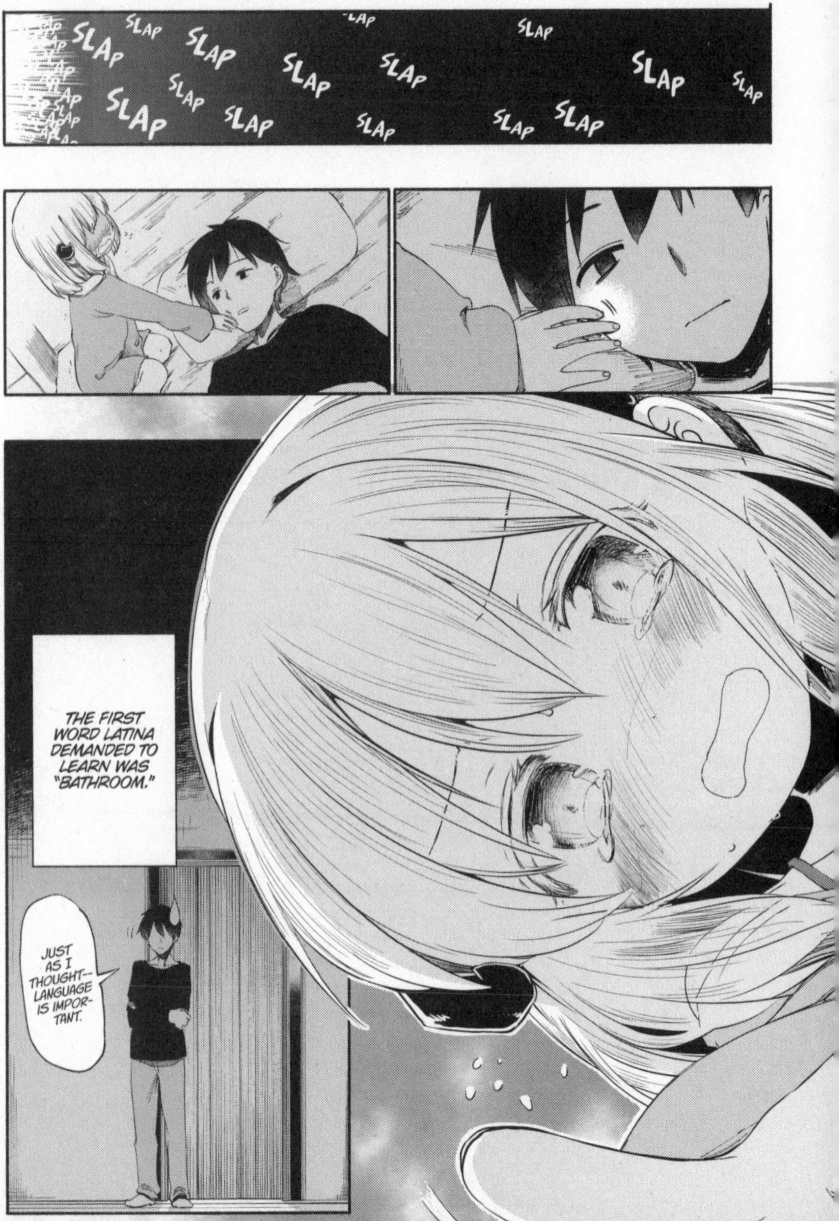
SLAP
SLAP
SLAP
SLAP
SLAP
SLAP
SLAP
SLAP
SLAP
SLAP
SLAP
SLAP
SLAP
SLAP
THE FIRST WORD LATINA DEMANDED TO LEARN WAS "BATHROOM."
JUST AS I THOUGHT-- LANGUAGE IS IMPOR-TANT.

IF It's
For My
Daughter
I'd Even Defeat
a Demon
Lord

2. Little Girl Begins a New Life

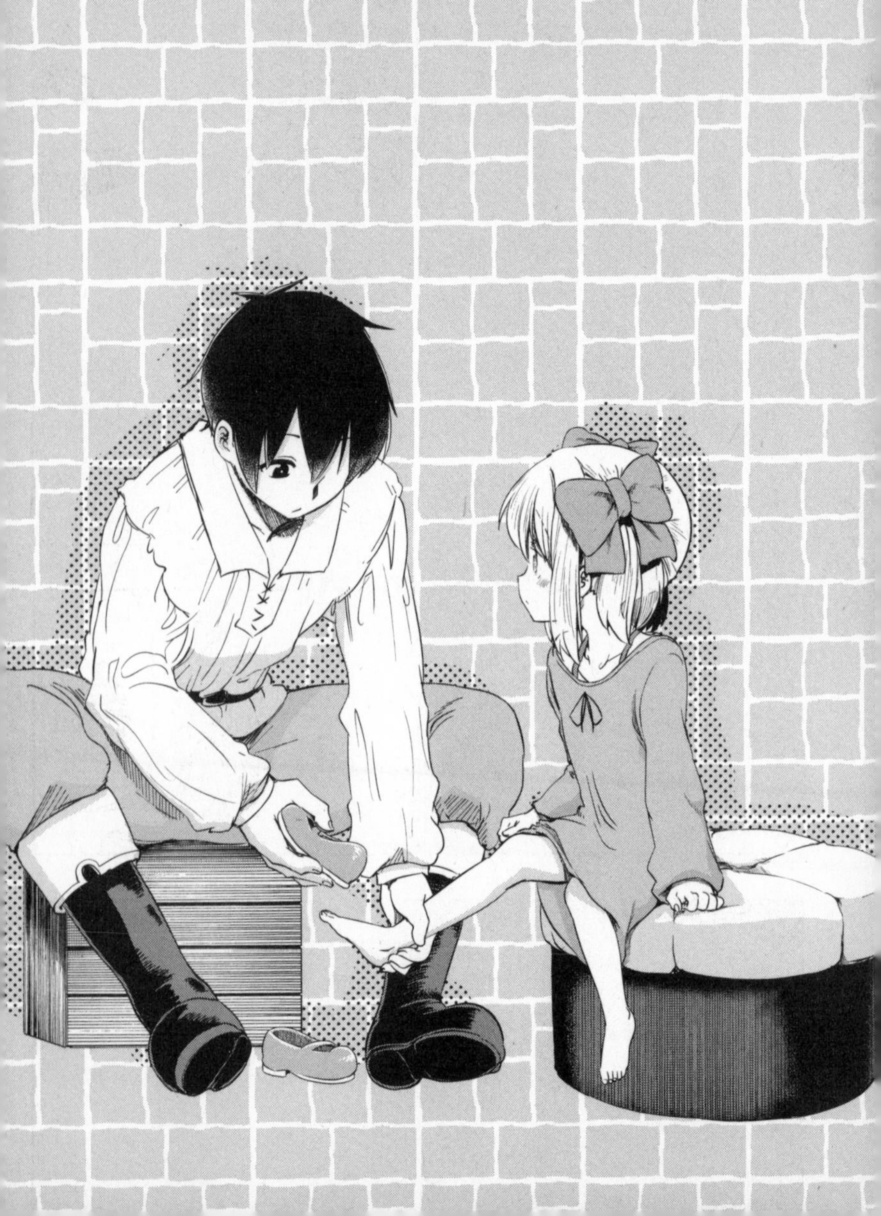

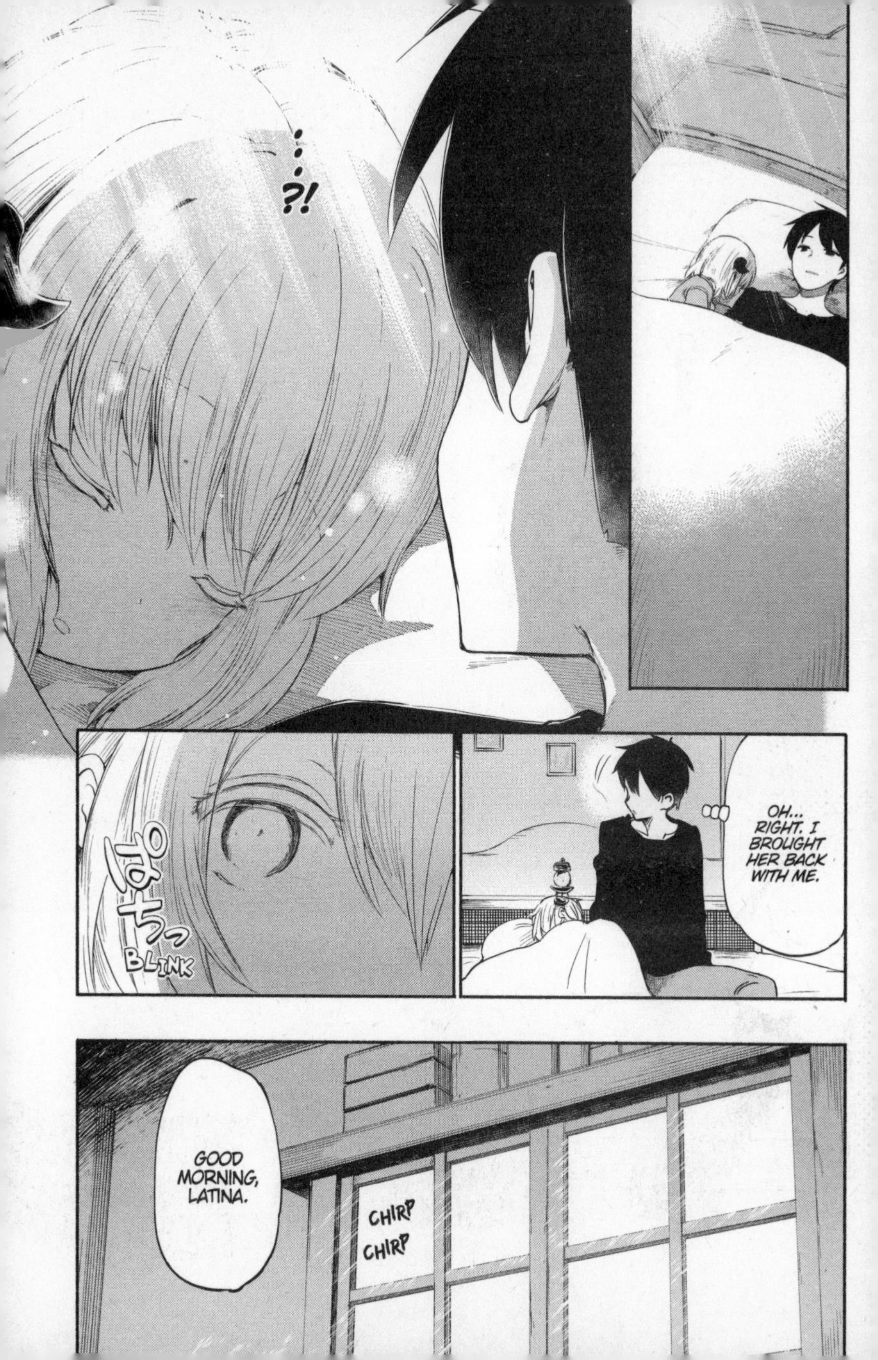
...?!
OH... RIGHT. I BROUGHT HER BACK WITH ME.
ぱちっ
BLINK
GOOD MORNING, LATINA.
CHIRP
CHIRP

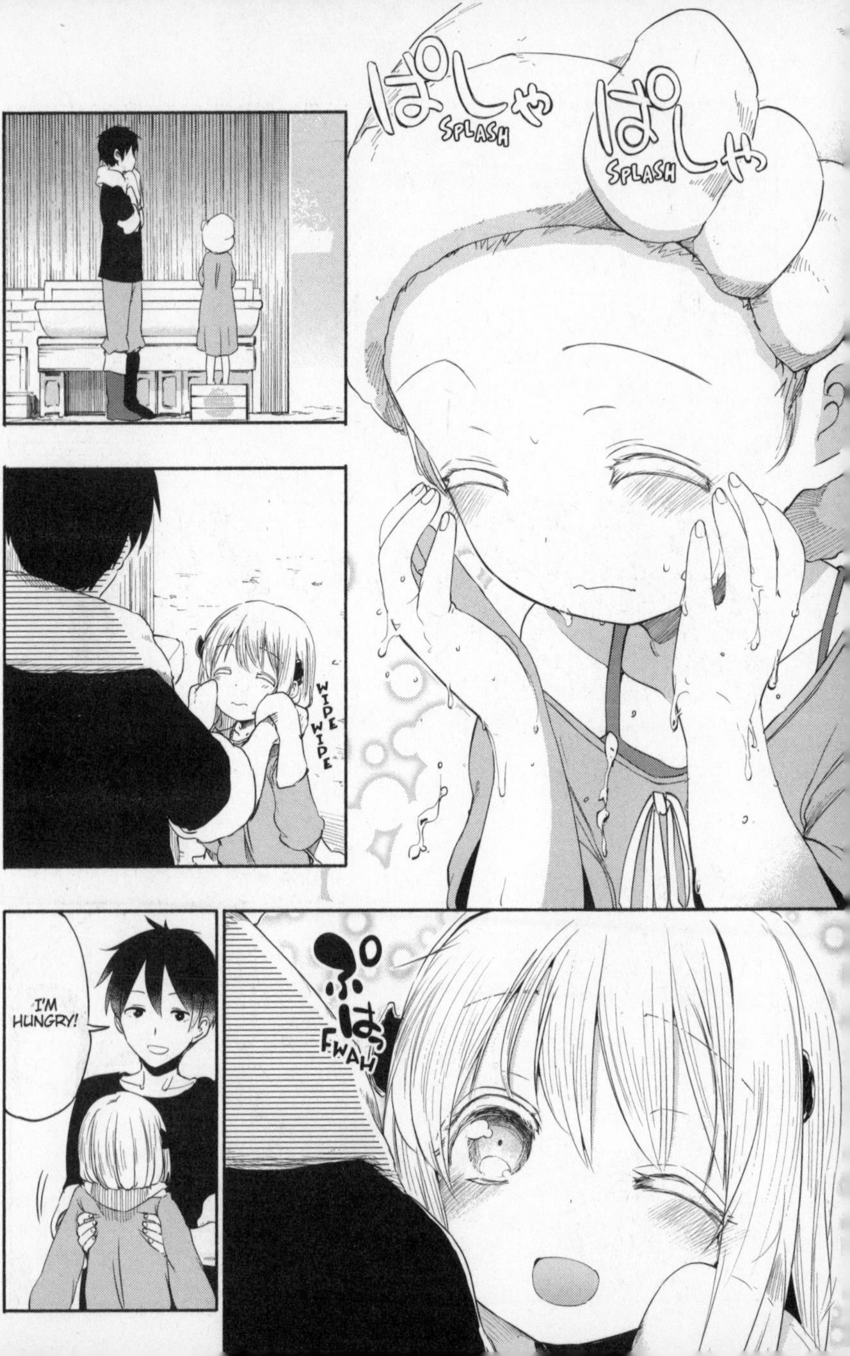

ぱしゃ
SPLASH
ぱしゃ
SPLASH
WIPE WIPE
ぷはっ
FWAH
I'M HUNGRY!

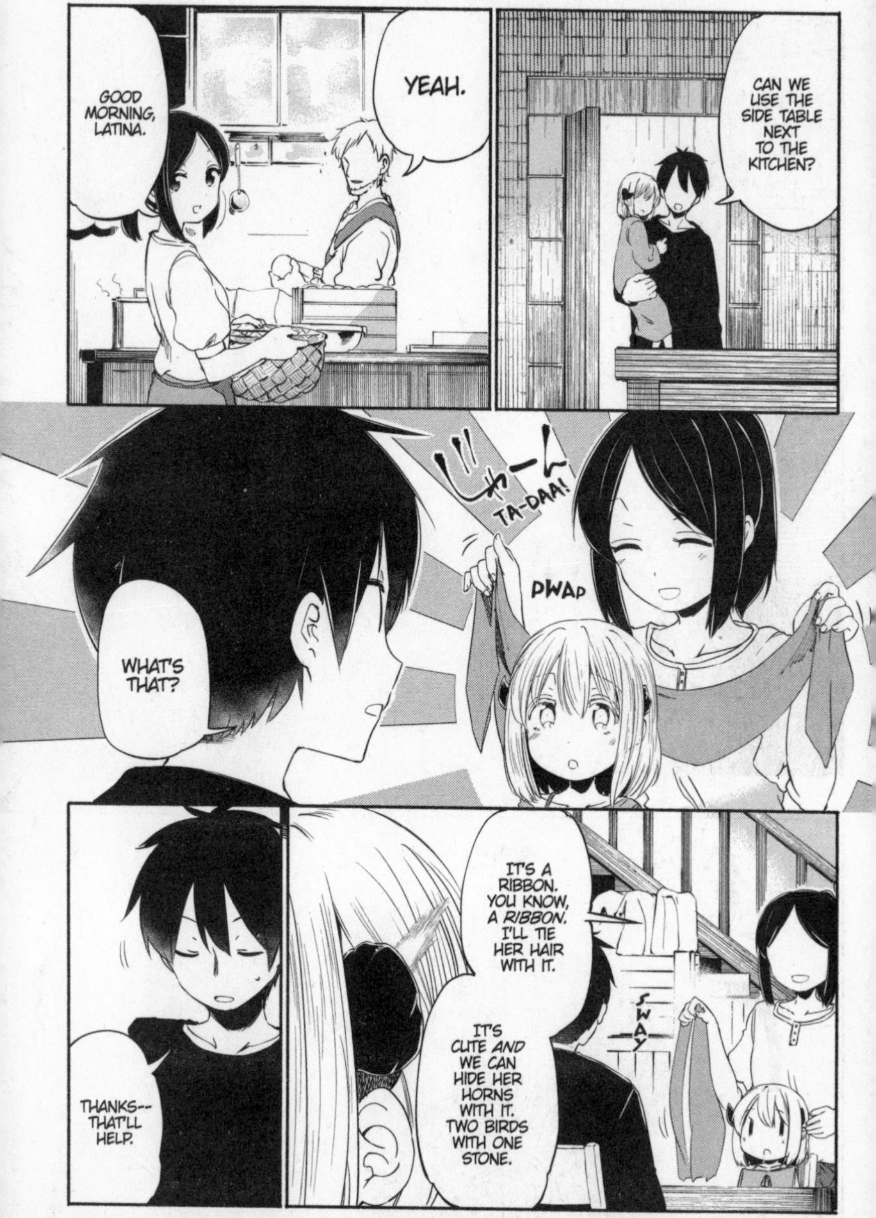

CAN WE USE THE SIDE TABLE NEXT TO THE KITCHEN?
YEAH.
GOOD MORNING, LATINA.
じゃーん
TA-DAA!
PWAP
WHAT'S THAT?
IT'S A RIBBON. YOU KNOW, A *RIBBON*. I'LL TIE HER HAIR WITH IT.
IT'S CUTE *AND* WE CAN HIDE HER HORNS WITH IT. TWO BIRDS WITH ONE STONE.
SWAY
THANKS--THAT'LL HELP.

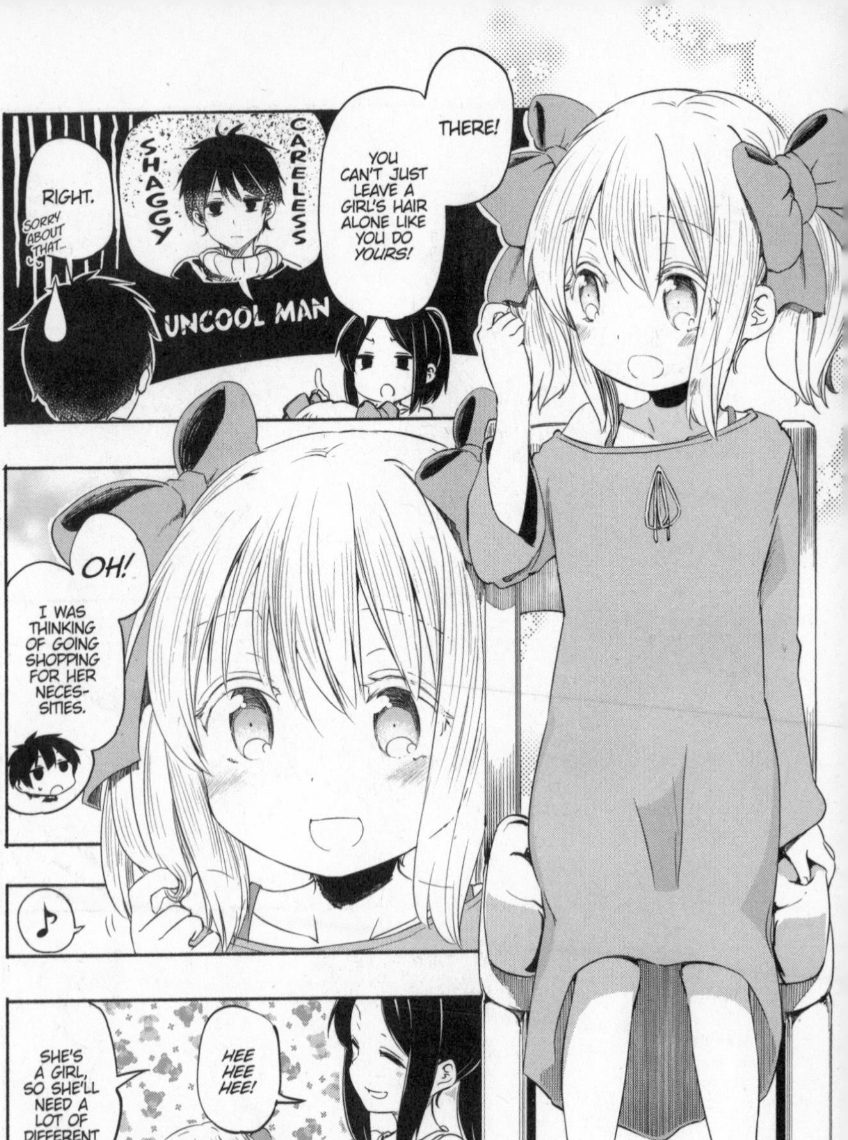
THERE!
YOU CAN'T JUST LEAVE A GIRL'S HAIR ALONE LIKE YOU DO YOURS!
CARELESS
SHAGGY
UNCOOL MAN
RIGHT.
SORRY ABOUT THAT...
OH!
I WAS THINKING OF GOING SHOPPING FOR HER NECES-SITIES.
♪
HEE HEE HEE!
SHE'S A GIRL, SO SHE'LL NEED A LOT OF DIFFERENT THINGS!

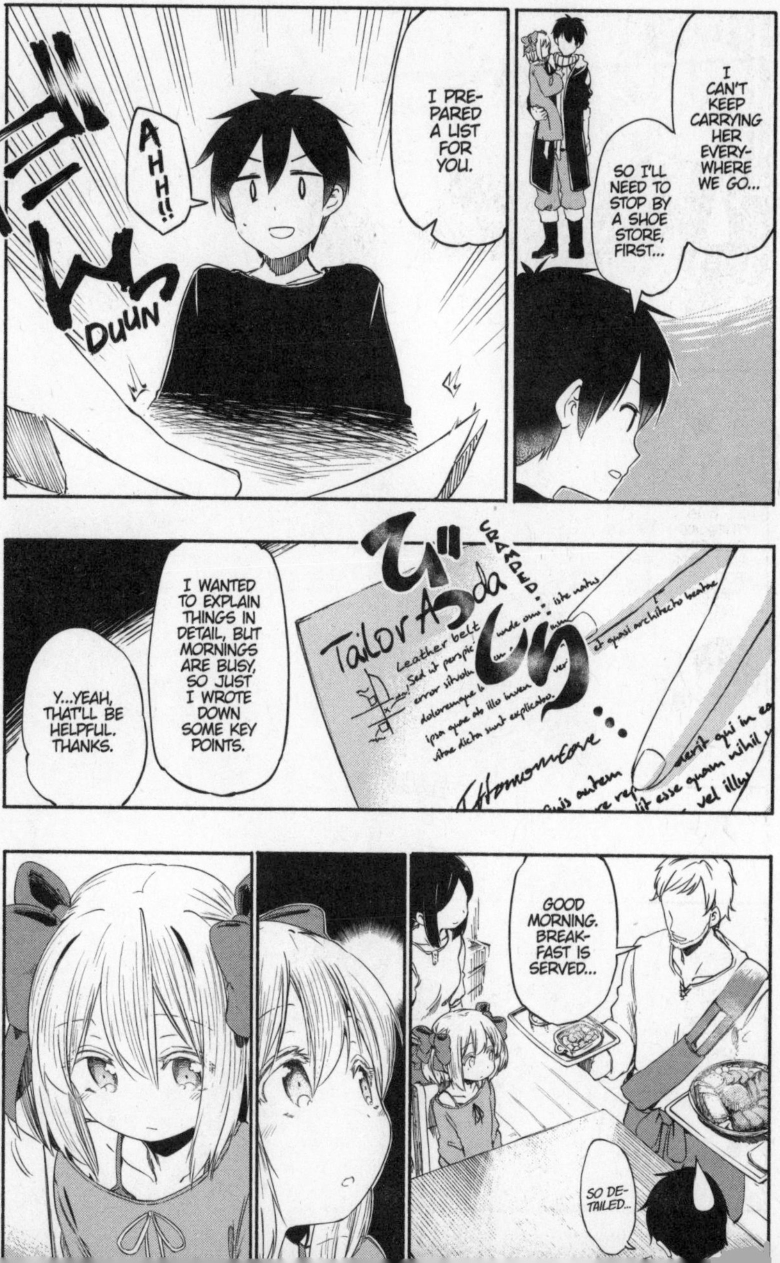
I CAN'T KEEP CARRYING HER EVERY-WHERE WE GO...
SO I'LL NEED TO STOP BY A SHOE STORE, FIRST...
I PRE-PARED A LIST FOR YOU.
AHH!!
だーん
DUUN
びっしり
CRAMPED...
Tailor Asda
Leather belt
I WANTED TO EXPLAIN THINGS IN DETAIL, BUT MORNINGS ARE BUSY, SO JUST I WROTE DOWN SOME KEY POINTS.
Y...YEAH, THAT'LL BE HELPFUL. THANKS.
GOOD MORNING. BREAK-FAST IS SERVED...
SO DE-TAILED...

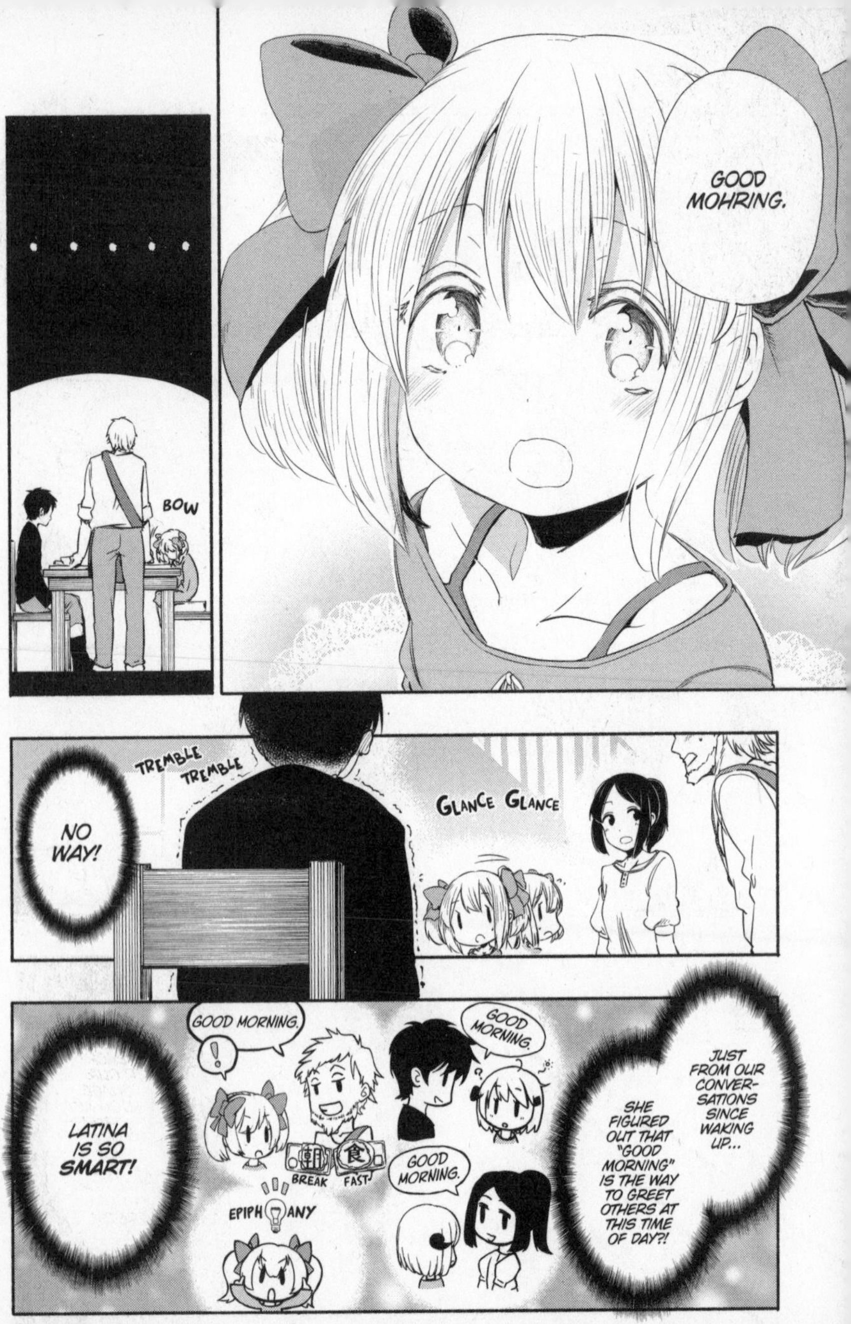
GOOD MOHRING.
. . . . .
BOW
GLANCE GLANCE
TREMBLE TREMBLE
NO WAY!
JUST FROM OUR CONVER-SATIONS SINCE WAKING UP...
SHE FIGURED OUT THAT "GOOD MORNING" IS THE WAY TO GREET OTHERS AT THIS TIME OF DAY?!
GOOD MORNING.
GOOD MORNING.
!
BREAK FAST
GOOD MORNING.
EPIPHANY
LATINA IS SO SMART!

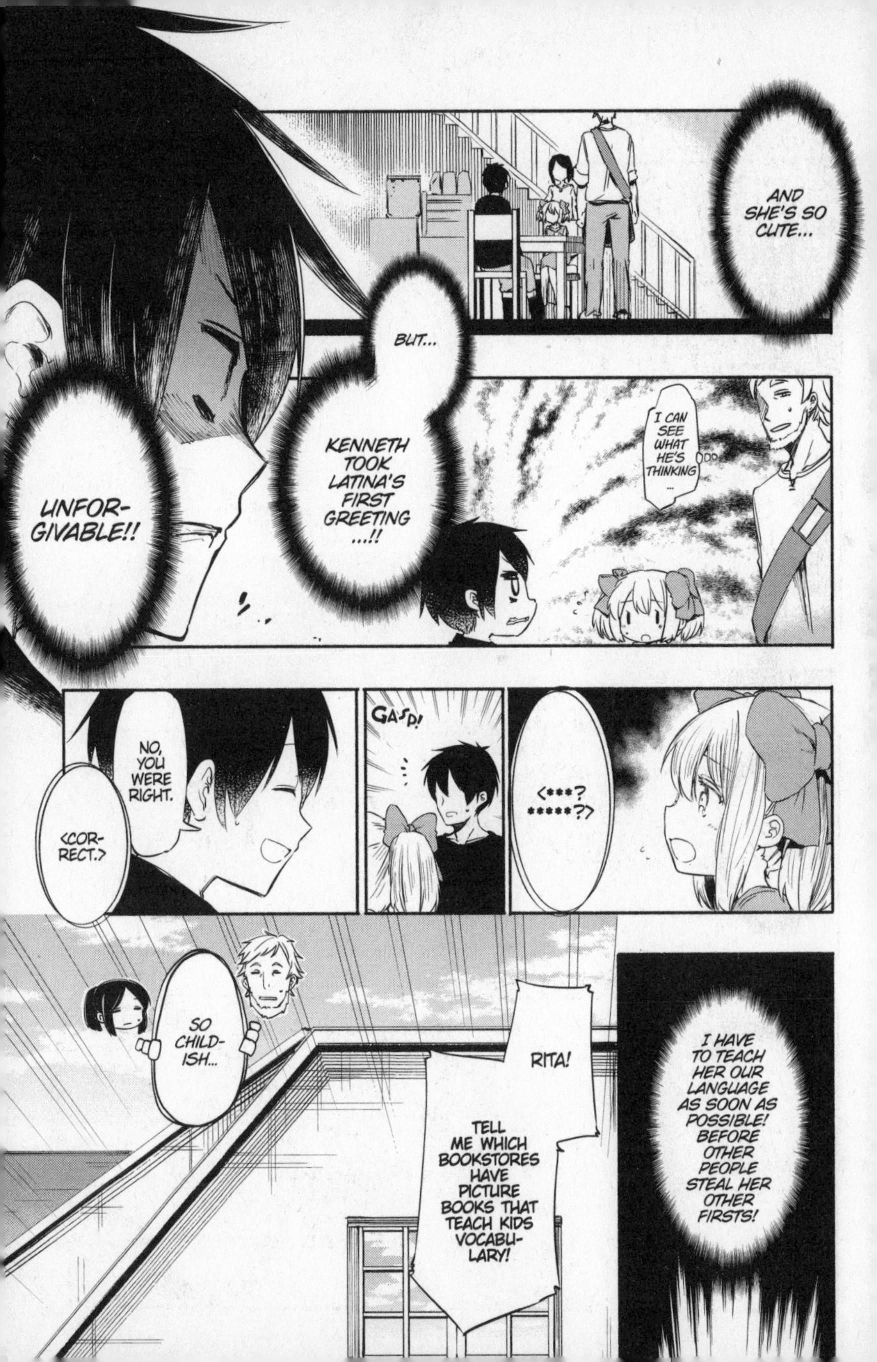
AND SHE'S SO CUTE...
BUT...
I CAN SEE WHAT HE'S THINKING...
KENNETH TOOK LATINA'S FIRST GREETING...!!
UNFOR-GIVABLE!!
<***? *****?>
GASP!
NO, YOU WERE RIGHT.
<COR-RECT.>
I HAVE TO TEACH HER OUR LANGUAGE AS SOON AS POSSIBLE! BEFORE OTHER PEOPLE STEAL HER OTHER FIRSTS!
RITA!
TELL ME WHICH BOOKSTORES HAVE PICTURE BOOKS THAT TEACH KIDS VOCABU-LARY!
SO CHILD-ISH...

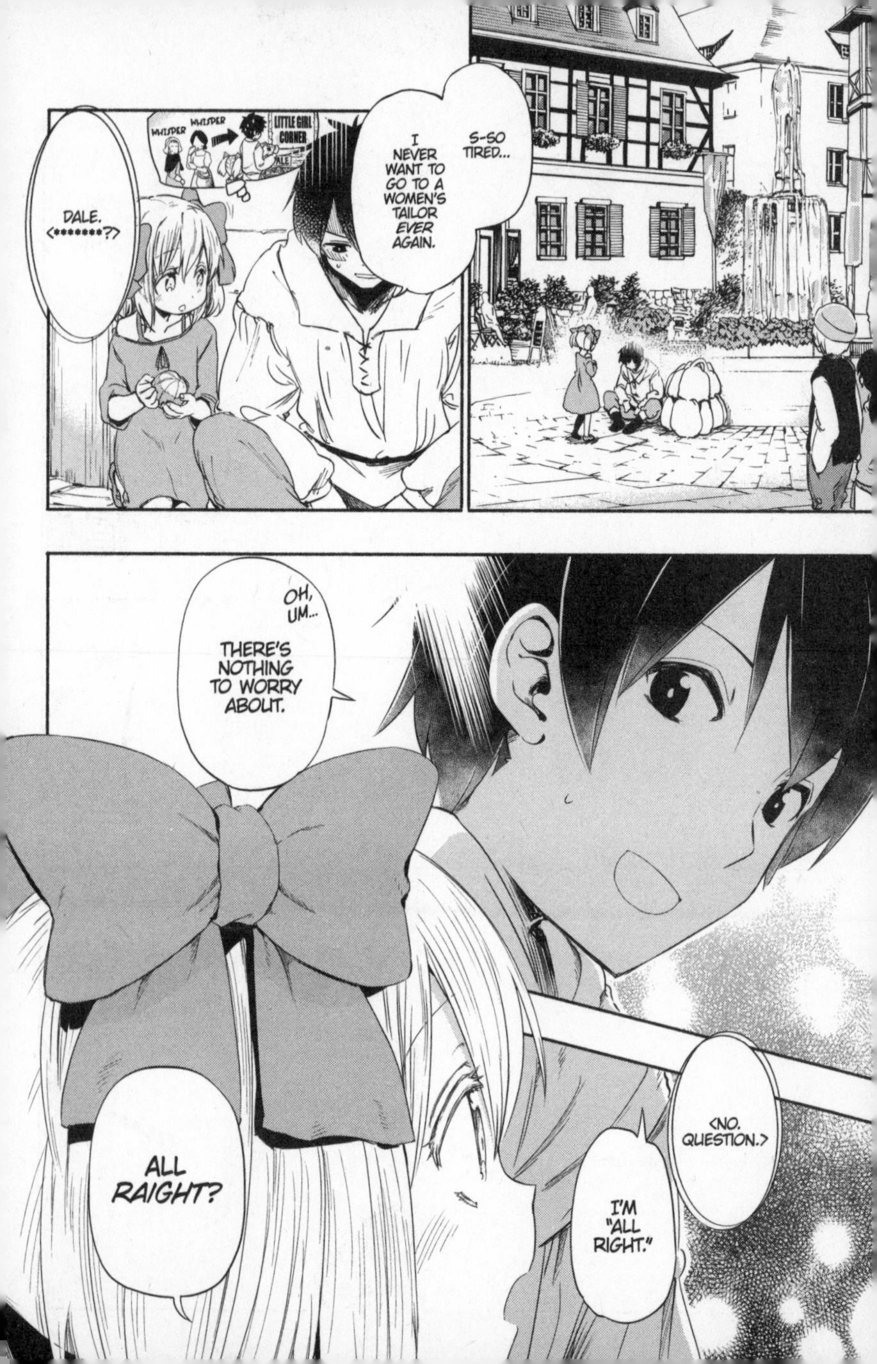
S-SO TIRED...
I NEVER WANT TO GO TO A WOMEN'S TAILOR EVER AGAIN.
WHISPER
WHISPER
LITTLE GIRL CORNER
DALE. <*******?>
OH, UM...
THERE'S NOTHING TO WORRY ABOUT.
ALL RAIGHT?
<NO. QUESTION.>
I'M "ALL RIGHT."

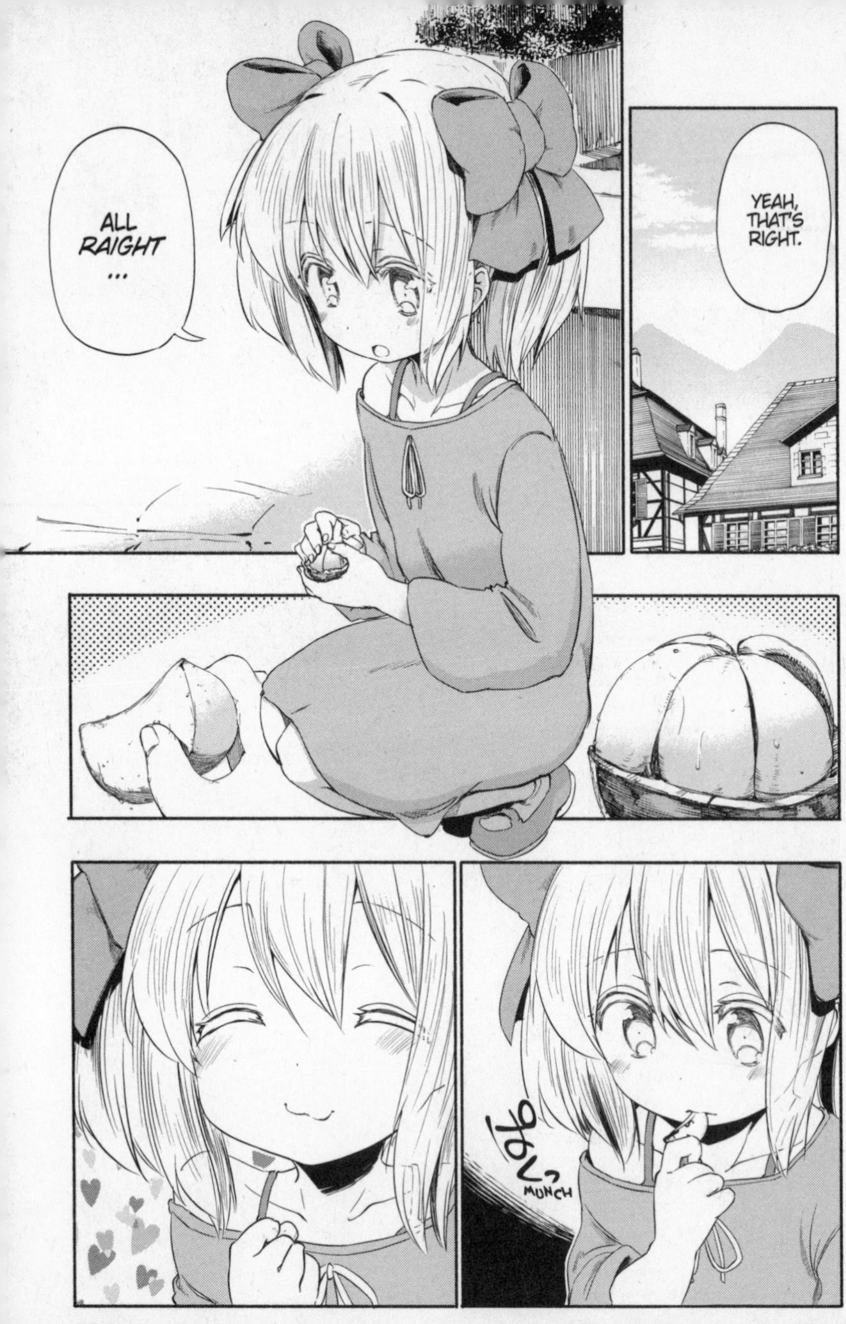
YEAH, THAT'S RIGHT.
ALL RAIGHT ...
MUNCH

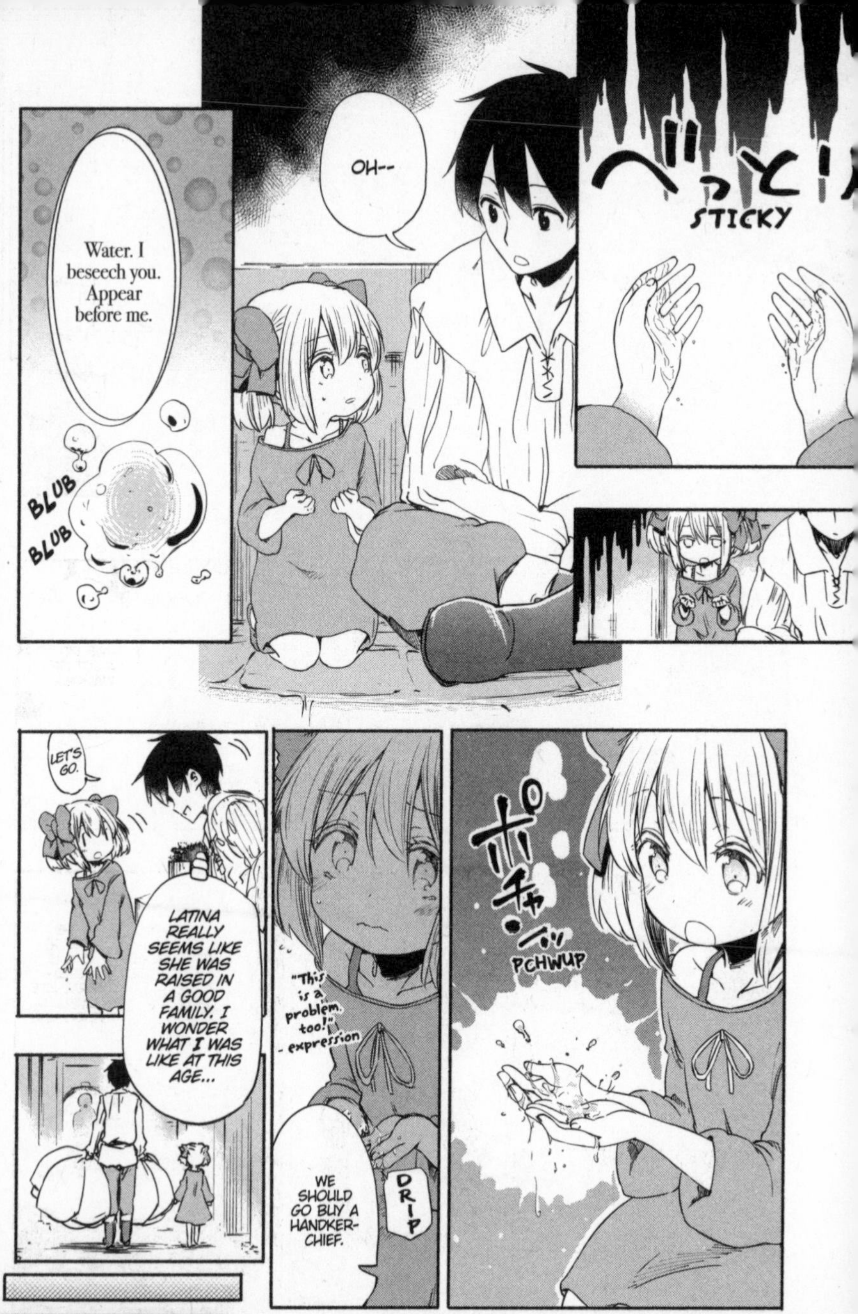

べっと!
STICKY
OH--
Water. I beseech you. Appear before me.
BLUB
BLUB
ポチャッ
PCHWUP
"This is a problem, too!" - expression
DRIP
WE SHOULD GO BUY A HANDKERCHIEF.
LET'S GO.
LATINA REALLY SEEMS LIKE SHE WAS RAISED IN A GOOD FAMILY. I WONDER WHAT I WAS LIKE AT THIS AGE...

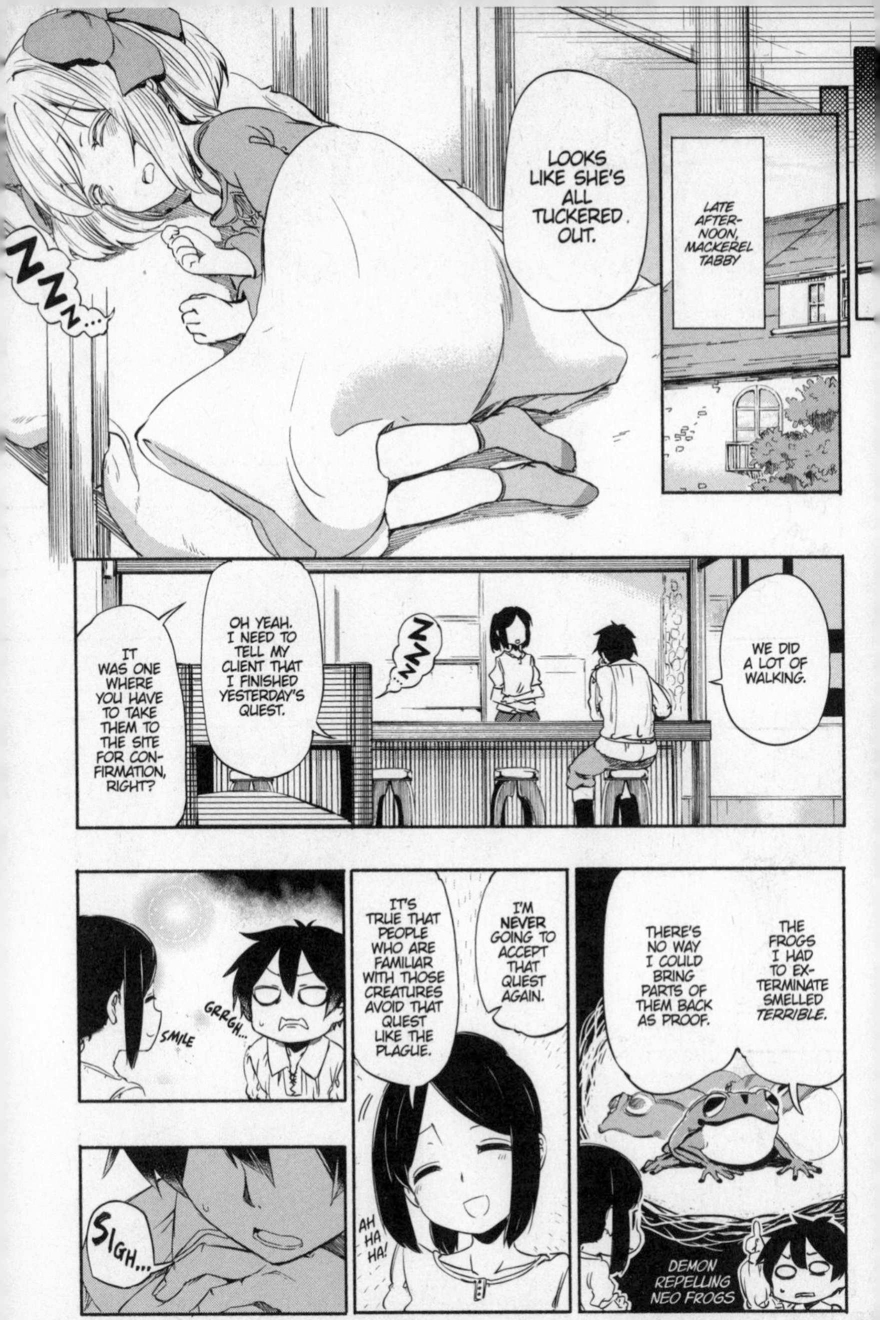
LATE AFTERNOON, MACKEREL TABBY
LOOKS LIKE SHE'S ALL TUCKERED OUT.
NNN...
WE DID A LOT OF WALKING.
NNN
OH YEAH. I NEED TO TELL MY CLIENT THAT I FINISHED YESTERDAY'S QUEST.
IT WAS ONE WHERE YOU HAVE TO TAKE THEM TO THE SITE FOR CONFIRMATION, RIGHT?
THE FROGS I HAD TO EXTERMINATE SMELLED TERRIBLE.
THERE'S NO WAY I COULD BRING PARTS OF THEM BACK AS PROOF.
DEMON REPELLING NEO FROGS
I'M NEVER GOING TO ACCEPT THAT QUEST AGAIN.
IT'S TRUE THAT PEOPLE WHO ARE FAMILIAR WITH THOSE CREATURES AVOID THAT QUEST LIKE THE PLAGUE.
AH HA HA!
GRRGH...
SMILE
SIGH...

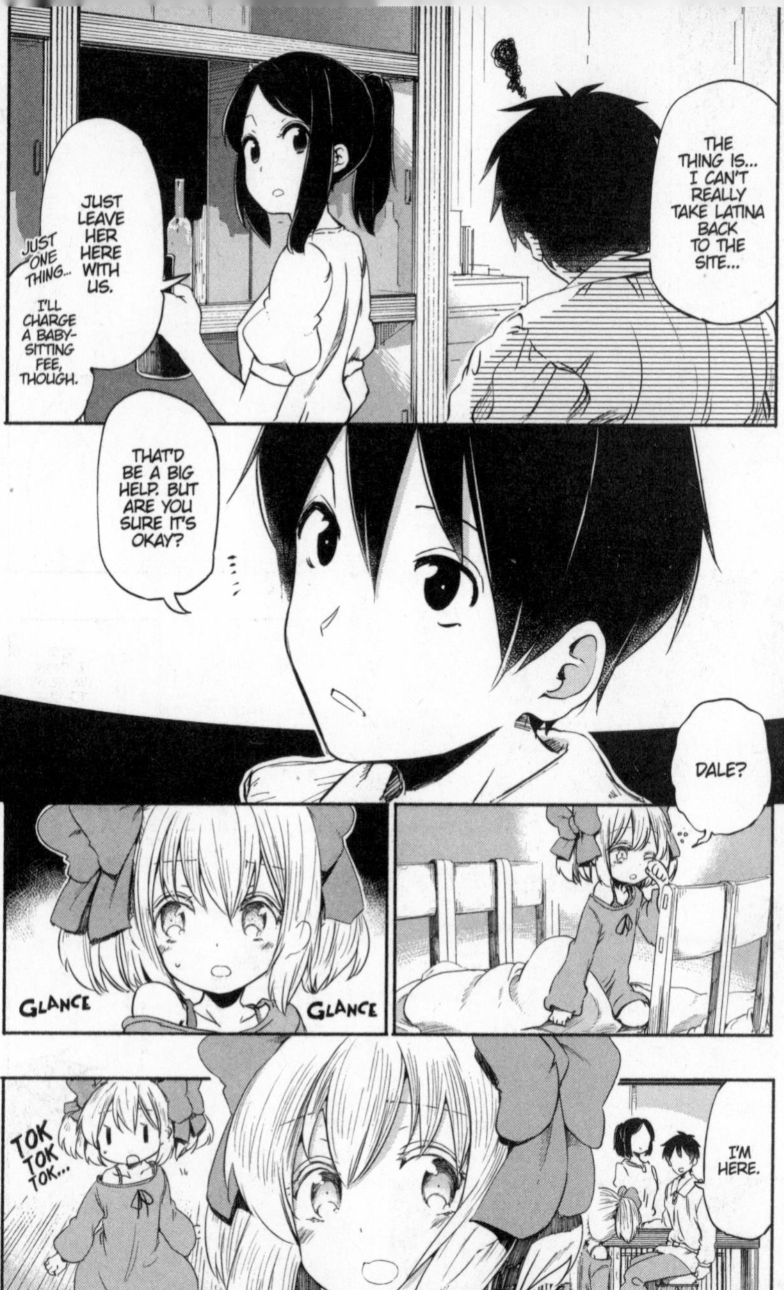
THE THING IS... I CAN'T REALLY TAKE LATINA BACK TO THE SITE...
JUST LEAVE HER HERE WITH US.
JUST ONE THING...
I'LL CHARGE A BABY-SITTING FEE, THOUGH.
THAT'D BE A BIG HELP. BUT ARE YOU SURE IT'S OKAY?
DALE?
GLANCE
GLANCE
I'M HERE.
TOK TOK TOK...

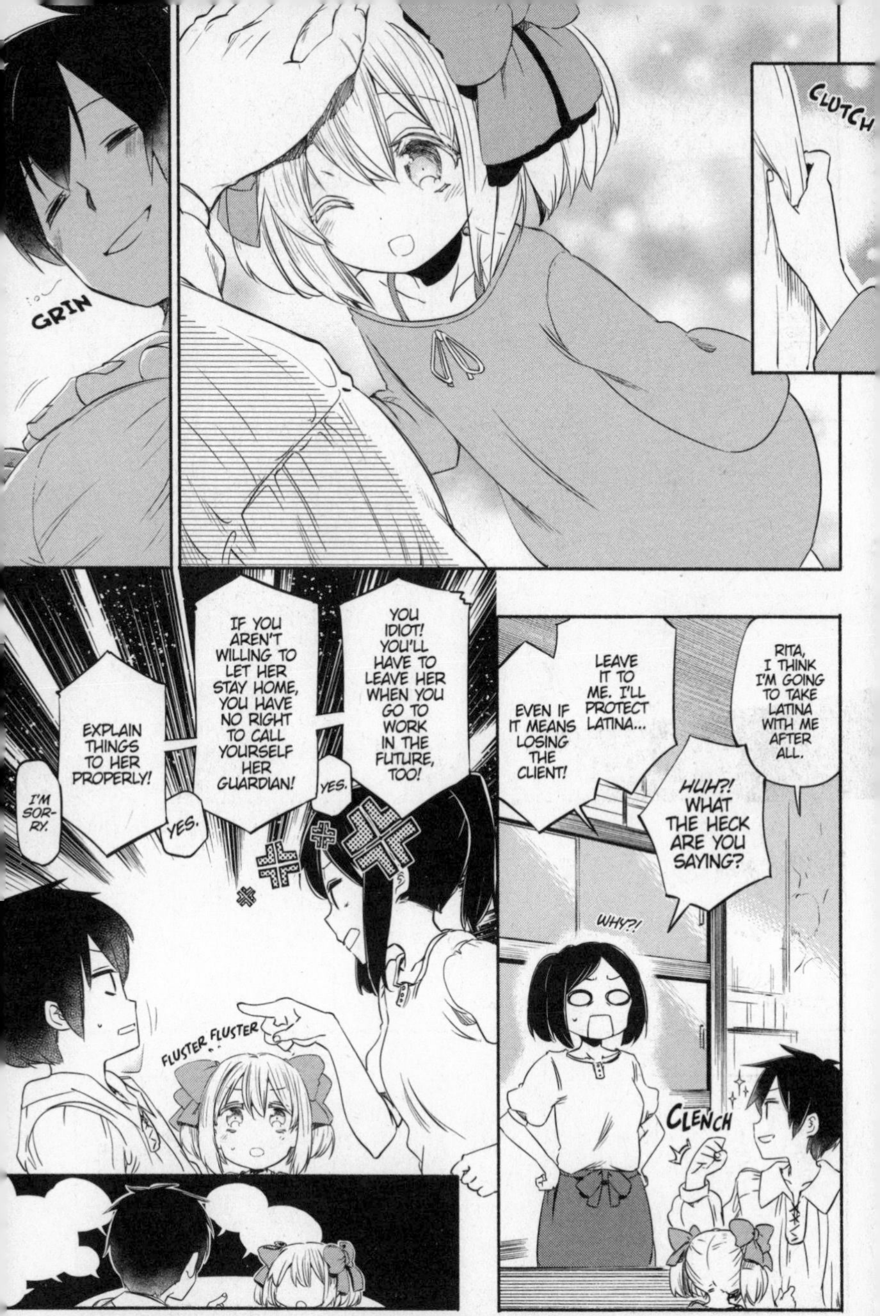
CLUTCH
GRIN
RITA, I THINK I'M GOING TO TAKE LATINA WITH ME AFTER ALL.
HUH?! WHAT THE HECK ARE YOU SAYING?
LEAVE IT TO ME. I'LL PROTECT LATINA...
EVEN IF IT MEANS LOSING THE CLIENT!
WHY?!
CLENCH
YOU IDIOT! YOU'LL HAVE TO LEAVE HER WHEN YOU GO TO WORK IN THE FUTURE, TOO!
YES.
IF YOU AREN'T WILLING TO LET HER STAY HOME, YOU HAVE NO RIGHT TO CALL YOURSELF HER GUARDIAN!
YES.
EXPLAIN THINGS TO HER PROPERLY!
I'M SORRY.
FLUSTER FLUSTER

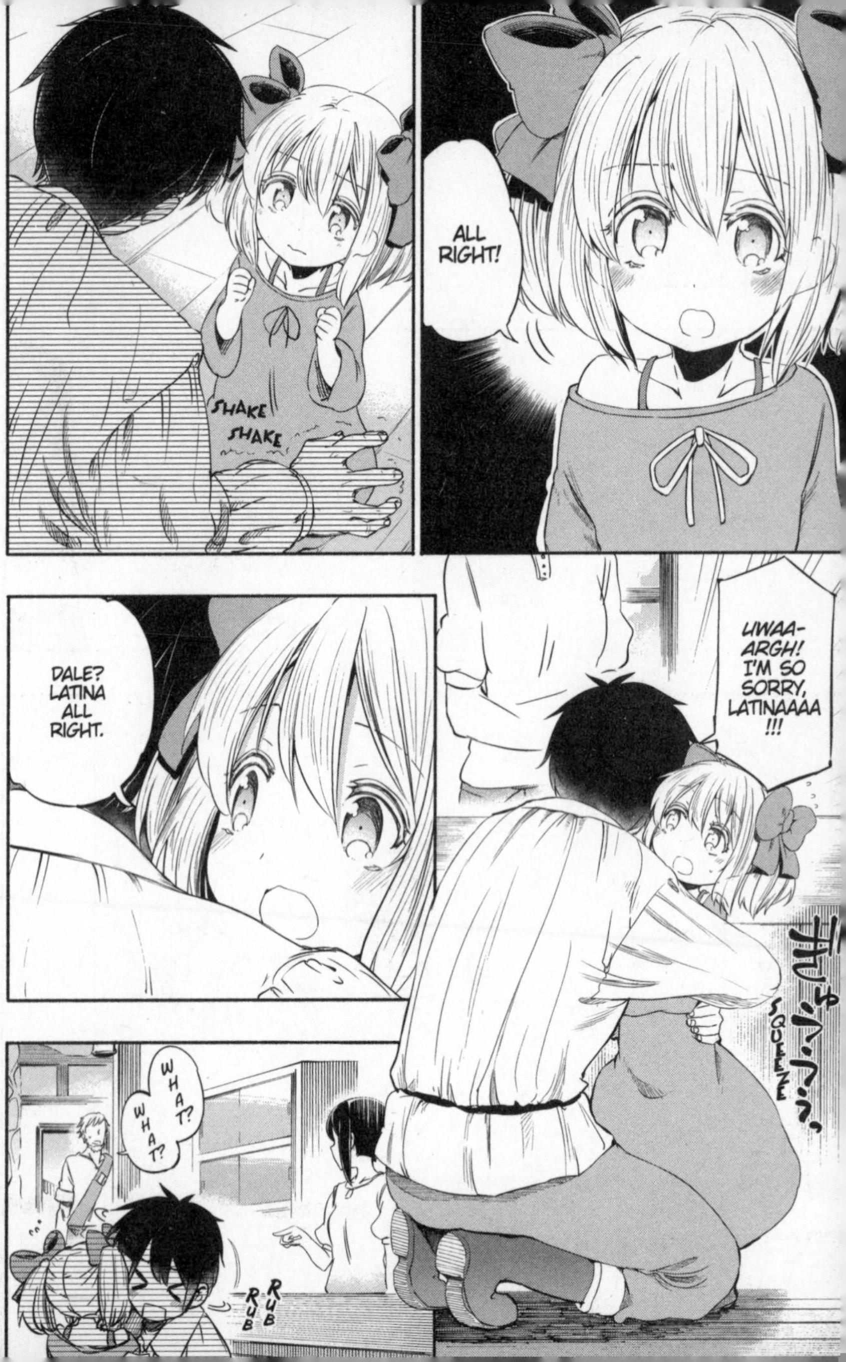
ALL RIGHT!
SHAKE SHAKE
UWAA-ARGH! I'M SO SORRY, LATINAAAA!!!
SQUEEZE
DALE? LATINA ALL RIGHT.
WHAT? WHAT?
RUB RUB

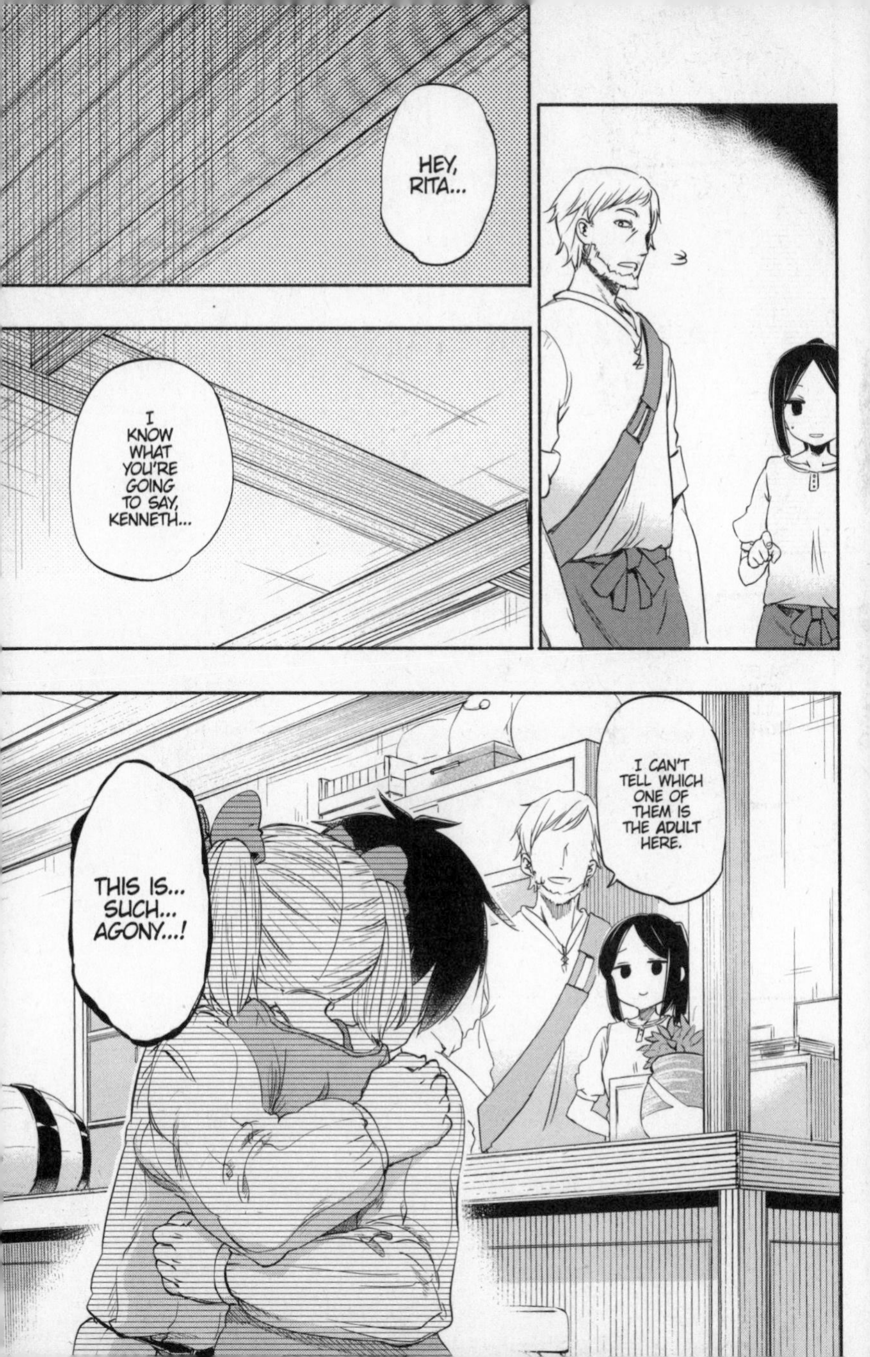
HEY, RITA...
I KNOW WHAT YOU'RE GOING TO SAY, KENNETH...
I CAN'T TELL WHICH ONE OF THEM IS THE ADULT HERE.
THIS IS... SUCH... AGONY...!

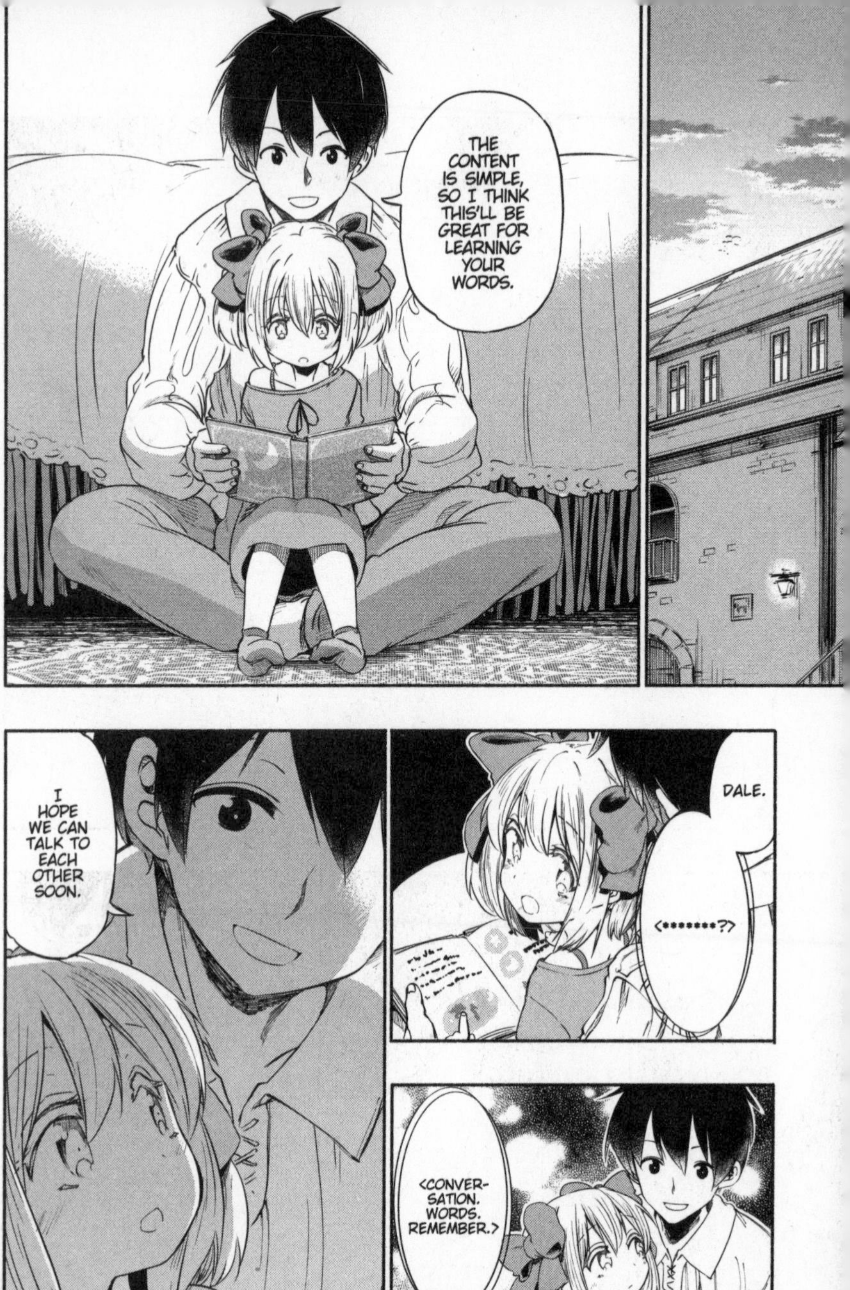
THE CONTENT IS SIMPLE, SO I THINK THIS'LL BE GREAT FOR LEARNING YOUR WORDS.
DALE.
<*******?>
<CONVER-SATION. WORDS. REMEMBER.>
I HOPE WE CAN TALK TO EACH OTHER SOON.

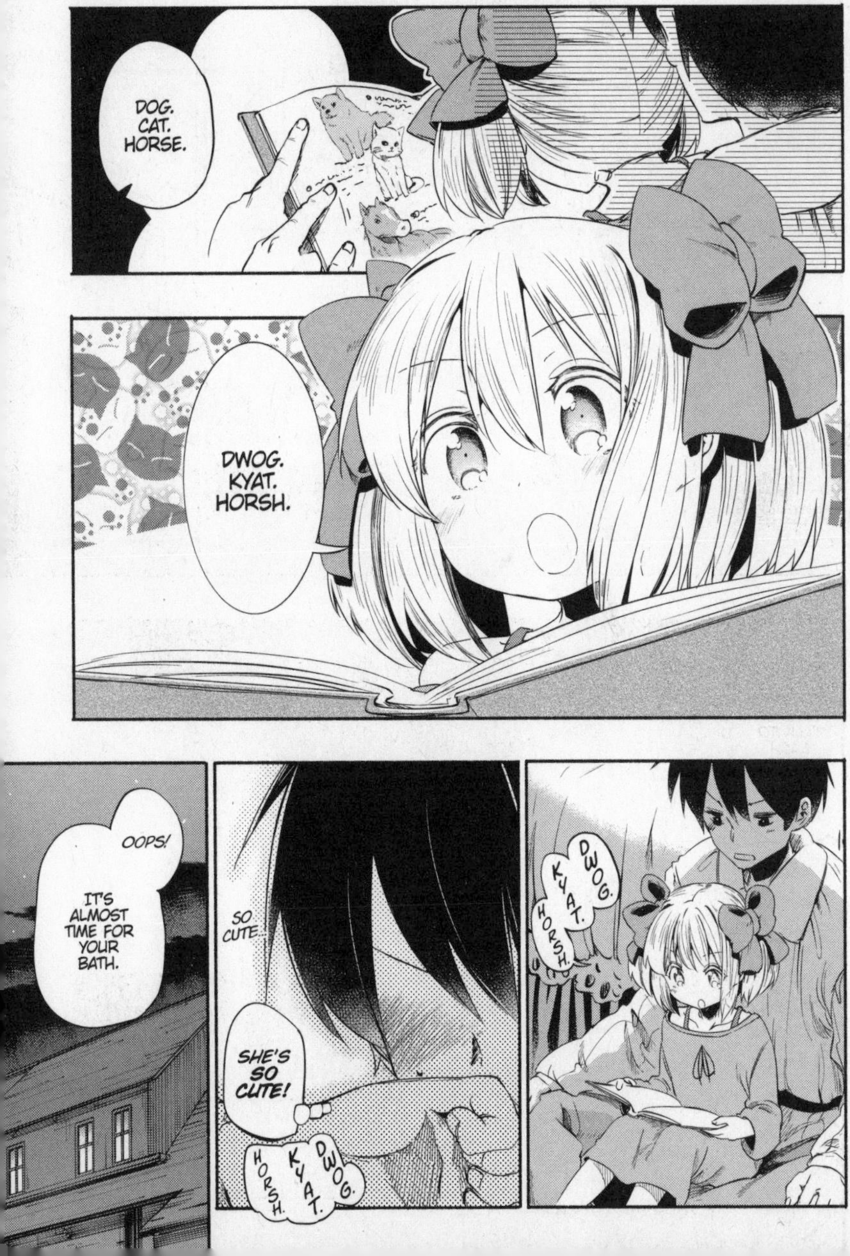
DOG. CAT. HORSE.
DWOG. KYAT. HORSH.
DWOG. KYAT. HORSH.
SO CUTE...
SHE'S SO CUTE!
DWOG. KYAT. HORSH.
OOPS!
IT'S ALMOST TIME FOR YOUR BATH.

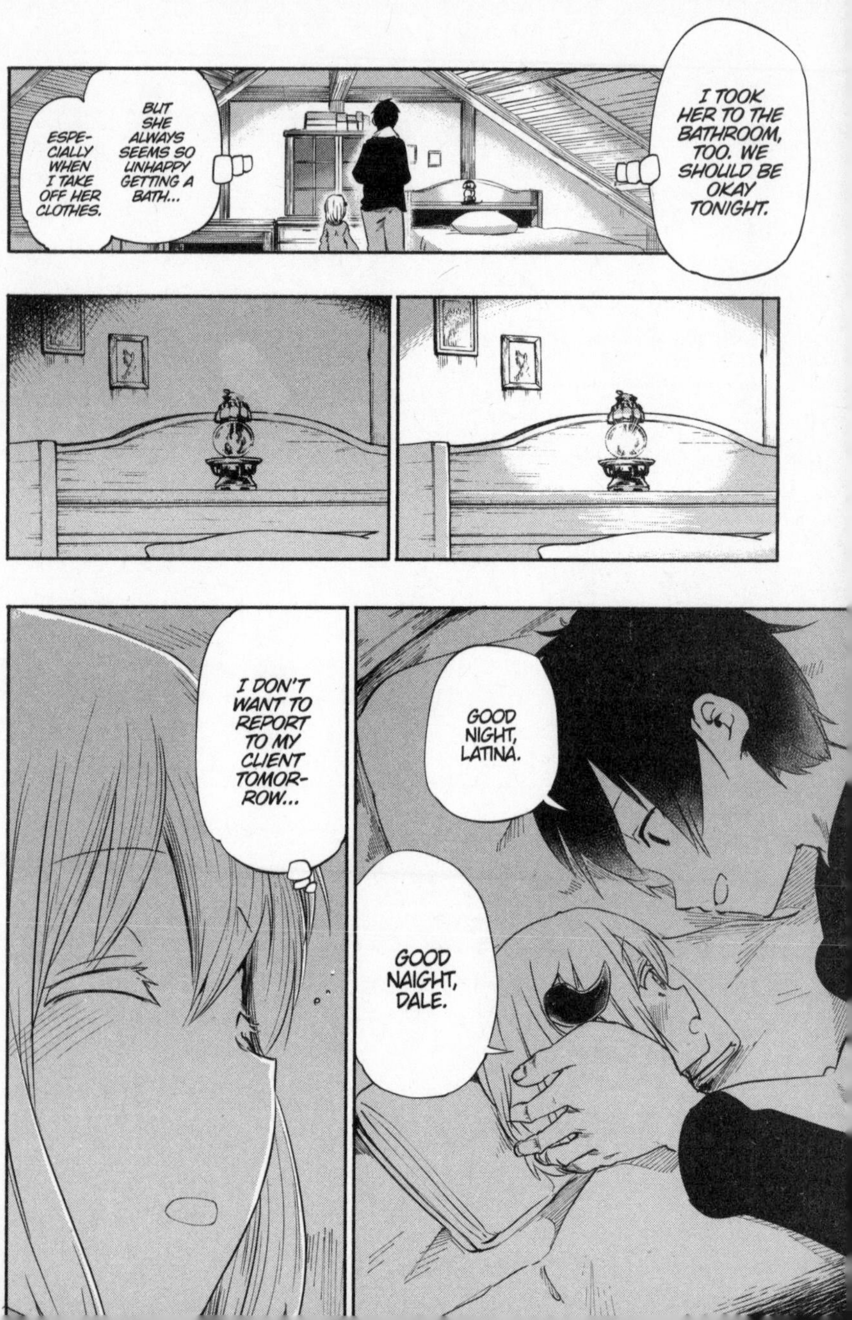
I TOOK HER TO THE BATHROOM, TOO. WE SHOULD BE OKAY TONIGHT.
BUT SHE ALWAYS SEEMS SO UNHAPPY GETTING A BATH...
ESPE-CIALLY WHEN I TAKE OFF HER CLOTHES.
GOOD NIGHT, LATINA.
GOOD NAIGHT, DALE.
I DON'T WANT TO REPORT TO MY CLIENT TOMOR-ROW...

IF It's
For My
Daughter,
I'd Even Defeat
a Demon
Lord

If It's For My Daughter, I'd Even Defeat a Demon Lord.

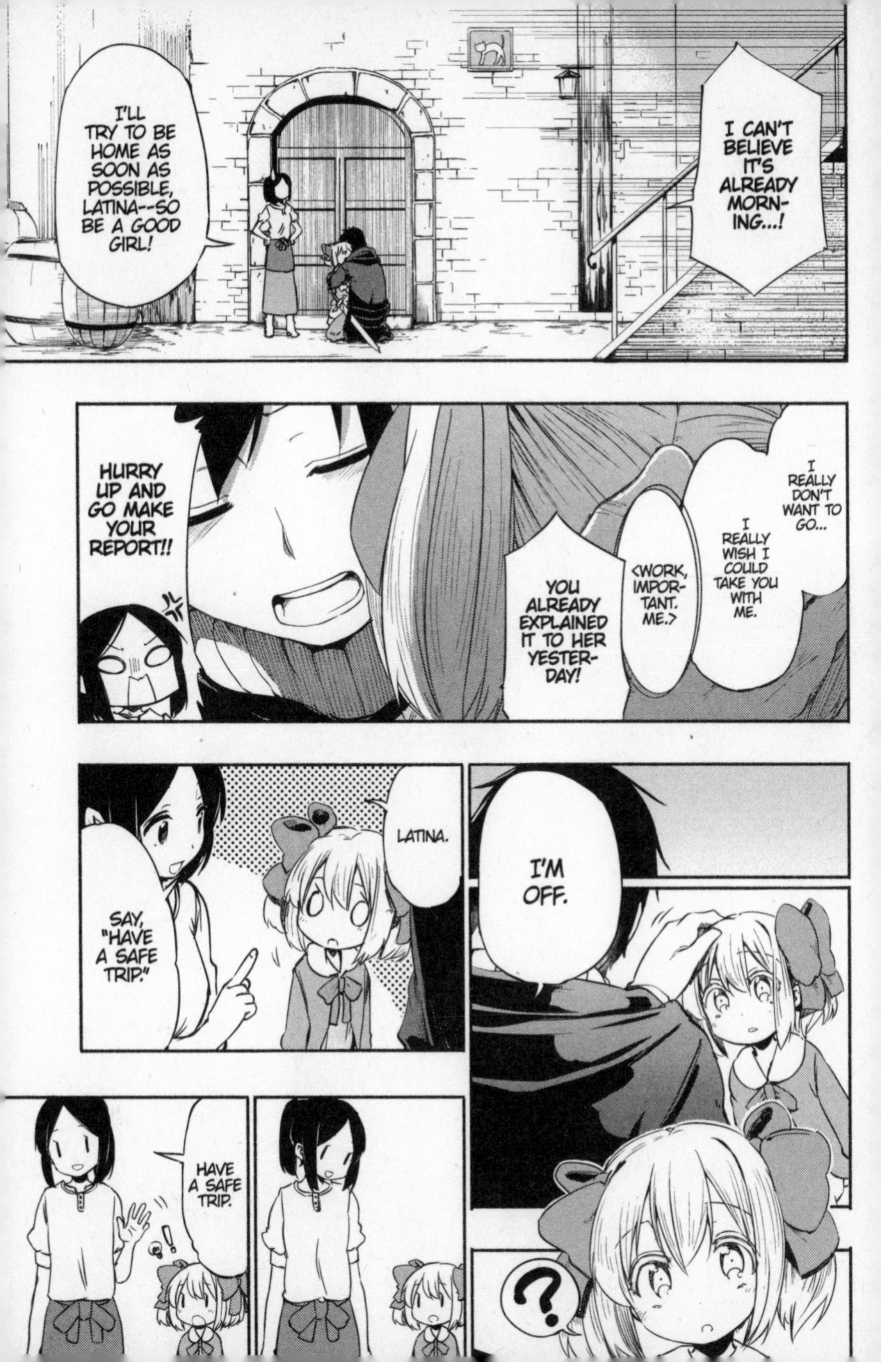
I CAN'T BELIEVE IT'S ALREADY MORNING...!
I'LL TRY TO BE HOME AS SOON AS POSSIBLE, LATINA--SO BE A GOOD GIRL!
I REALLY DON'T WANT TO GO...
I REALLY WISH I COULD TAKE YOU WITH ME.
<WORK, IMPORTANT. ME.>
YOU ALREADY EXPLAINED IT TO HER YESTERDAY!
HURRY UP AND GO MAKE YOUR REPORT!!
I'M OFF.
?
LATINA.
SAY, "HAVE A SAFE TRIP."
HAVE A SAFE TRIP.

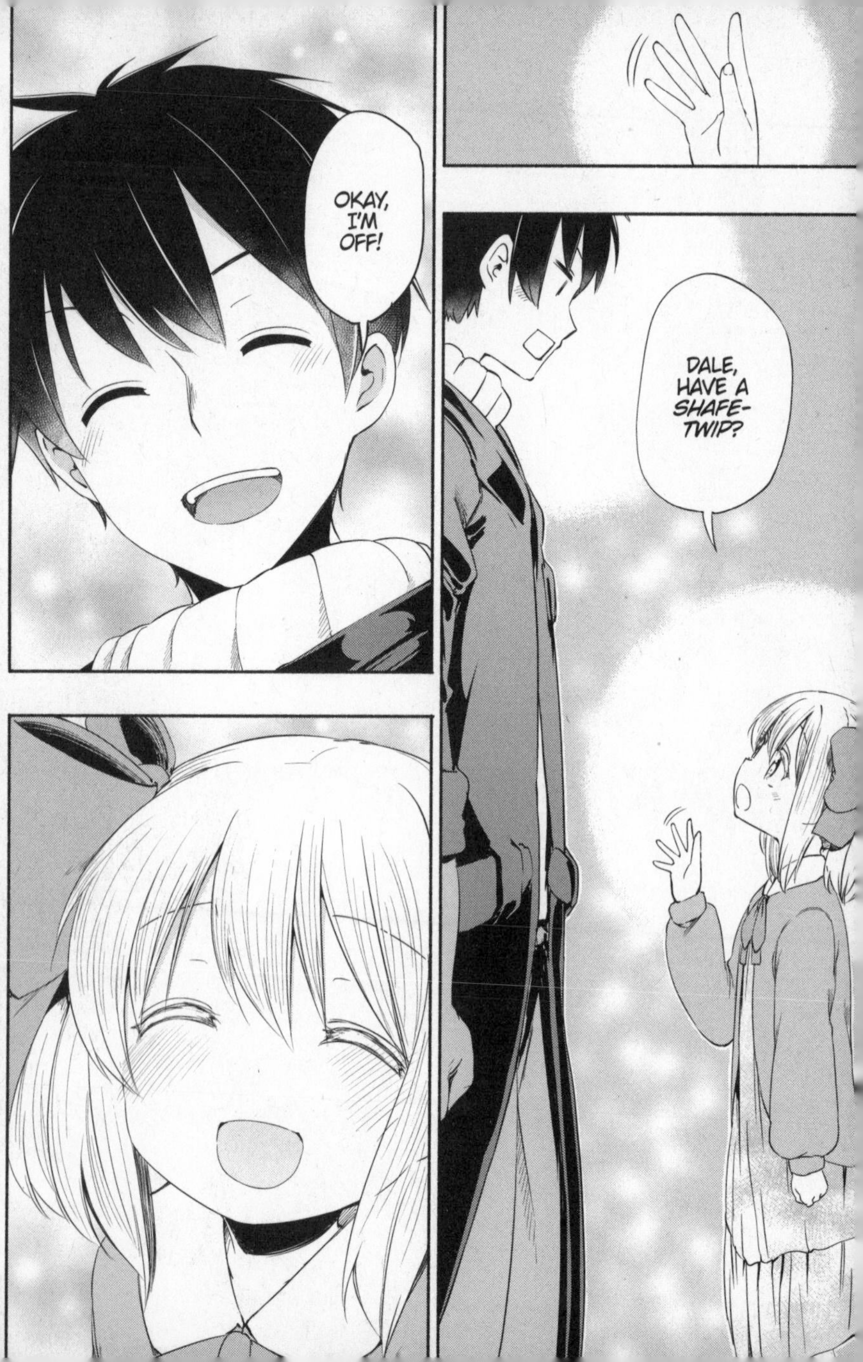
DALE, HAVE A SHAFE-TWIP?
OKAY, I'M OFF!

3. Little Girl's First Time Staying at Home

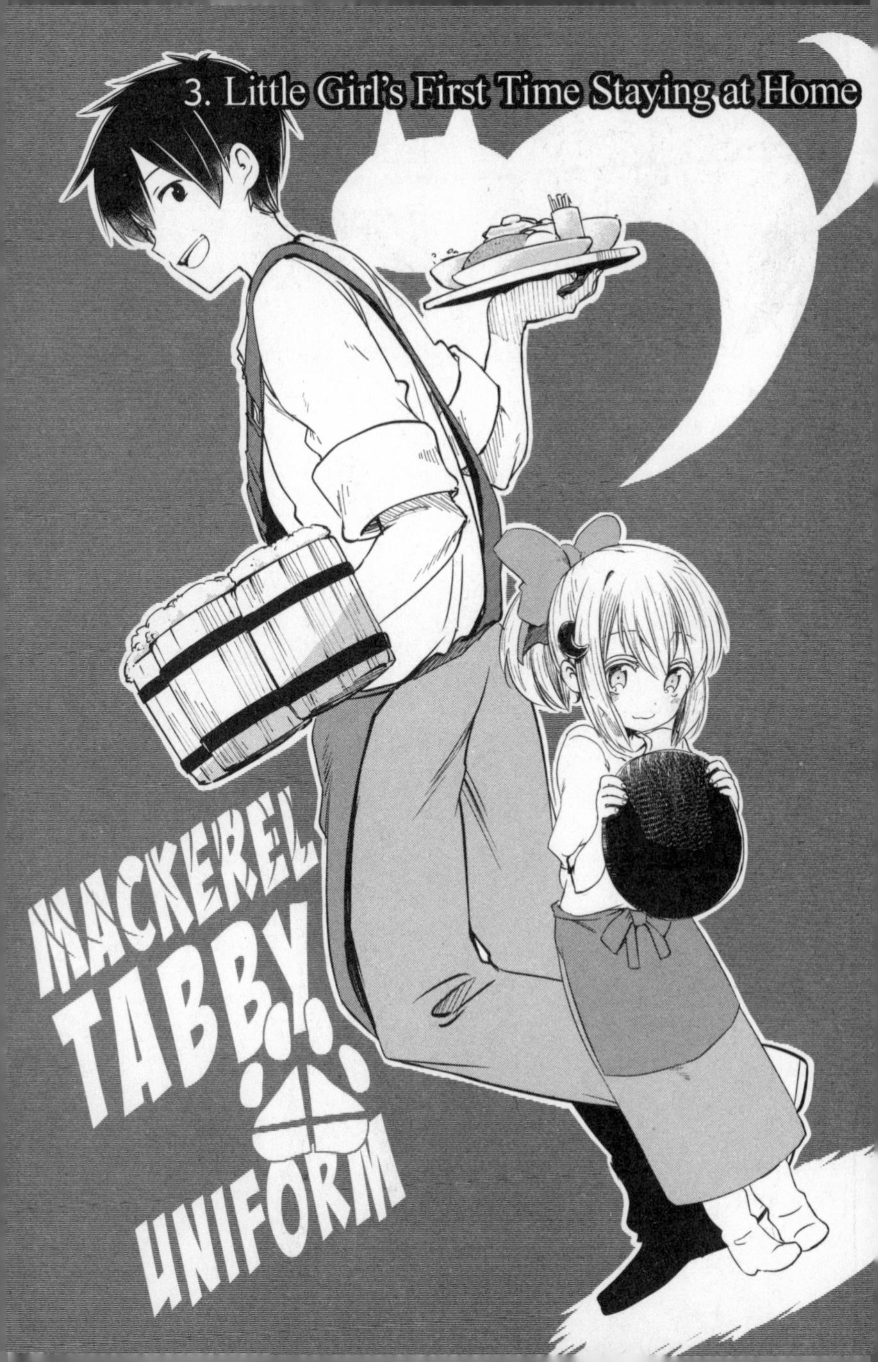
MACKEREL
TABBY
UNIFORM

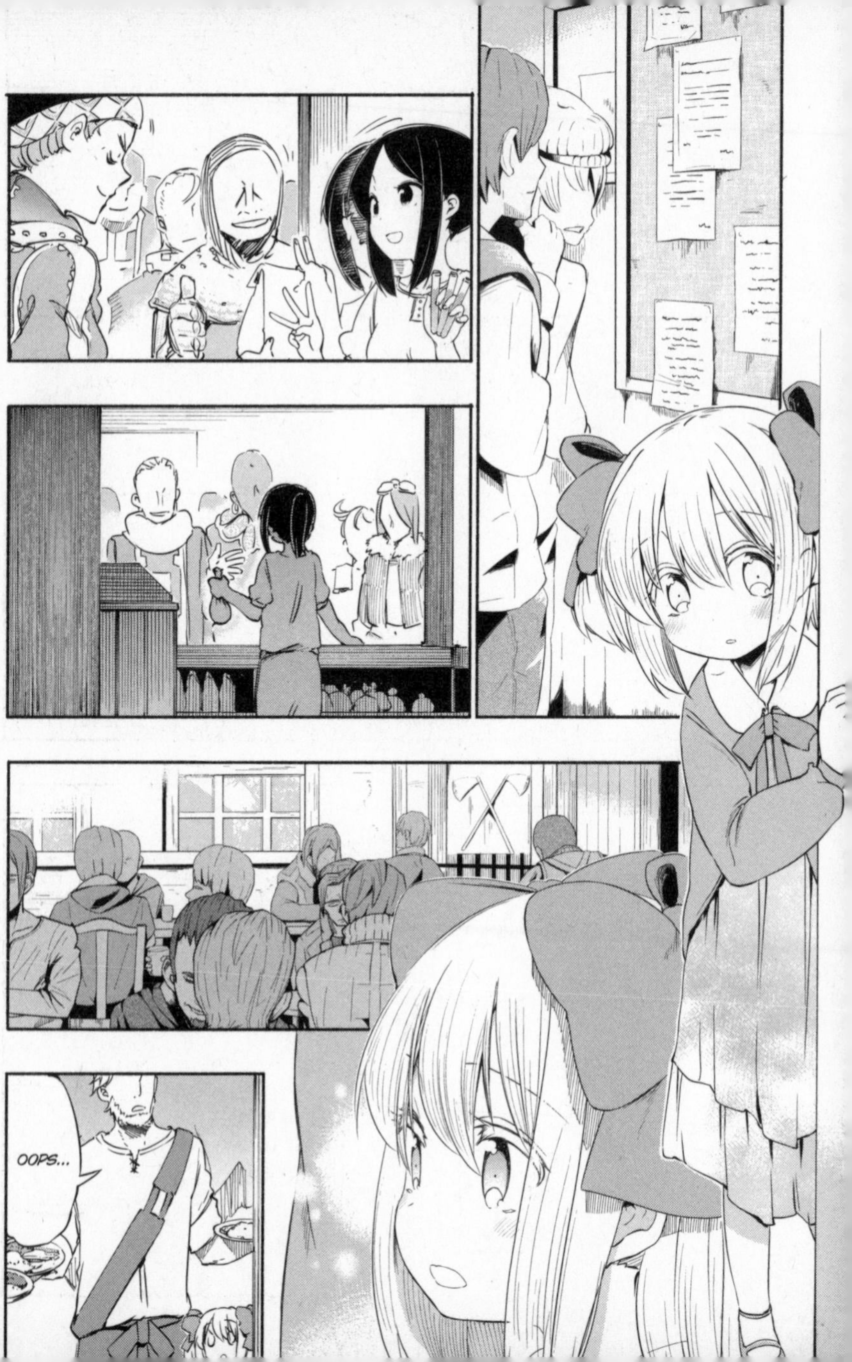
OOPS...

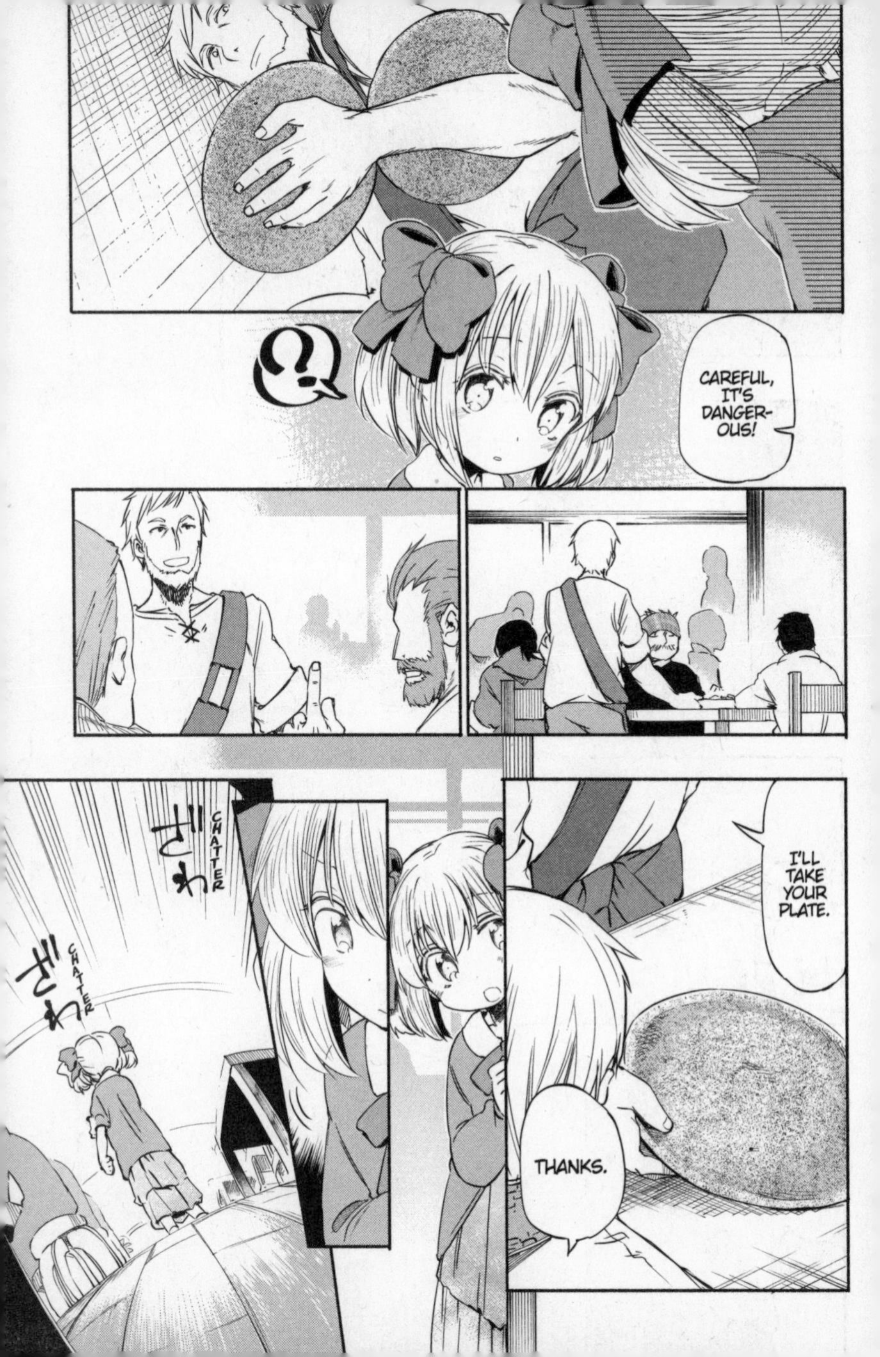
CAREFUL, IT'S DANGEROUS!
?
I'LL TAKE YOUR PLATE.
THANKS.
ざわ CHATTER
ざわ CHATTER

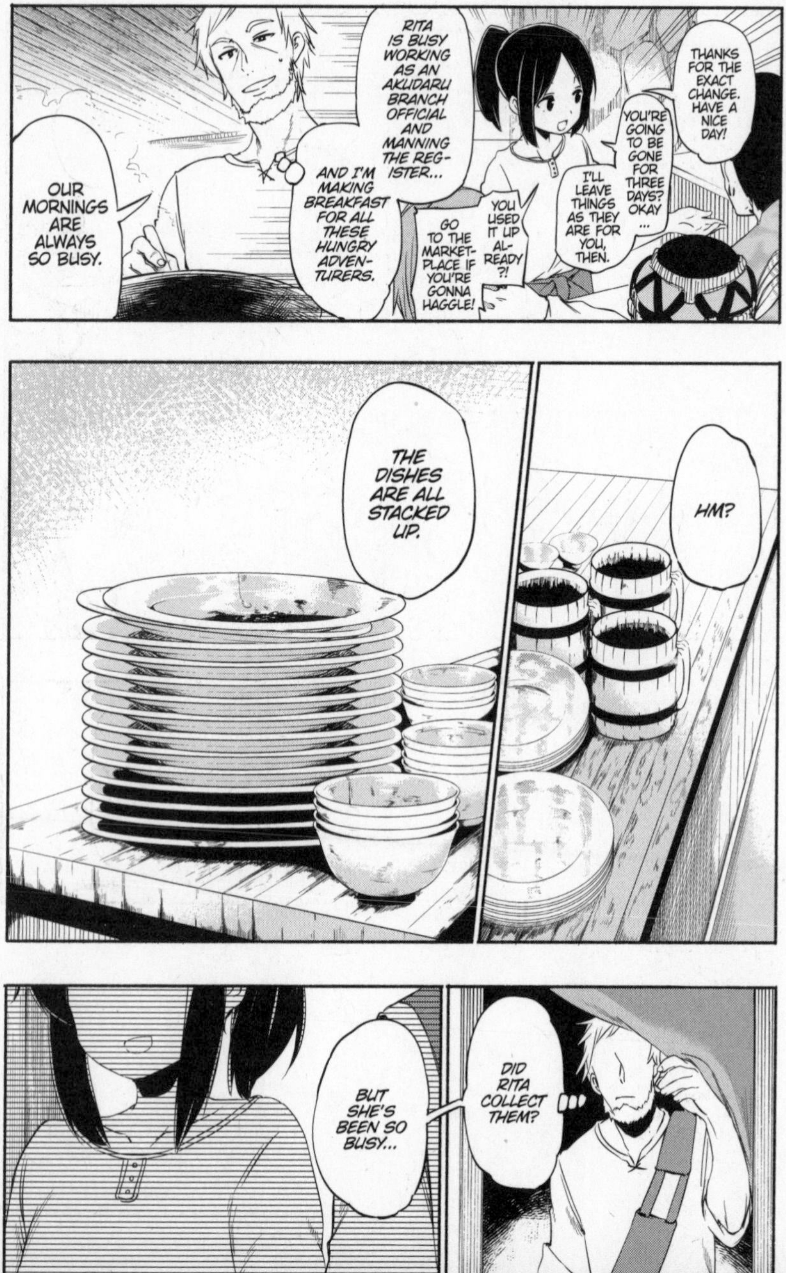
THANKS FOR THE EXACT CHANGE. HAVE A NICE DAY!
YOU'RE GOING TO BE GONE FOR THREE DAYS? OKAY ...
I'LL LEAVE THINGS AS THEY ARE FOR YOU, THEN.
YOU USED IT UP ALREADY?!
GO TO THE MARKETPLACE IF YOU'RE GONNA HAGGLE!
RITA IS BUSY WORKING AS AN AKUDARU BRANCH OFFICIAL AND MANNING THE REGISTER...
AND I'M MAKING BREAKFAST FOR ALL THESE HUNGRY ADVENTURERS.
OUR MORNINGS ARE ALWAYS SO BUSY.
HM?
THE DISHES ARE ALL STACKED UP.
DID RITA COLLECT THEM?
BUT SHE'S BEEN SO BUSY...

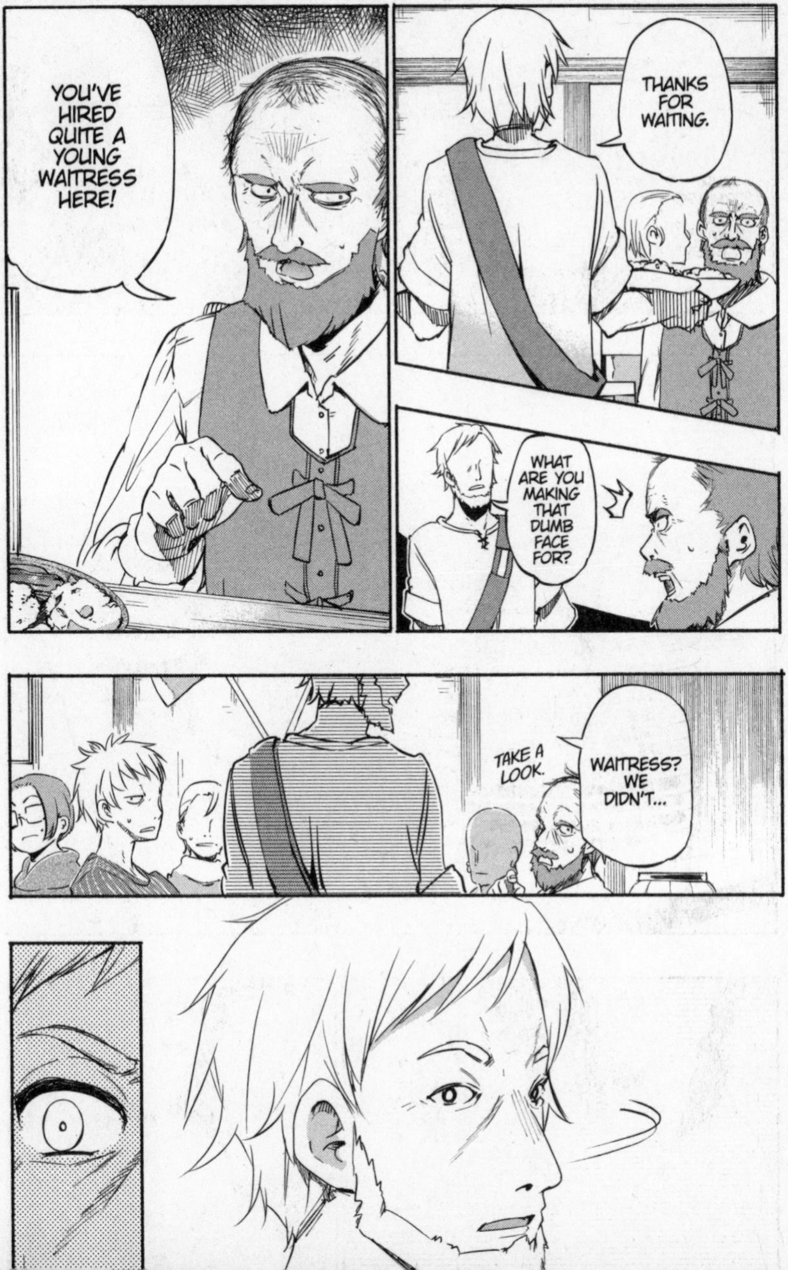
THANKS FOR WAITING.
WHAT ARE YOU MAKING THAT DUMB FACE FOR?
YOU'VE HIRED QUITE A YOUNG WAITRESS HERE!
WAITRESS? WE DIDN'T...
TAKE A LOOK.

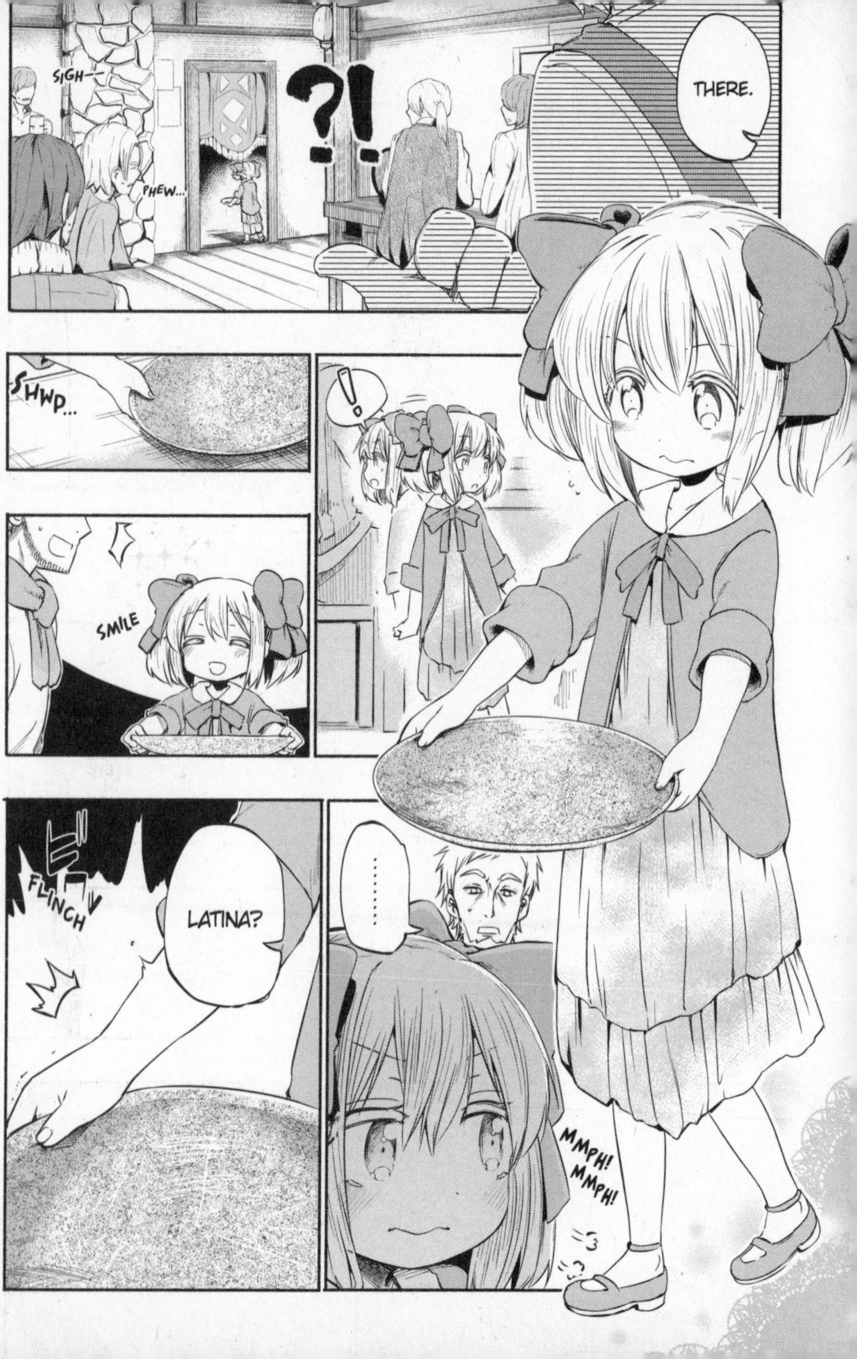
THERE.
?!
SIGH—
PHEW...
!
SHWP...
SMILE
......
MMPH! MMPH!
LATINA?
FLINCH

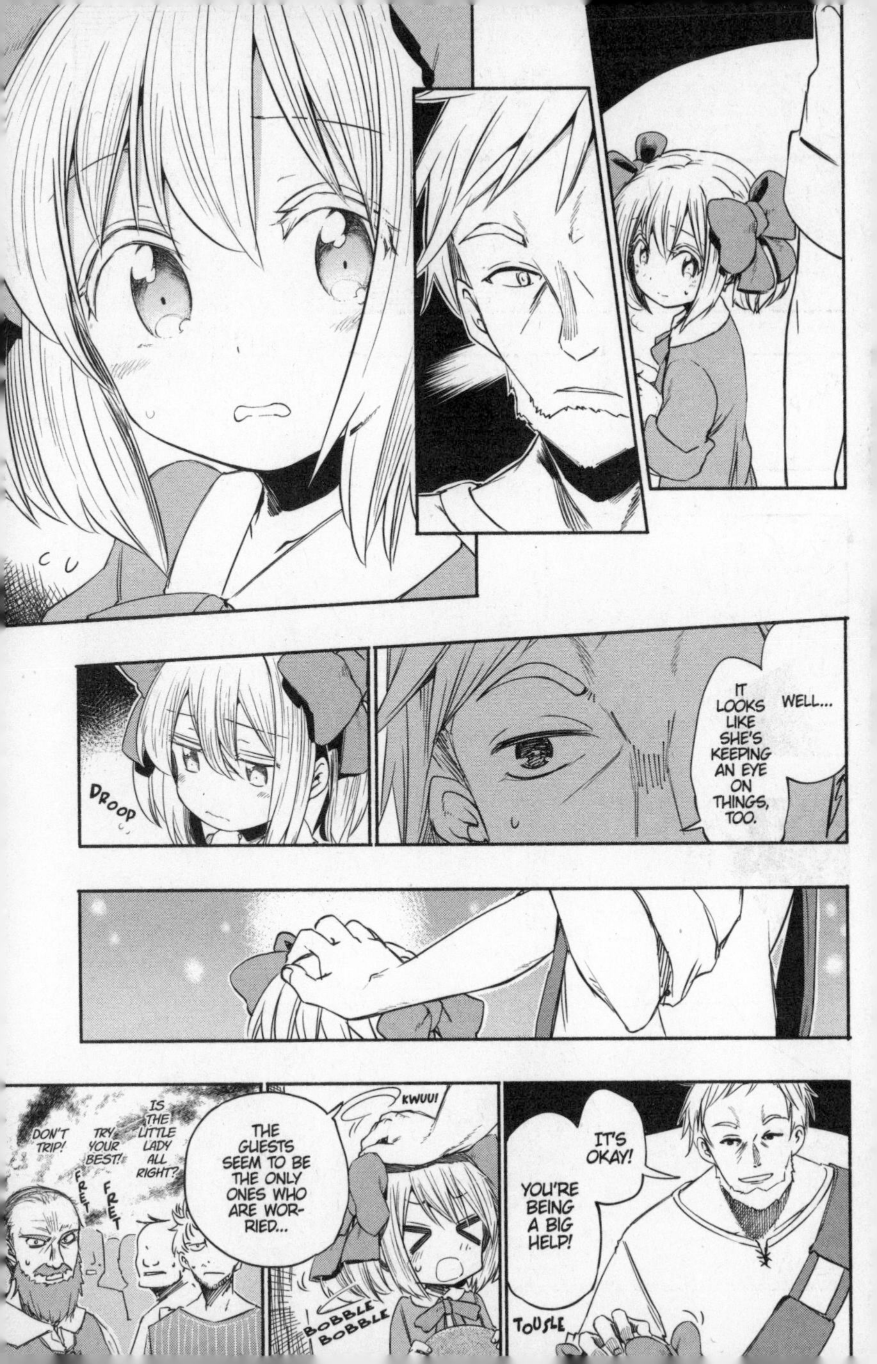
WELL...
IT LOOKS LIKE SHE'S KEEPING AN EYE ON THINGS, TOO.
DROOP
IT'S OKAY!
YOU'RE BEING A BIG HELP!
TOUSLE
KWUU!
THE GUESTS SEEM TO BE THE ONLY ONES WHO ARE WOR-RIED...
BOBBLE BOBBLE
IS THE LITTLE LADY ALL RIGHT?
TRY YOUR BEST!
DON'T TRIP!
FRET FRET

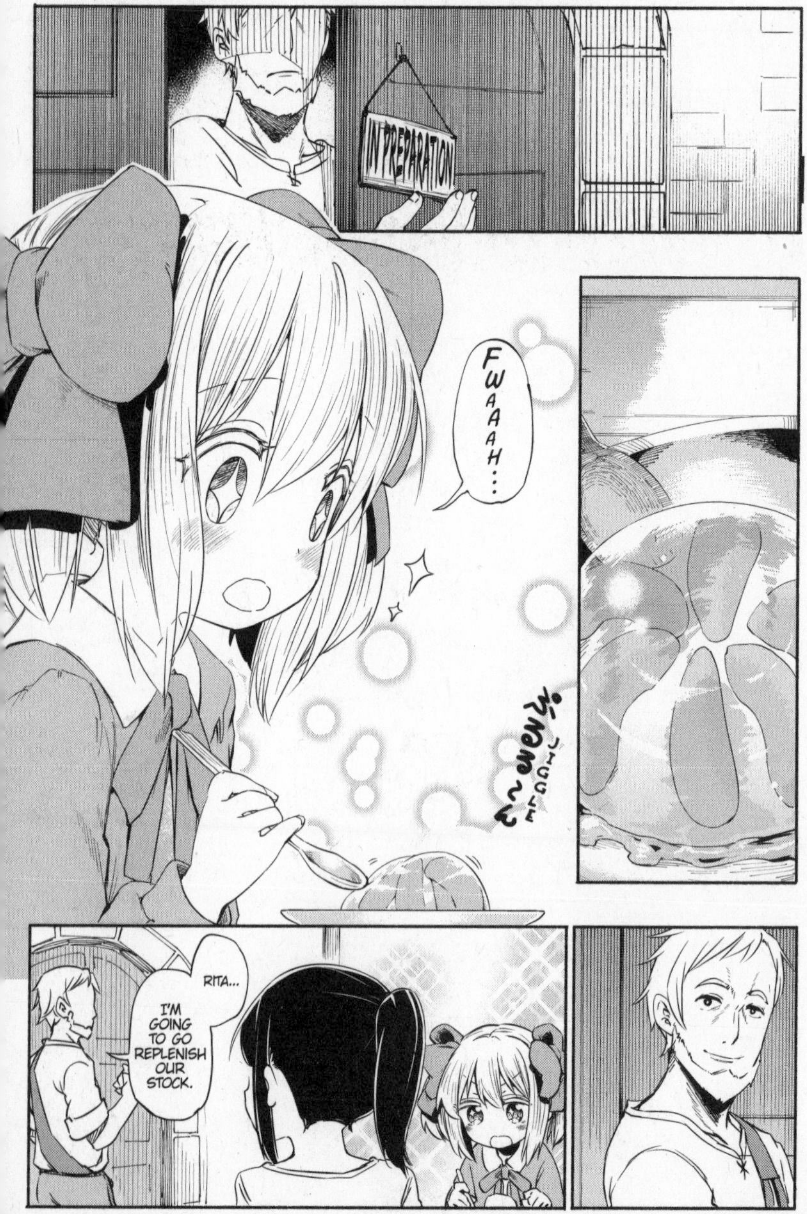
IN PREPARATION
FWAAAAH...
JIGGLE
RITA...
I'M GOING TO GO REPLENISH OUR STOCK.

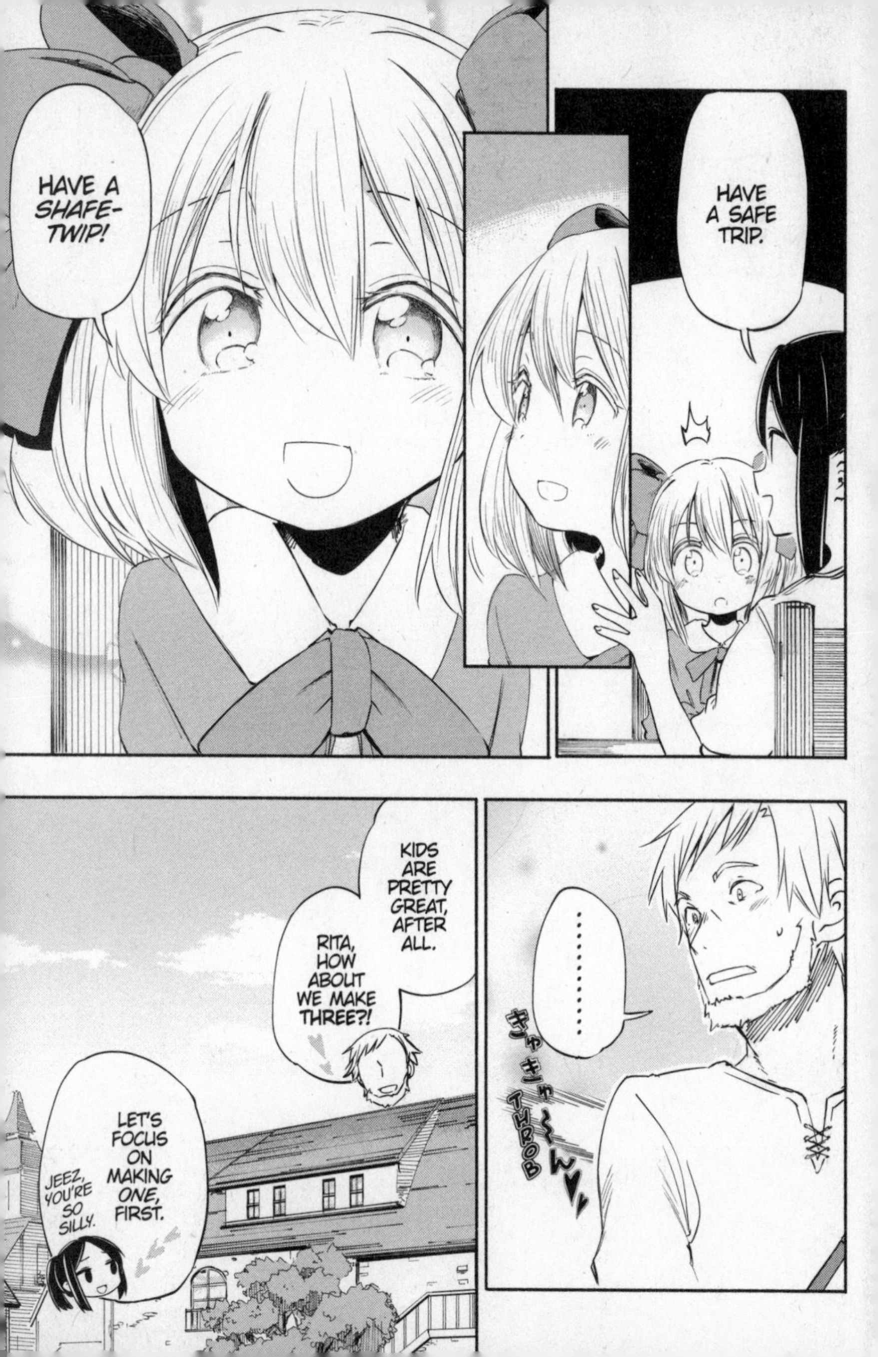
HAVE A SAFE TRIP.
HAVE A SHAFE-TWIP!
......
きゅきゅ~ん THROB
KIDS ARE PRETTY GREAT, AFTER ALL.
RITA, HOW ABOUT WE MAKE THREE?!
LET'S FOCUS ON MAKING ONE, FIRST.
JEEZ, YOU'RE SO SILLY.

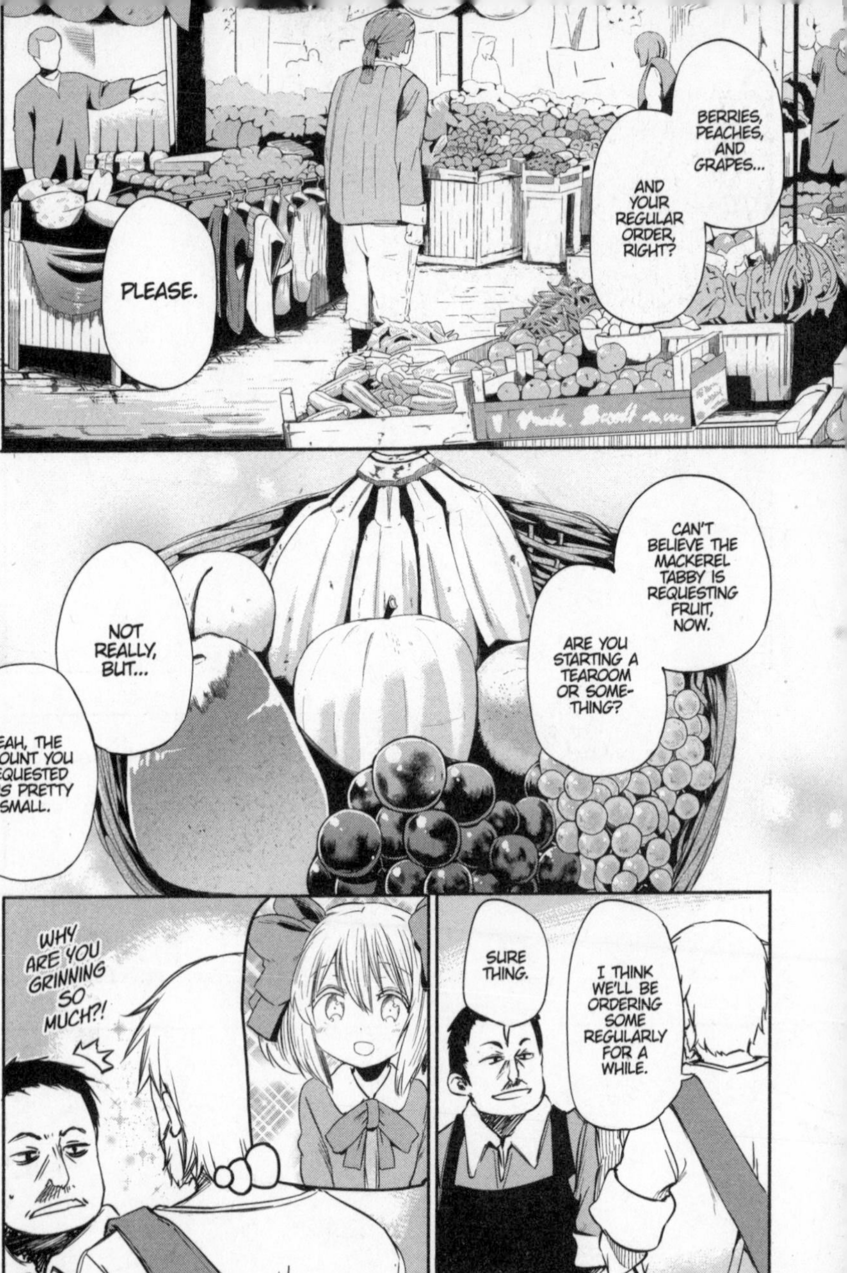
BERRIES, PEACHES, AND GRAPES...
AND YOUR REGULAR ORDER, RIGHT?
PLEASE.
CAN'T BELIEVE THE MACKEREL TABBY IS REQUESTING FRUIT, NOW.
ARE YOU STARTING A TEAROOM OR SOME-THING?
NOT REALLY, BUT...
YEAH, THE AMOUNT YOU REQUESTED WAS PRETTY SMALL.
I THINK WE'LL BE ORDERING SOME REGULARLY FOR A WHILE.
SURE THING.
WHY ARE YOU GRINNING SO MUCH?!

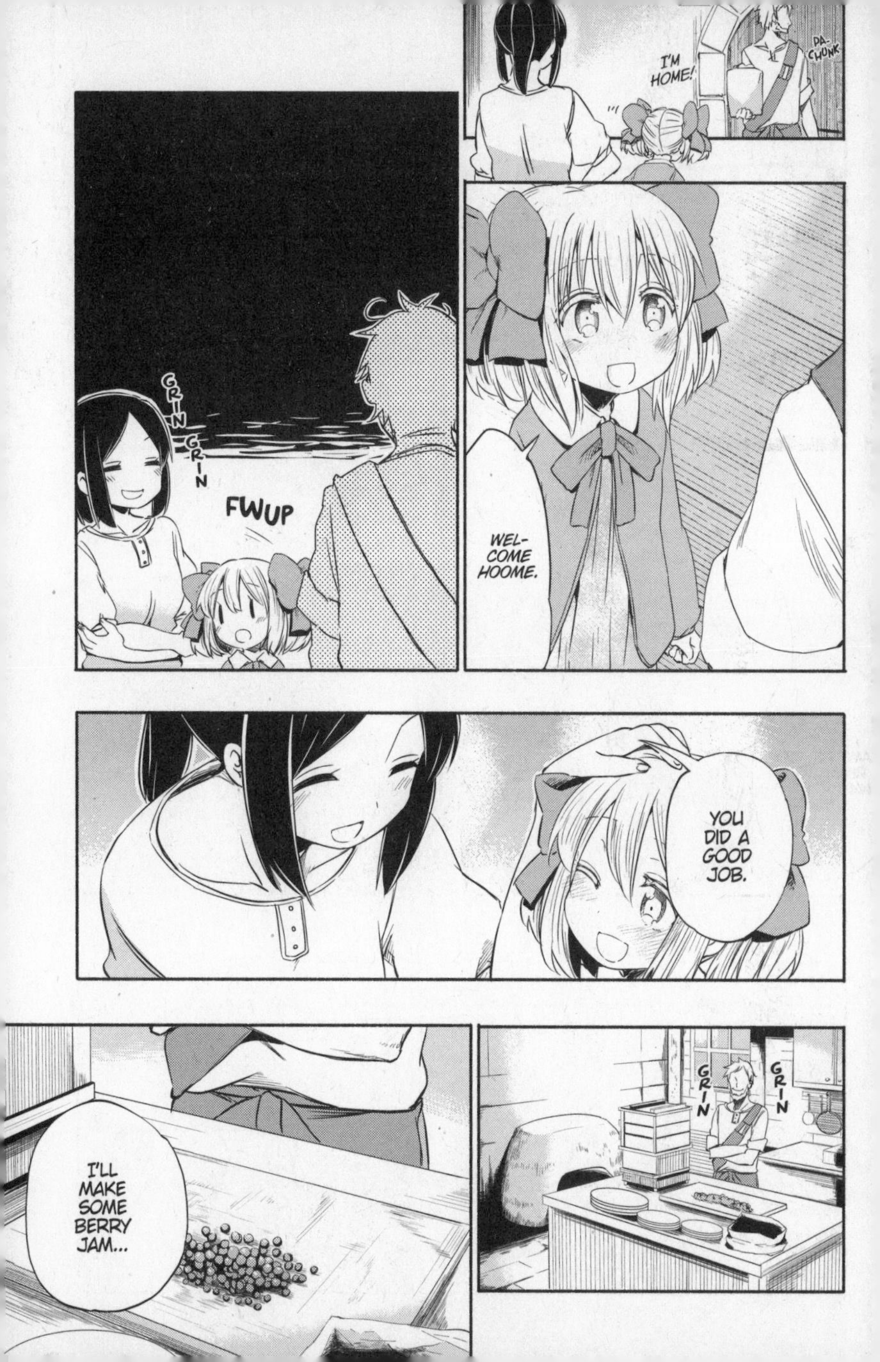
DA-CHUNK
I'M HOME!
WEL-COME HOOME.
GRIN GRIN
FWUP
YOU DID A GOOD JOB.
GRIN GRIN
I'LL MAKE SOME BERRY JAM...

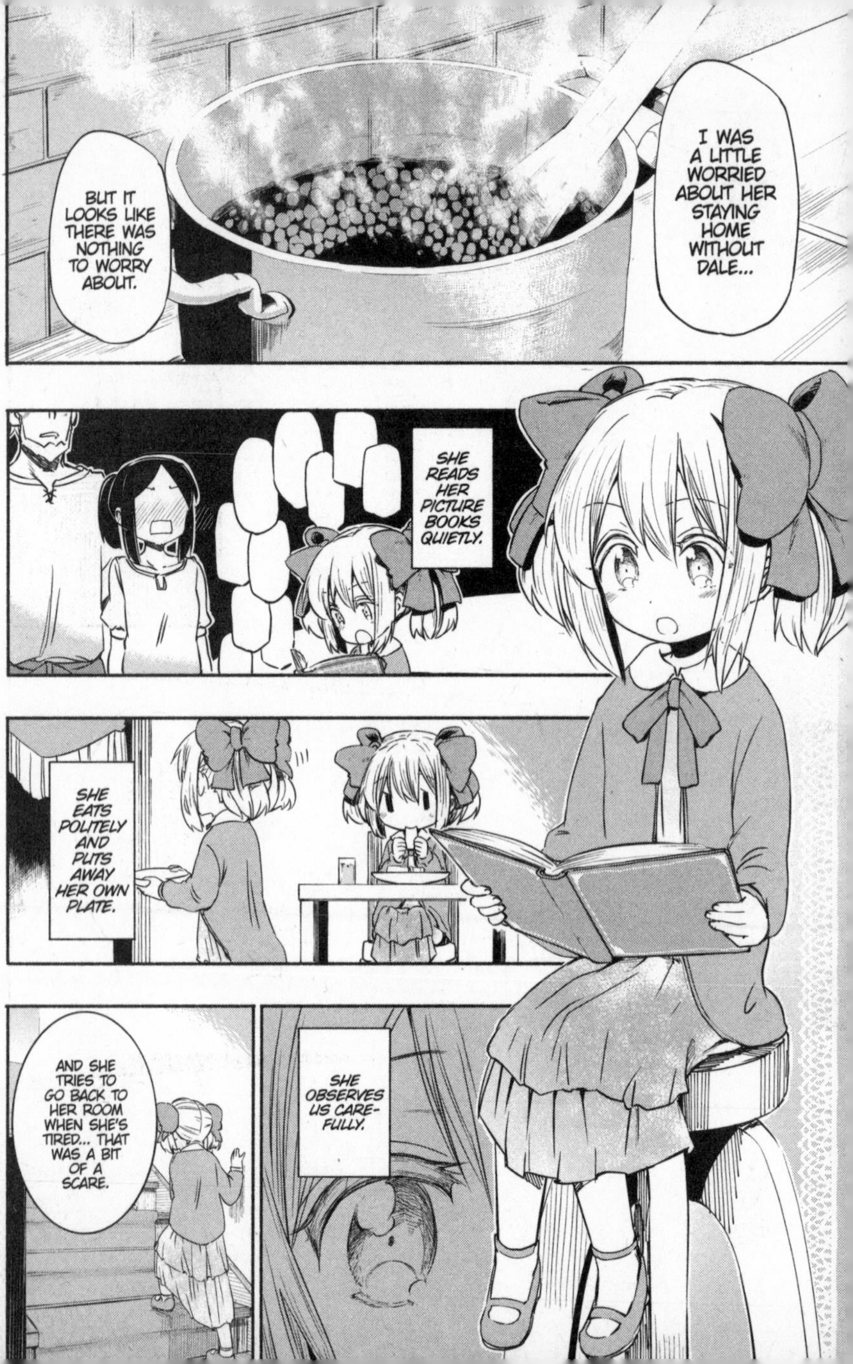
I WAS A LITTLE WORRIED ABOUT HER STAYING HOME WITHOUT DALE...
BUT IT LOOKS LIKE THERE WAS NOTHING TO WORRY ABOUT.
SHE READS HER PICTURE BOOKS QUIETLY.
SHE EATS POLITELY AND PUTS AWAY HER OWN PLATE.
SHE OBSERVES US CARE-FULLY.
AND SHE TRIES TO GO BACK TO HER ROOM WHEN SHE'S TIRED... THAT WAS A BIT OF A SCARE.

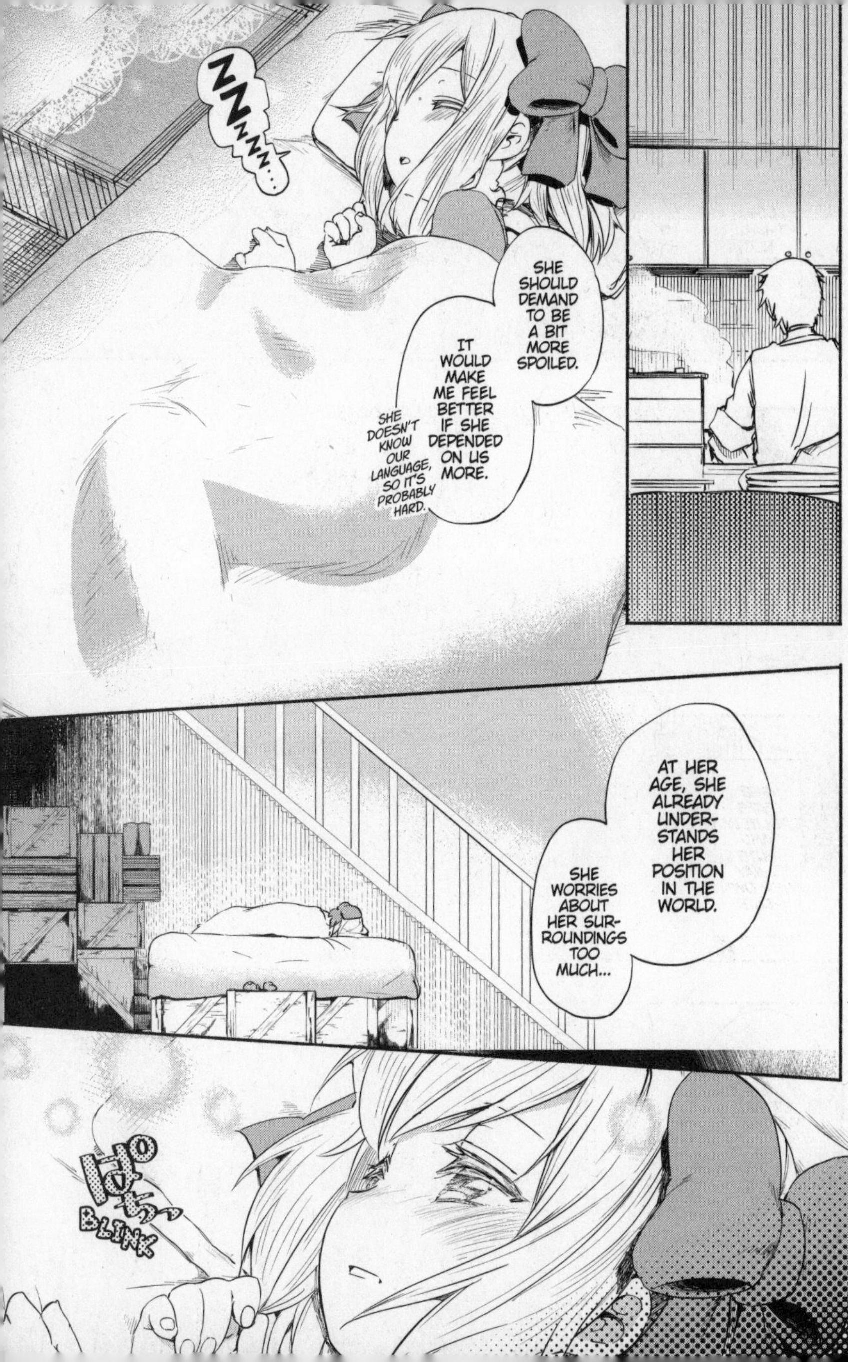
ZZZZZ...
SHE SHOULD DEMAND TO BE A BIT MORE SPOILED.
IT WOULD MAKE ME FEEL BETTER IF SHE DEPENDED ON US MORE.
SHE DOESN'T KNOW OUR LANGUAGE, SO IT'S PROBABLY HARD.
AT HER AGE, SHE ALREADY UNDER-STANDS HER POSITION IN THE WORLD.
SHE WORRIES ABOUT HER SUR-ROUNDINGS TOO MUCH...
BLINK

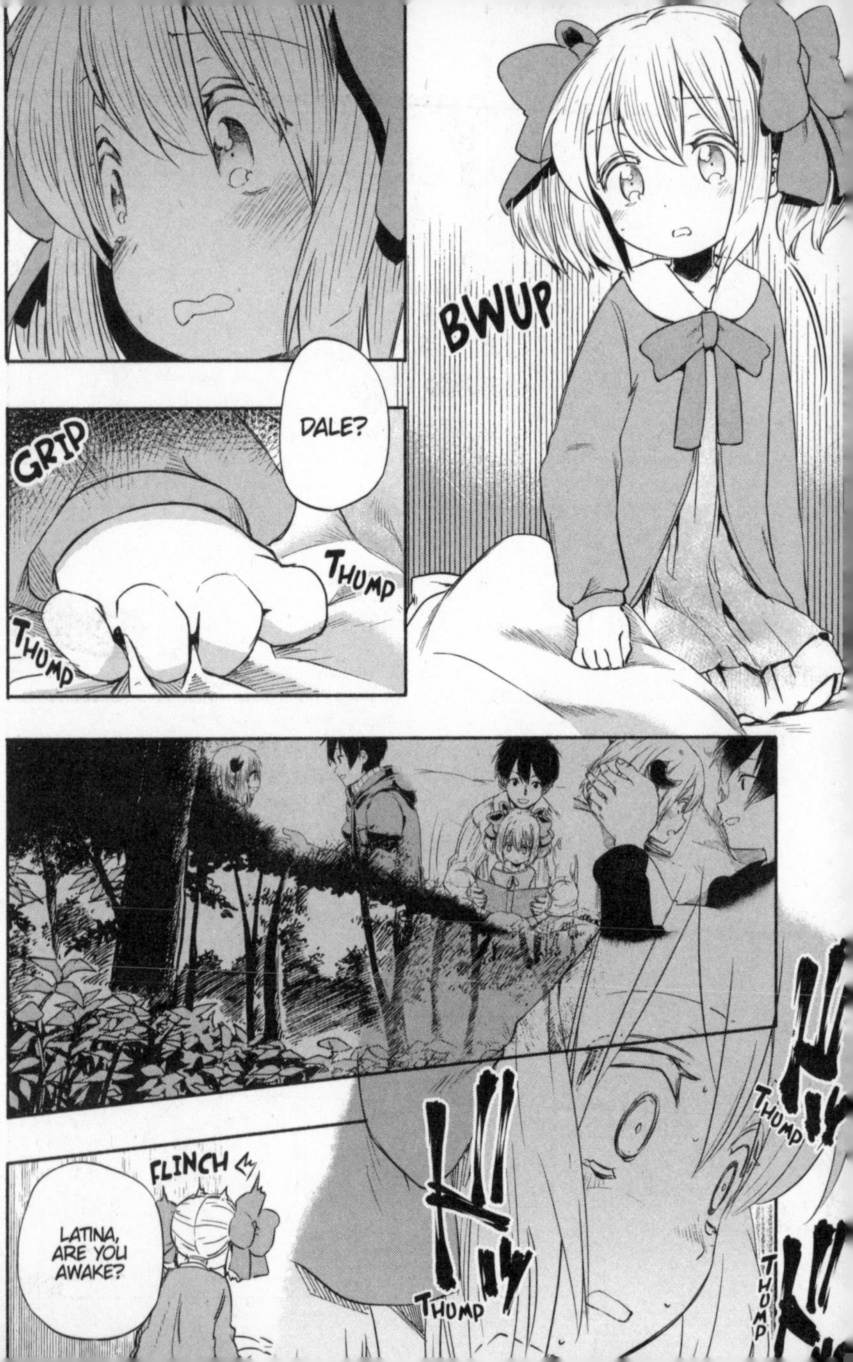
BWUP
DALE?
GRIP
THUMP
THUMP
THUMP
THUMP
THUMP
FLINCH
LATINA, ARE YOU AWAKE?

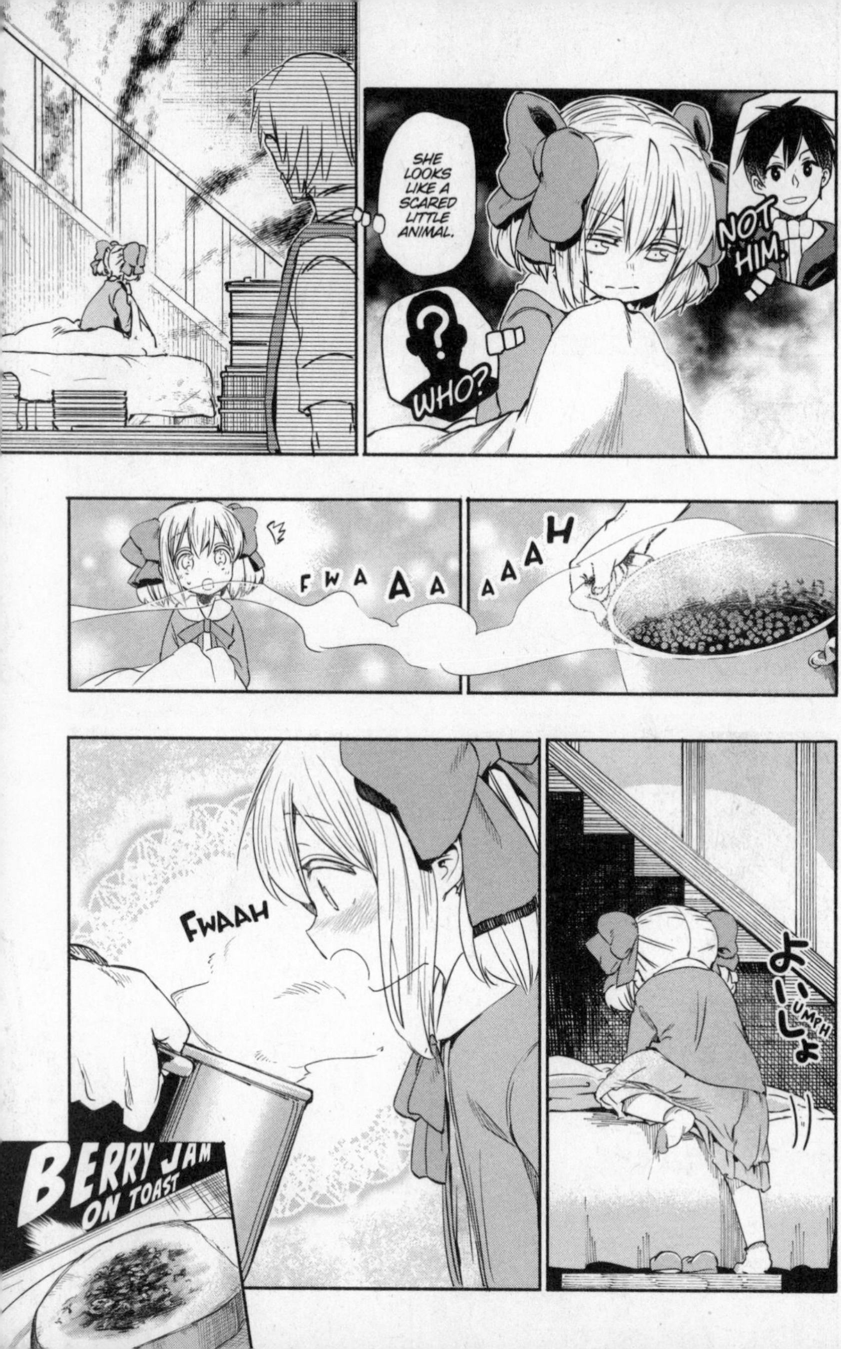
NOT HIM.
SHE LOOKS LIKE A SCARED LITTLE ANIMAL.
WHO?
FWA A A AAAH
よいしょ
UMPH
FWAAH
BERRY JAM ON TOAST

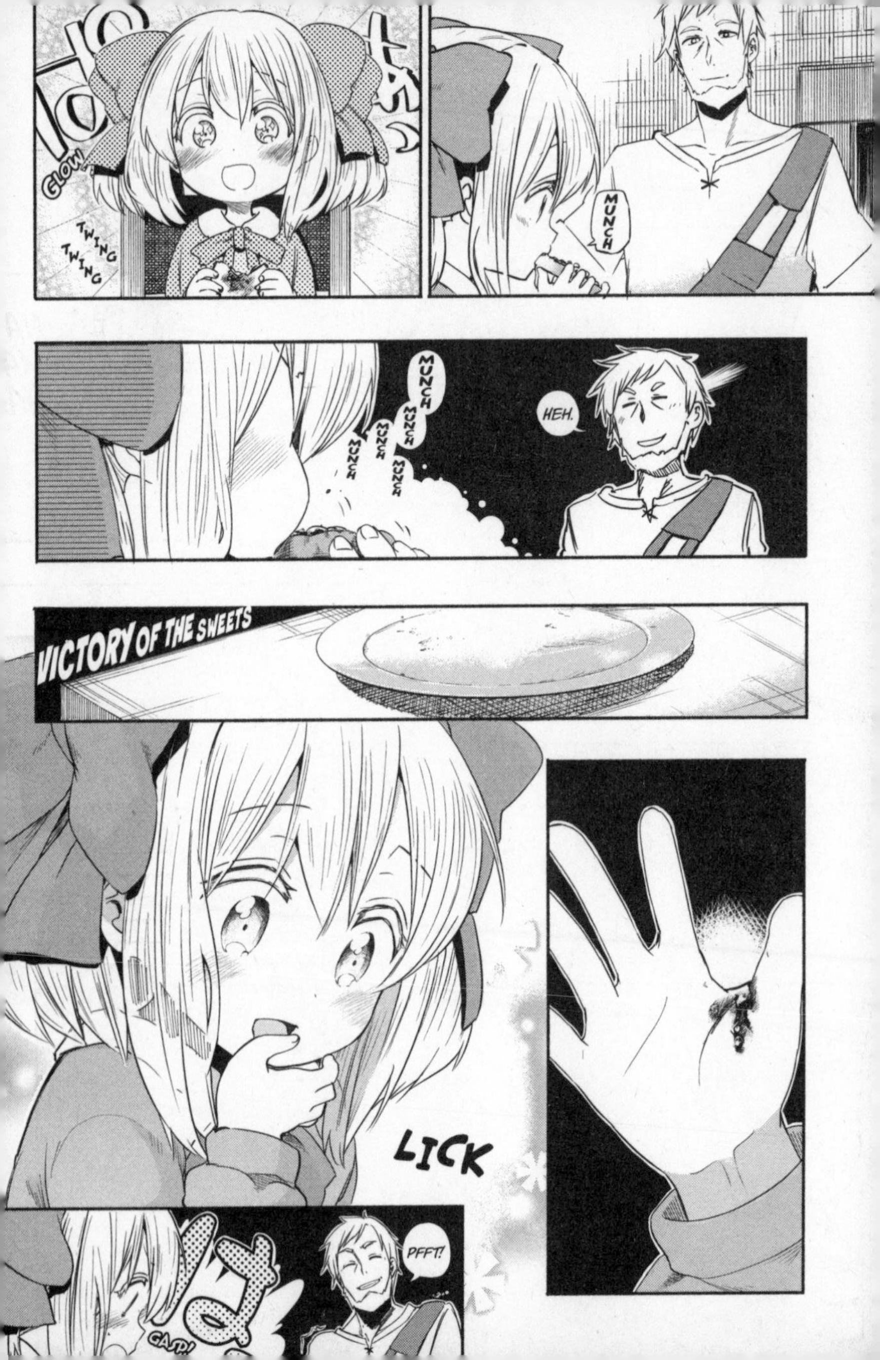
MUNCH
GLOW
TWING TWING
HEH.
MUNCH MUNCH MUNCH MUNCH MUNCH
VICTORY OF THE SWEETS
LICK
PFFT!
GASP!

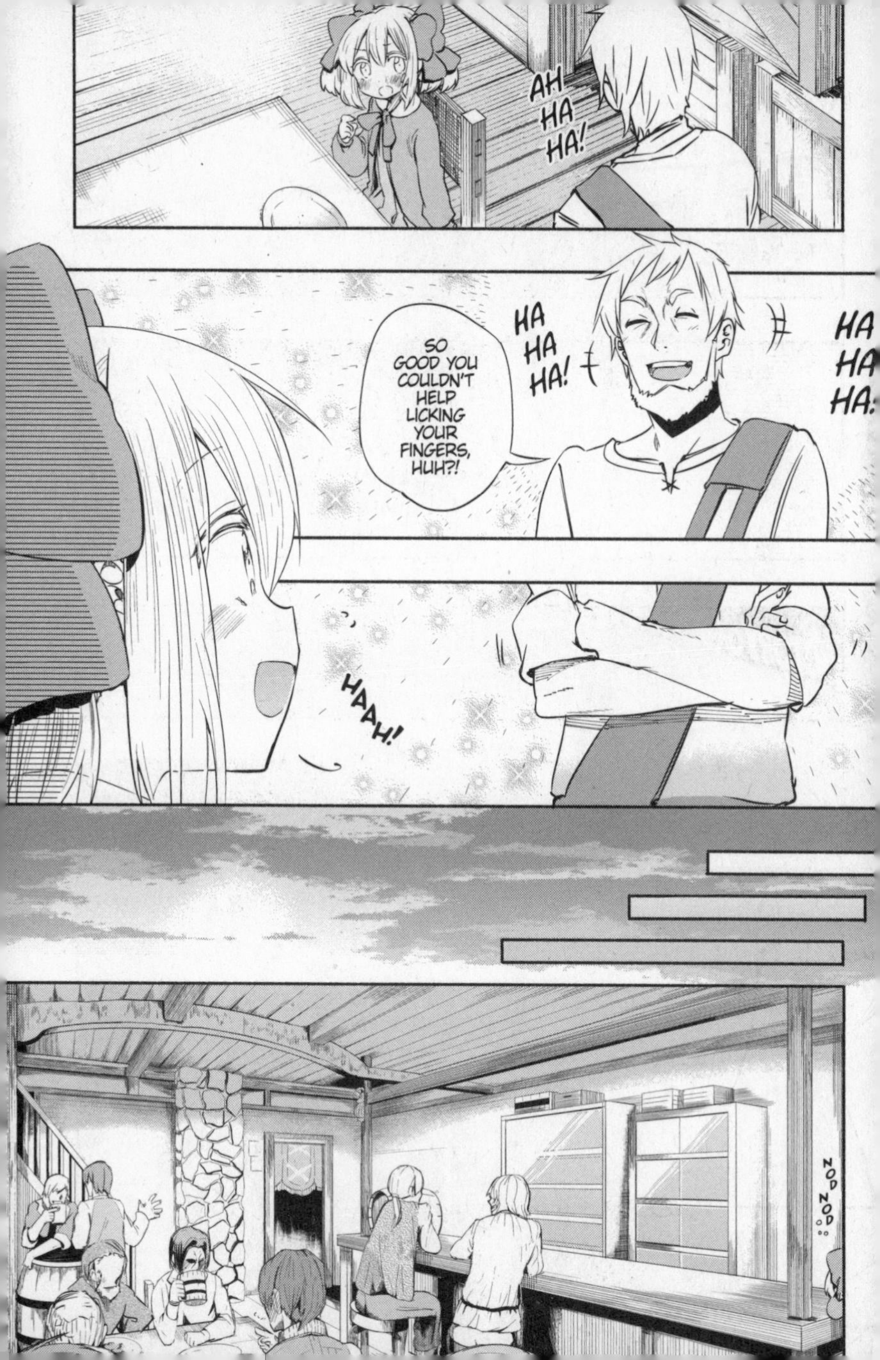
AH HA HA!
HA HA HA
HA HA HA!
SO GOOD YOU COULDN'T HELP LICKING YOUR FINGERS, HUH?!
HAAAH!
NOD NOD..

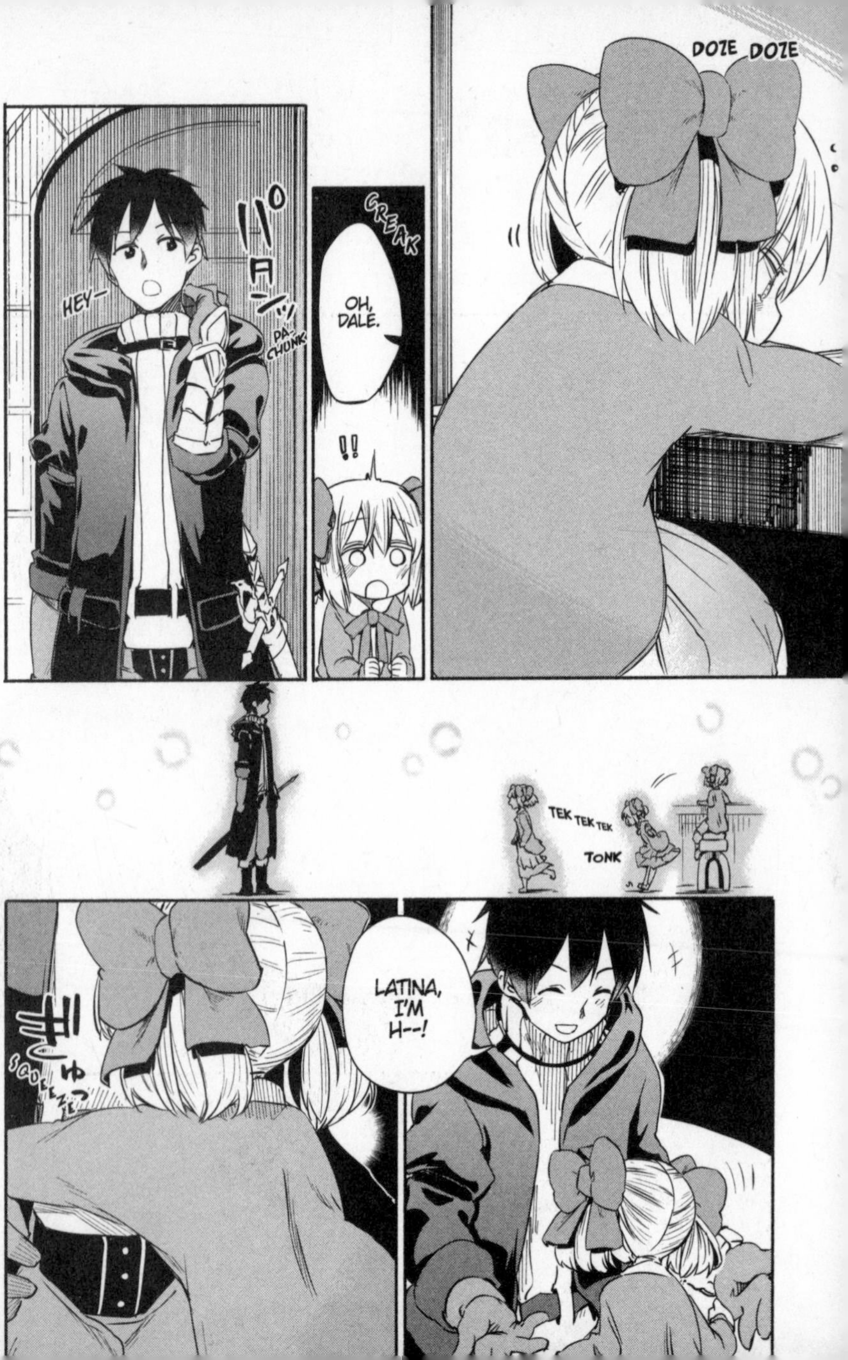
DOZE DOZE
CREAK
OH, DALE.
!!
HEY—
PA-CHUNK
TEK TEK TEK
TONK
LATINA, I'M H--!
SQUEEZE

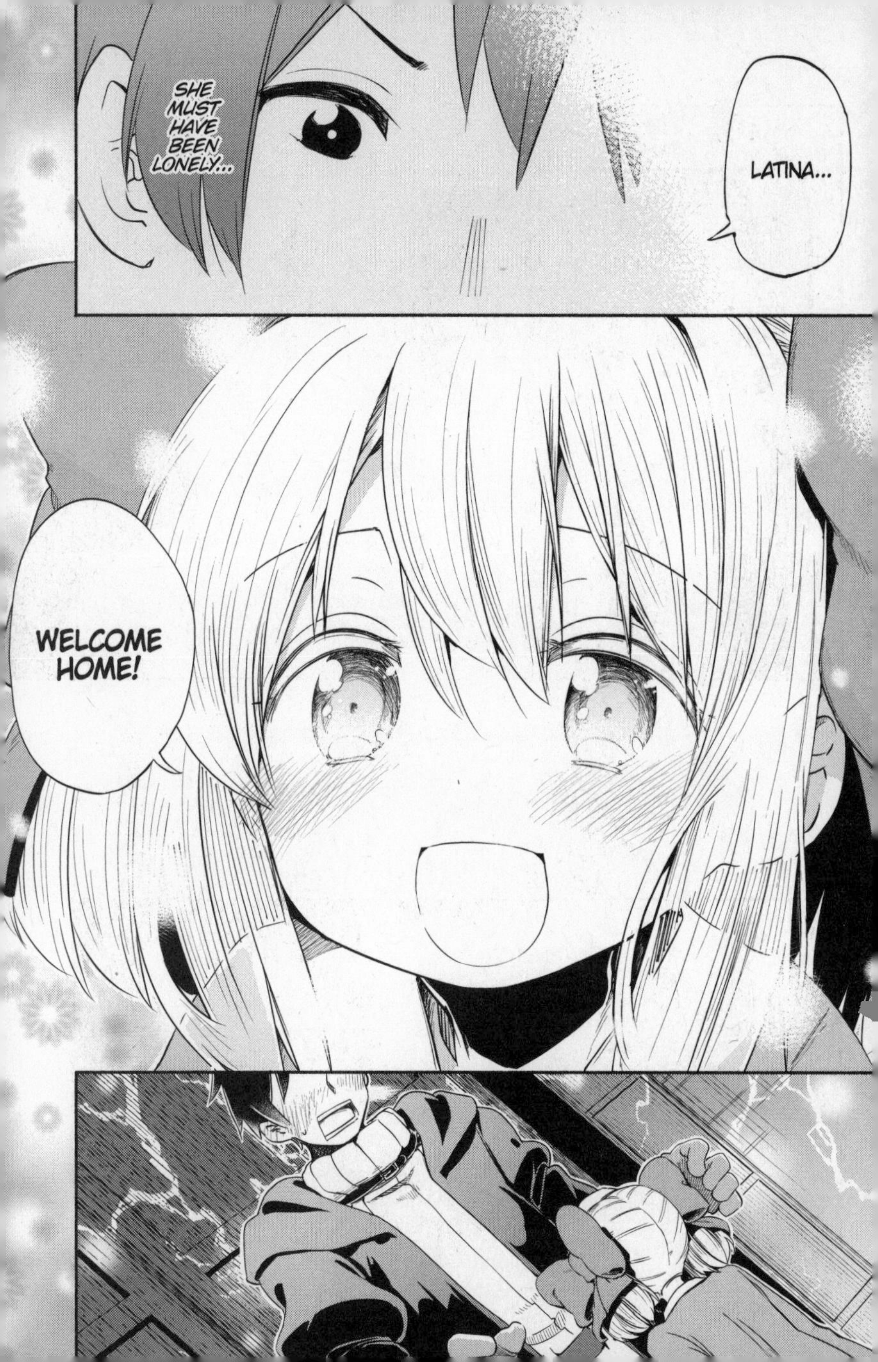
LATINA...
SHE MUST HAVE BEEN LONELY...
WELCOME HOME!

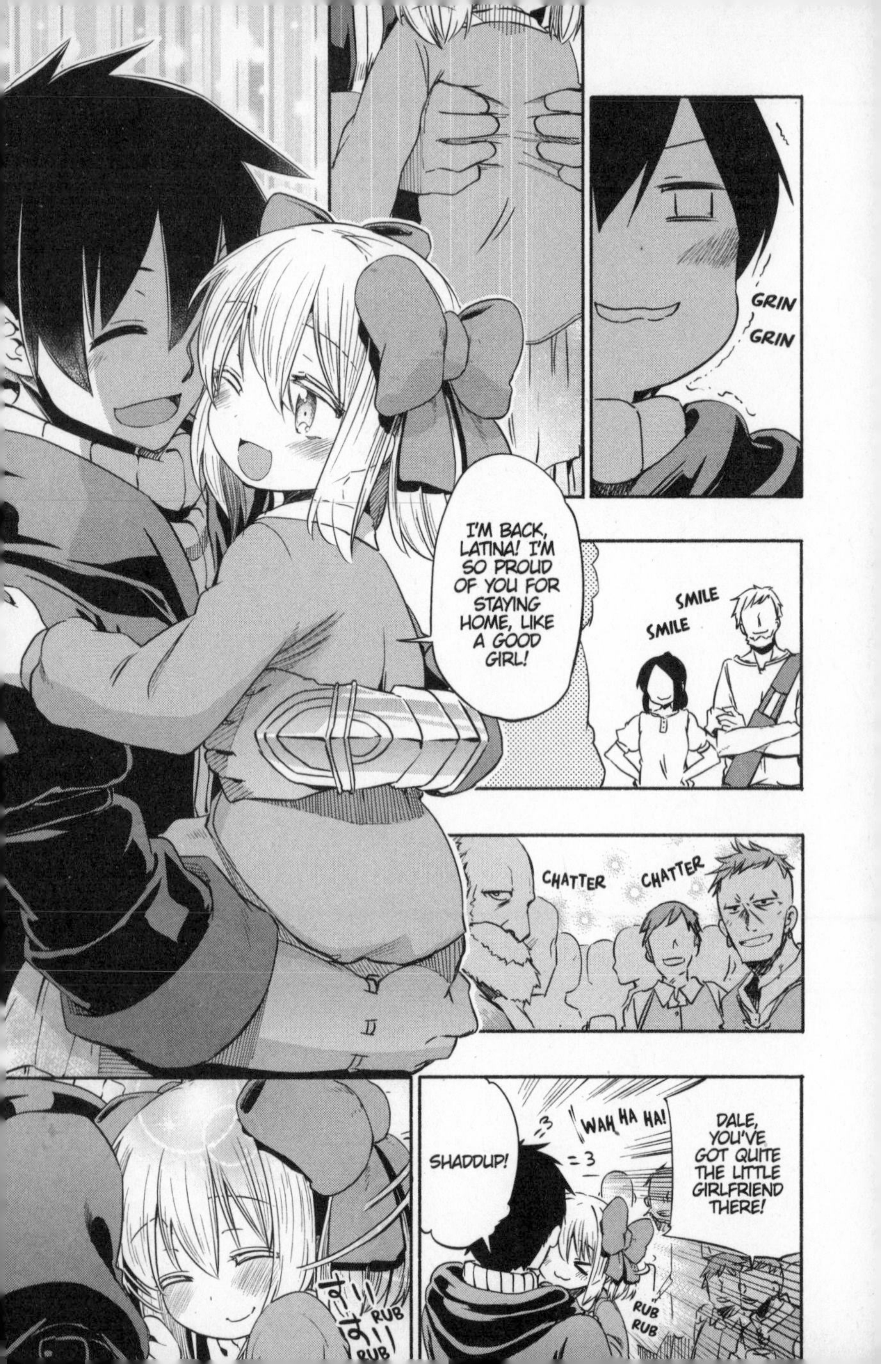
GRIN
GRIN
SMILE
SMILE
CHATTER
CHATTER
I'M BACK, LATINA! I'M SO PROUD OF YOU FOR STAYING HOME, LIKE A GOOD GIRL!
DALE, YOU'VE GOT QUITE THE LITTLE GIRLFRIEND THERE!
WAH HA HA!
SHADDUP!
RUB RUB
RUB RUB

IF It's
For My
Daughter
I'd Even Defeat
a Demon
Lord

4. Little Girl Helps

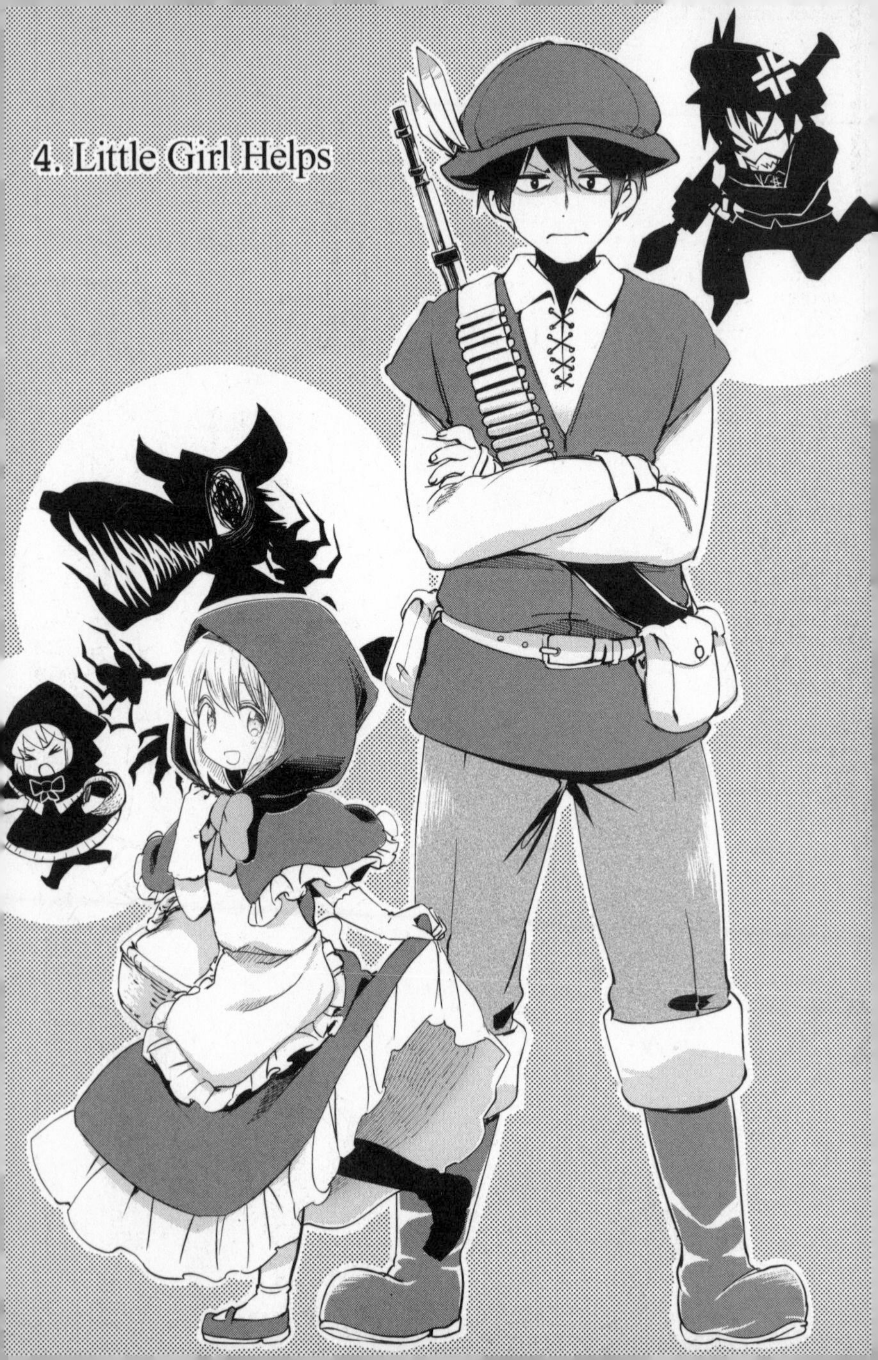

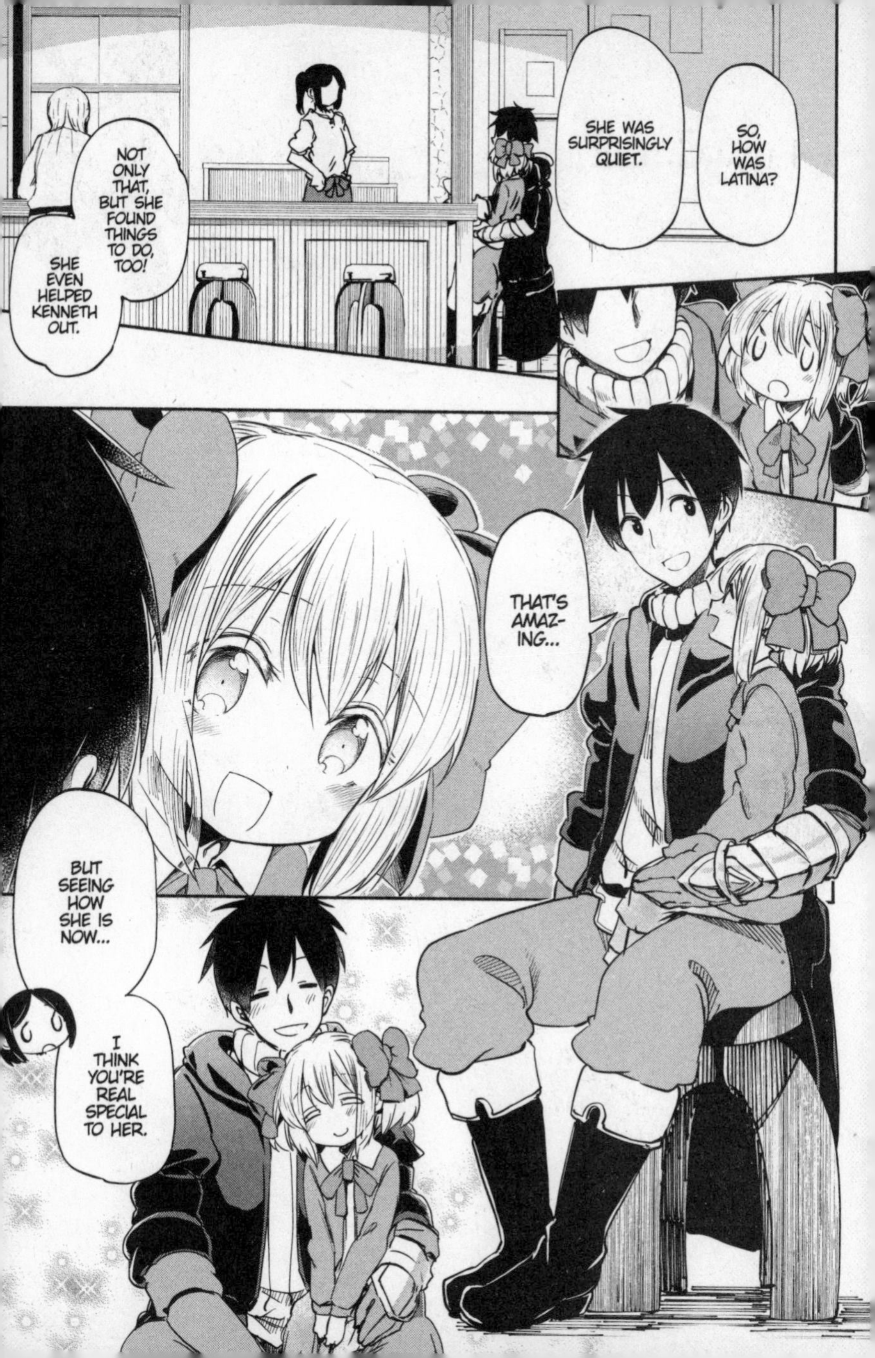
SO, HOW WAS LATINA?
SHE WAS SURPRISINGLY QUIET.
NOT ONLY THAT, BUT SHE FOUND THINGS TO DO, TOO!
SHE EVEN HELPED KENNETH OUT.
THAT'S AMAZ-ING...
BUT SEEING HOW SHE IS NOW...
I THINK YOU'RE REAL SPECIAL TO HER.

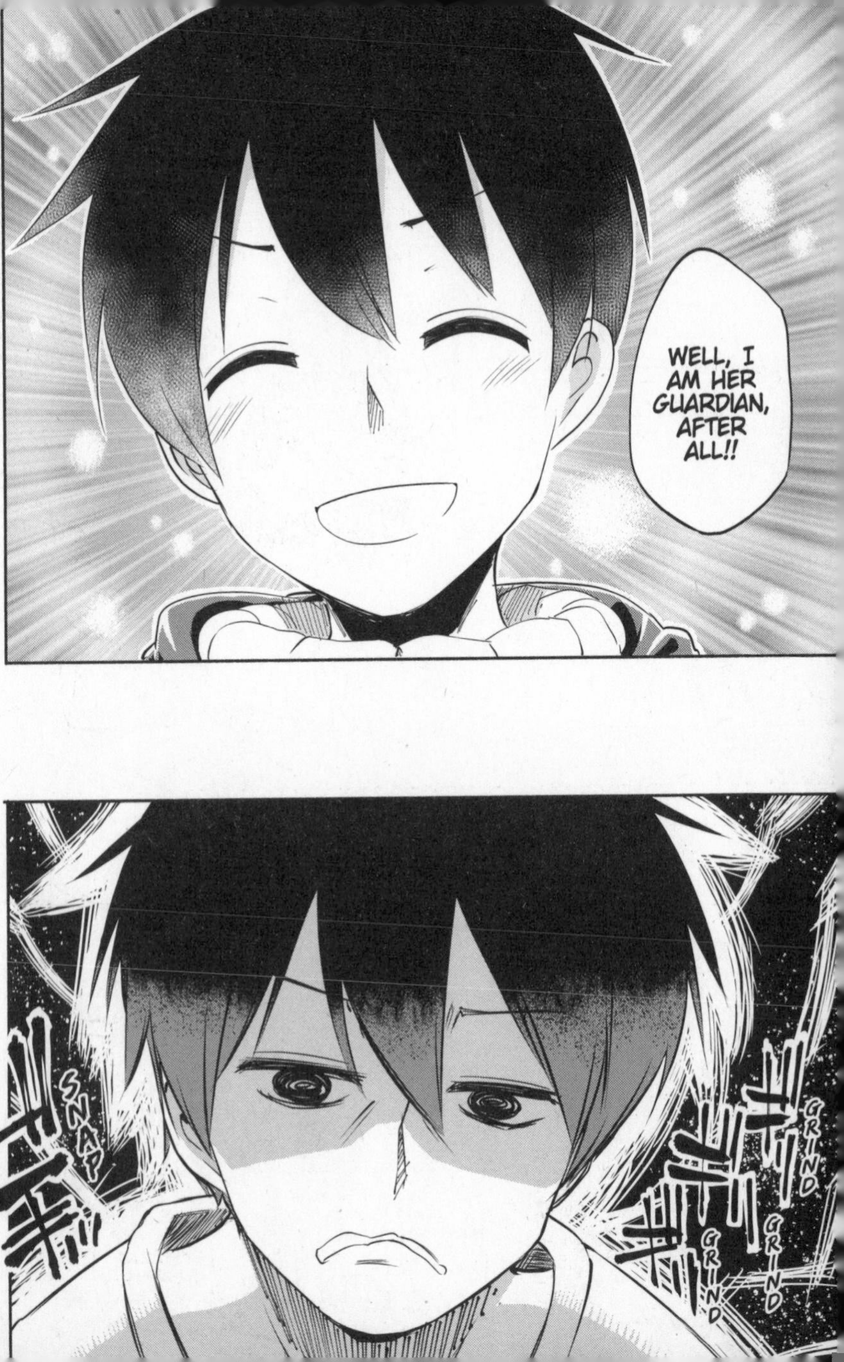
WELL, I AM HER GUARDIAN, AFTER ALL!!
GRIND
GRIND
GRIND
SNAP

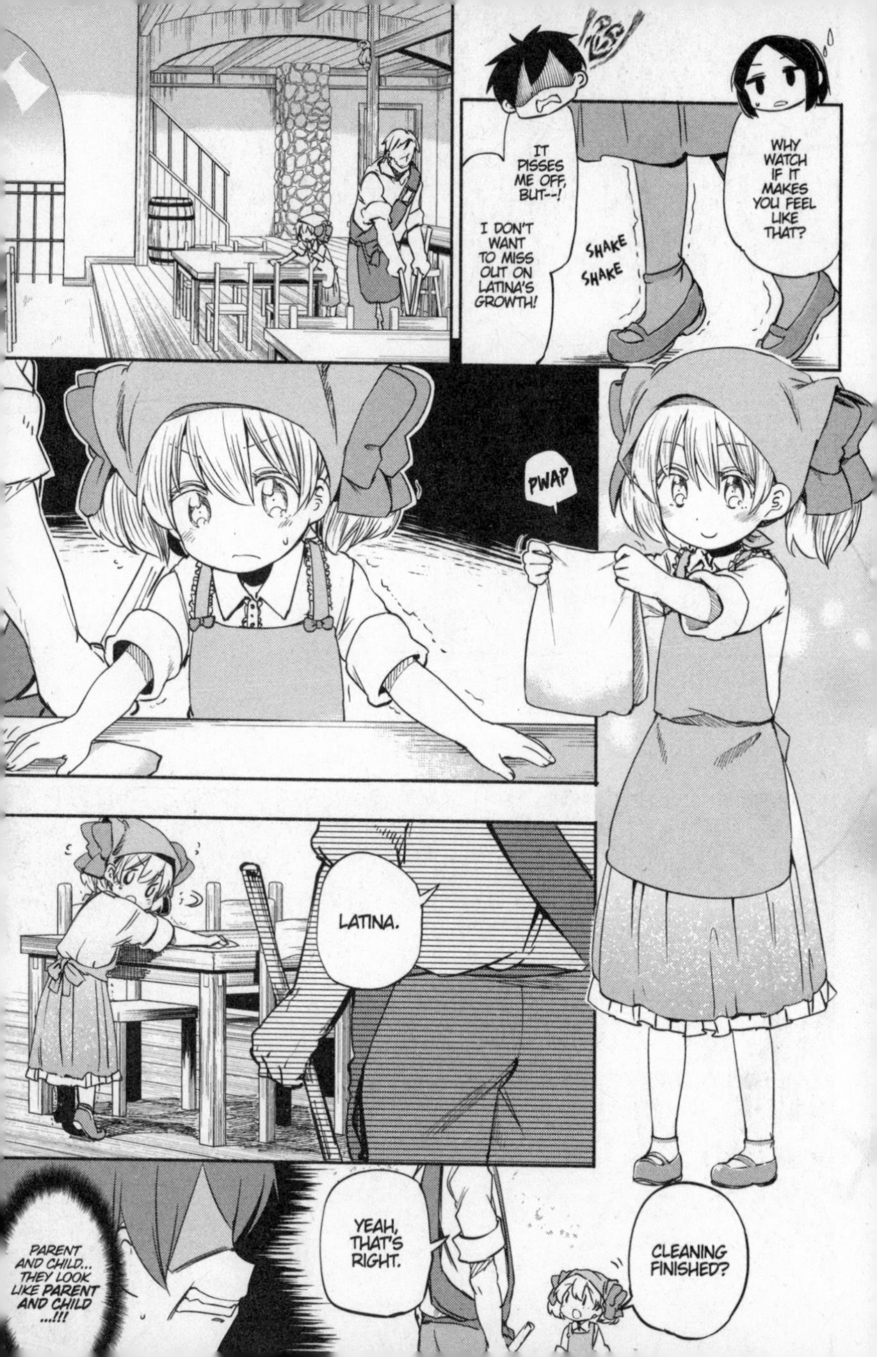
WHY WATCH IF IT MAKES YOU FEEL LIKE THAT?
IT PISSES ME OFF, BUT--!
I DON'T WANT TO MISS OUT ON LATINA'S GROWTH!
SHAKE SHAKE
PWAP
LATINA.
CLEANING FINISHED?
YEAH, THAT'S RIGHT.
PARENT AND CHILD... THEY LOOK LIKE PARENT AND CHILD ...!!!

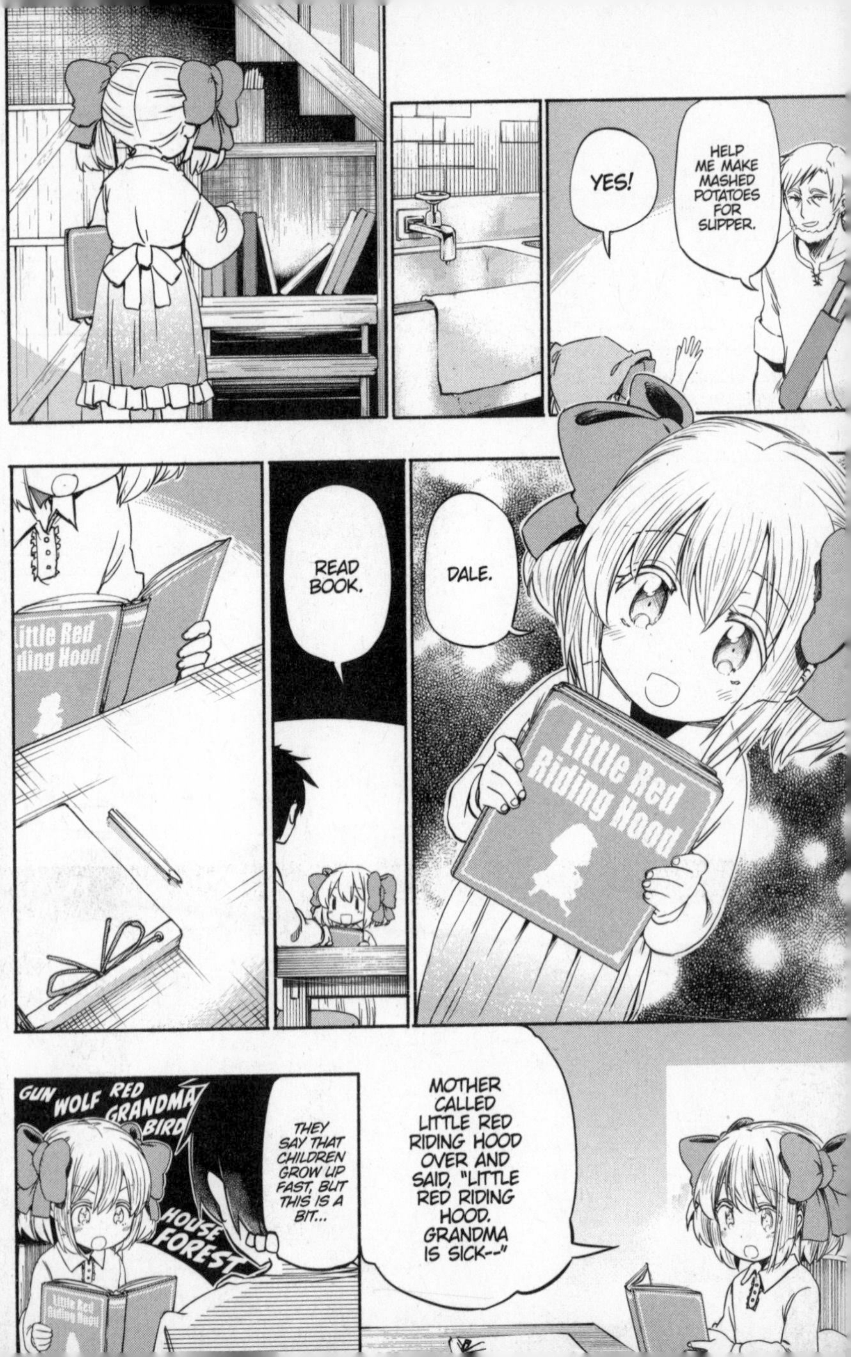
HELP ME MAKE MASHED POTATOES FOR SUPPER.
YES!
DALE.
Little Red Riding Hood
READ BOOK.
Little Red Riding Hood
MOTHER CALLED LITTLE RED RIDING HOOD OVER AND SAID, "LITTLE RED RIDING HOOD. GRANDMA IS SICK--"
GUN WOLF RED GRANDMA BIRD
HOUSE FOREST
THEY SAY THAT CHILDREN GROW UP FAST, BUT THIS IS A BIT...
Little Red Riding Hood

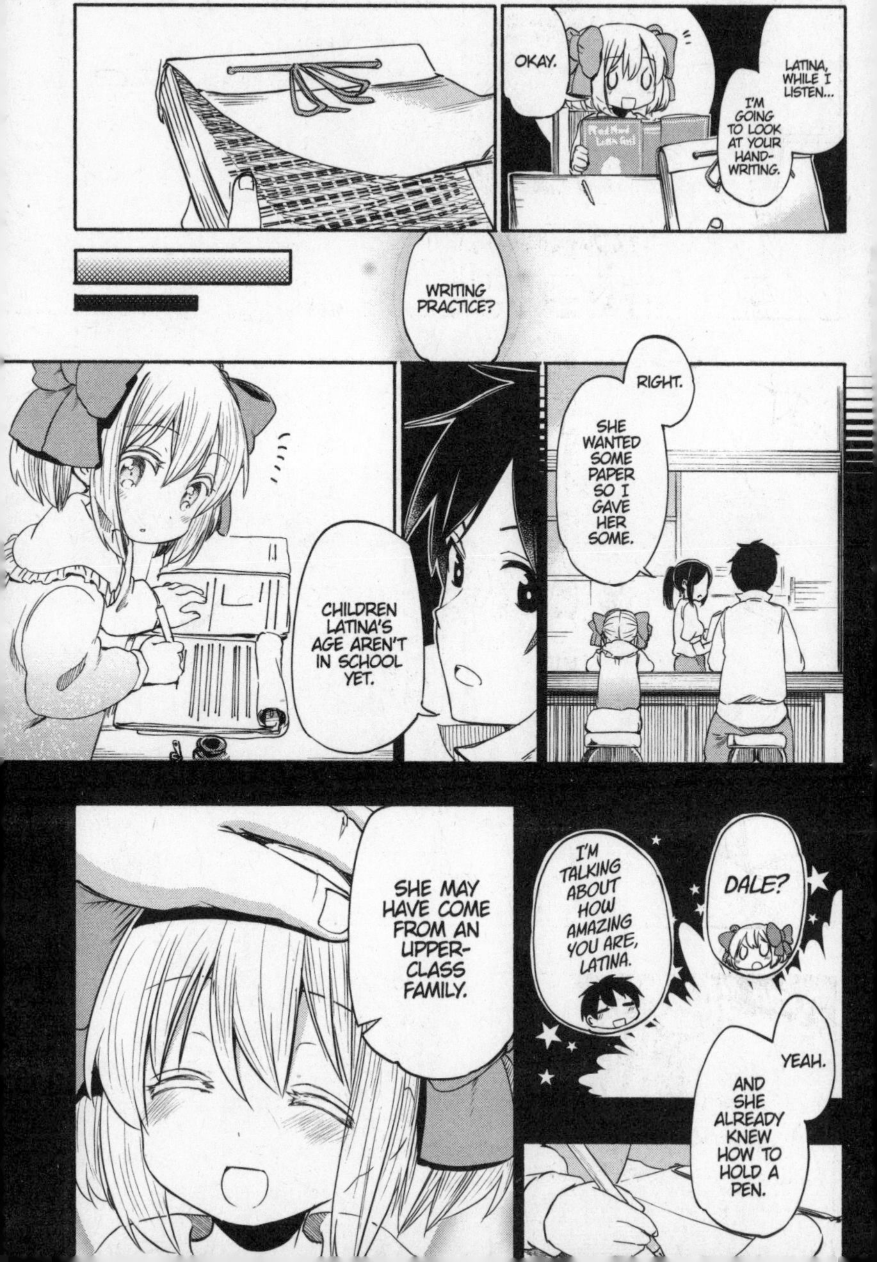
LATINA, WHILE I LISTEN...
I'M GOING TO LOOK AT YOUR HANDWRITING.
OKAY.
WRITING PRACTICE?
RIGHT.
SHE WANTED SOME PAPER SO I GAVE HER SOME.
CHILDREN LATINA'S AGE AREN'T IN SCHOOL YET.
DALE?
I'M TALKING ABOUT HOW AMAZING YOU ARE, LATINA.
YEAH.
AND SHE ALREADY KNEW HOW TO HOLD A PEN.
SHE MAY HAVE COME FROM AN UPPER-CLASS FAMILY.

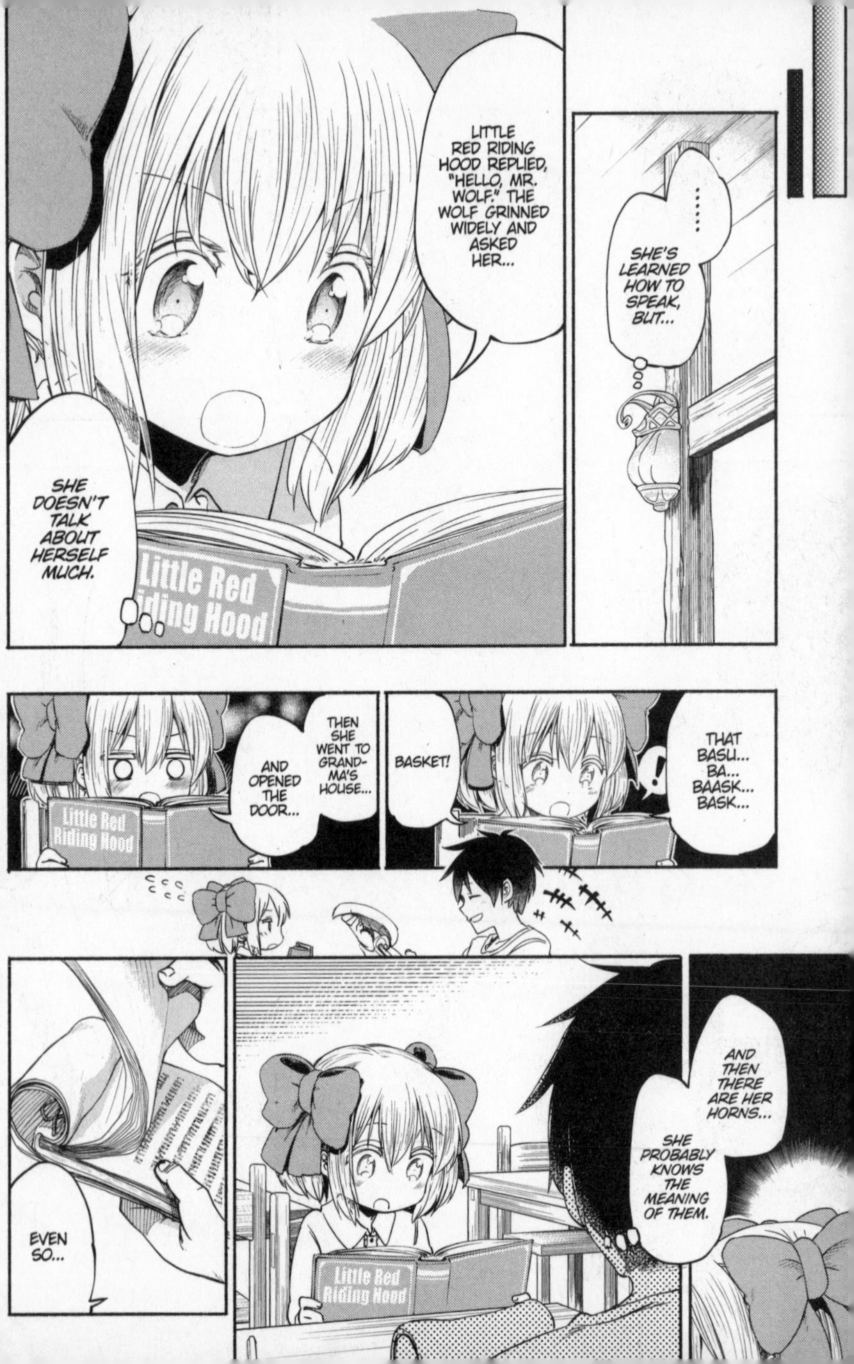

......
SHE'S LEARNED HOW TO SPEAK, BUT...
LITTLE RED RIDING HOOD REPLIED, "HELLO, MR. WOLF." THE WOLF GRINNED WIDELY AND ASKED HER...
Little Red Riding Hood
SHE DOESN'T TALK ABOUT HERSELF MUCH.
THAT BASU... BA... BAASK... BASK...
!
BASKET!
THEN SHE WENT TO GRAND-MA'S HOUSE...
AND OPENED THE DOOR...
Little Red Riding Hood
AND THEN THERE ARE HER HORNS...
SHE PROBABLY KNOWS THE MEANING OF THEM.
Little Red Riding Hood
EVEN SO...

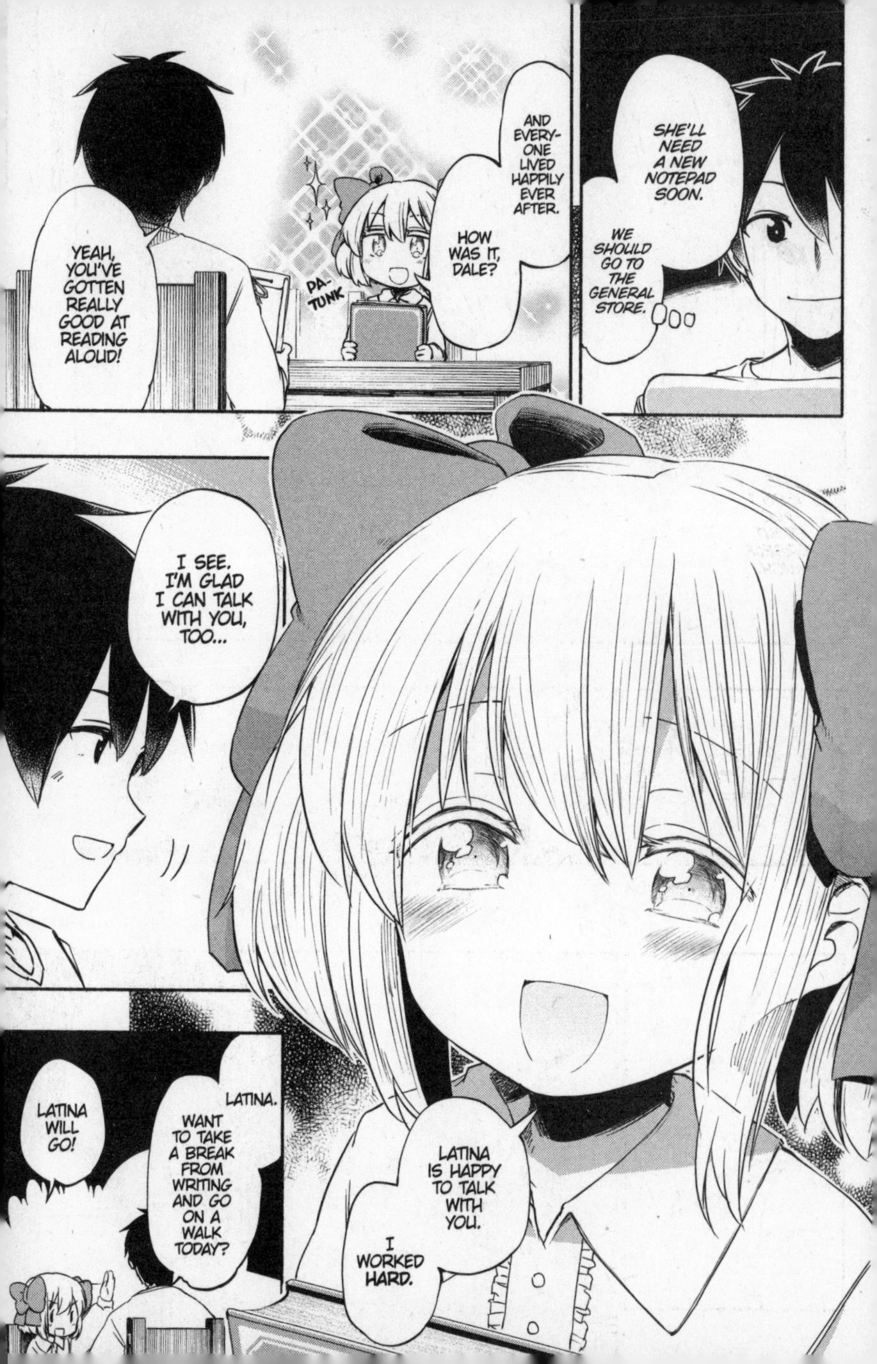
SHE'LL NEED A NEW NOTEPAD SOON.
WE SHOULD GO TO THE GENERAL STORE.
AND EVERY-ONE LIVED HAPPILY EVER AFTER.
HOW WAS IT, DALE?
PA-TUNK
YEAH, YOU'VE GOTTEN REALLY GOOD AT READING ALOUD!
LATINA IS HAPPY TO TALK WITH YOU.
I WORKED HARD.
I SEE. I'M GLAD I CAN TALK WITH YOU, TOO...
LATINA.
WANT TO TAKE A BREAK FROM WRITING AND GO ON A WALK TODAY?
LATINA WILL GO!

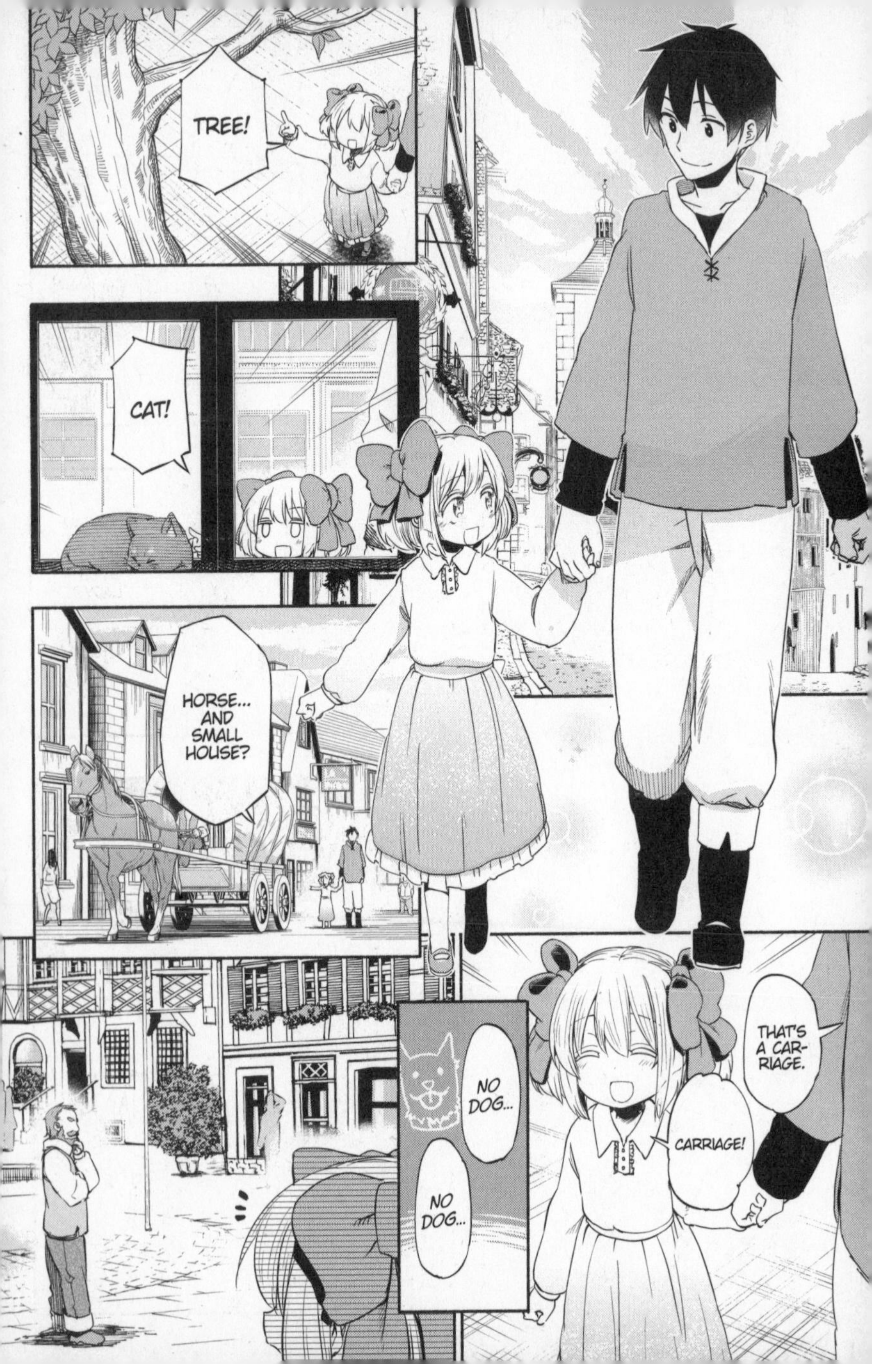
TREE!
CAT!
HORSE... AND SMALL HOUSE?
THAT'S A CARRIAGE.
CARRIAGE!
NO DOG...
NO DOG...

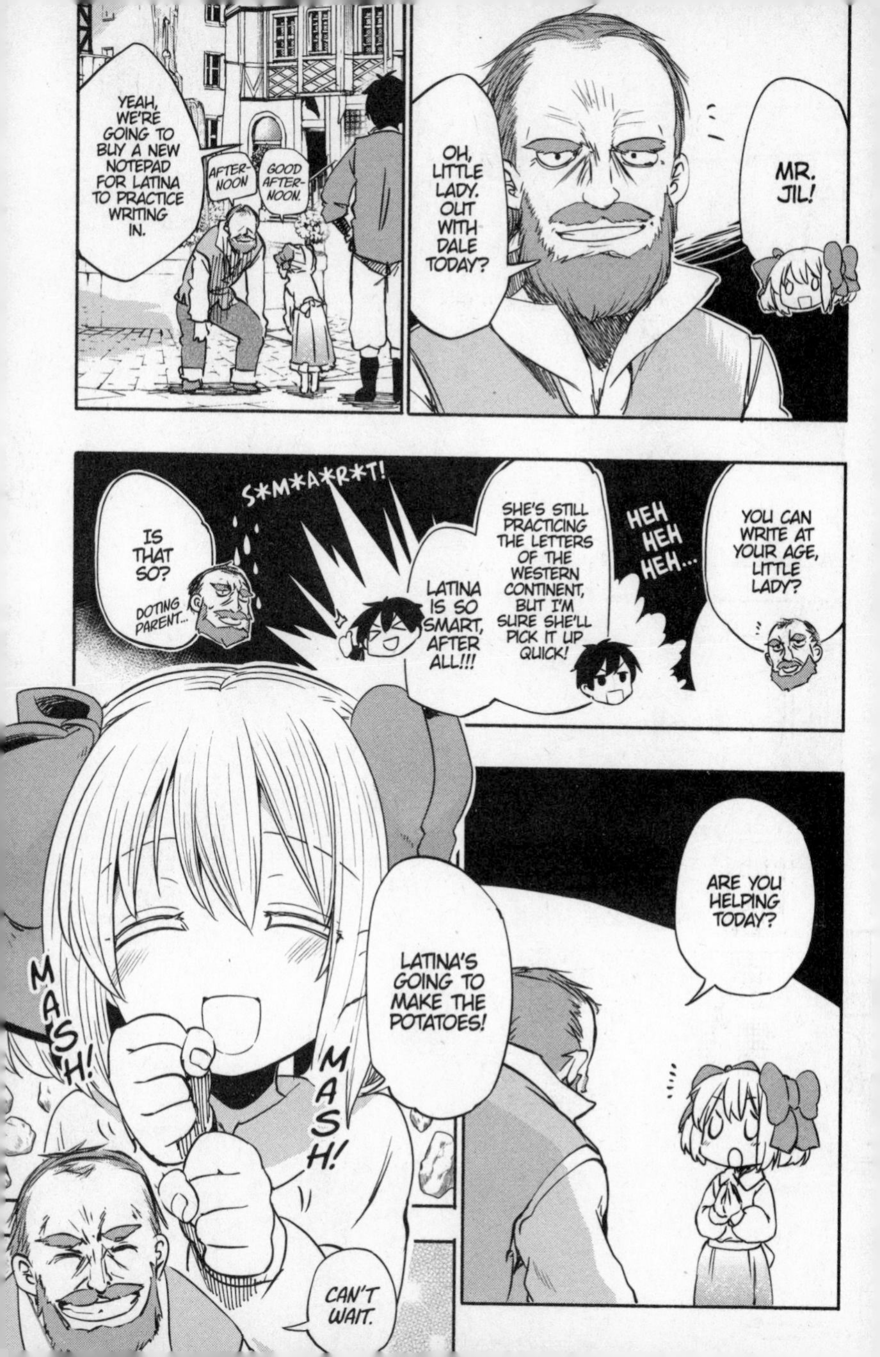
MR. JIL!
OH, LITTLE LADY. OUT WITH DALE TODAY?
GOOD AFTER-NOON.
AFTER-NOON
YEAH, WE'RE GOING TO BUY A NEW NOTEPAD FOR LATINA TO PRACTICE WRITING IN.
YOU CAN WRITE AT YOUR AGE, LITTLE LADY?
HEH HEH HEH...
SHE'S STILL PRACTICING THE LETTERS OF THE WESTERN CONTINENT, BUT I'M SURE SHE'LL PICK IT UP QUICK!
LATINA IS SO SMART, AFTER ALL!!!
S*M*A*R*T!
IS THAT SO?
DOTING PARENT...
ARE YOU HELPING TODAY?
LATINA'S GOING TO MAKE THE POTATOES!
MASH!
MASH!
CAN'T WAIT.

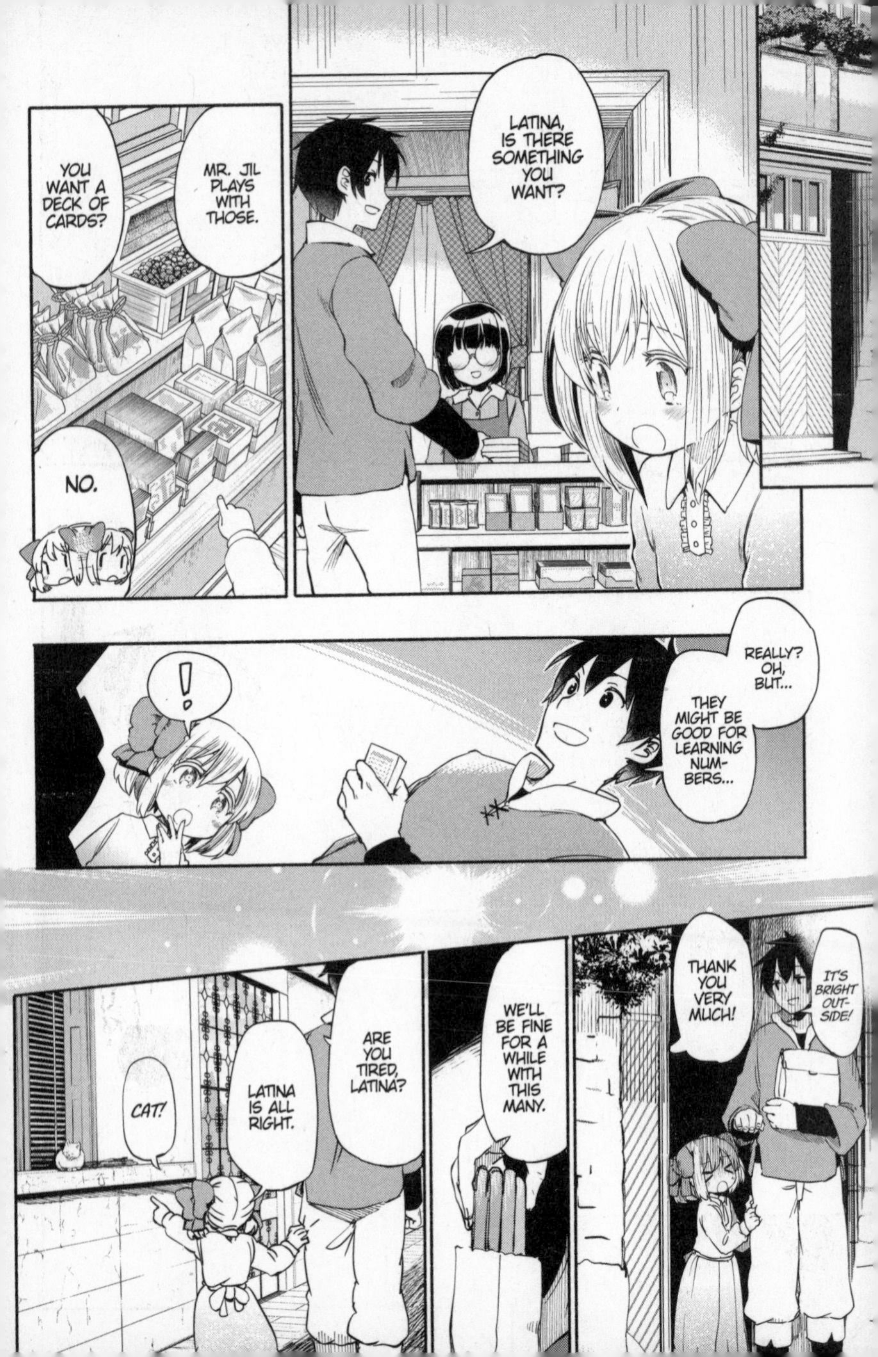
LATINA, IS THERE SOMETHING YOU WANT?
MR. JIL PLAYS WITH THOSE.
YOU WANT A DECK OF CARDS?
NO.
REALLY? OH, BUT...
THEY MIGHT BE GOOD FOR LEARNING NUMBERS...
!
IT'S BRIGHT OUTSIDE!
THANK YOU VERY MUCH!
WE'LL BE FINE FOR A WHILE WITH THIS MANY.
ARE YOU TIRED, LATINA?
LATINA IS ALL RIGHT.
CAT!

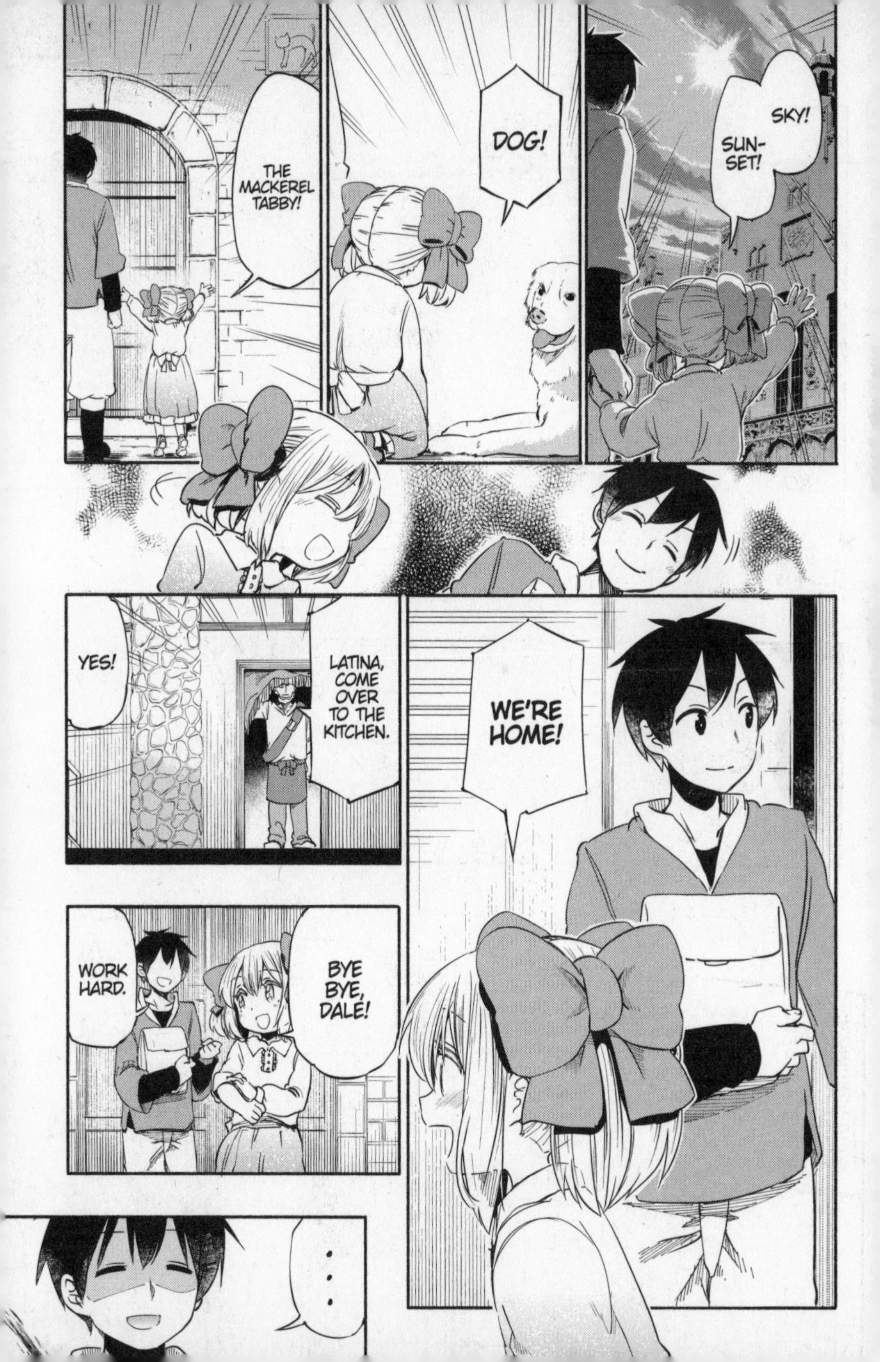
SKY! SUN-SET!
DOG!
THE MACKEREL TABBY!
WE'RE HOME!
LATINA, COME OVER TO THE KITCHEN.
YES!
BYE BYE, DALE!
WORK HARD.
...

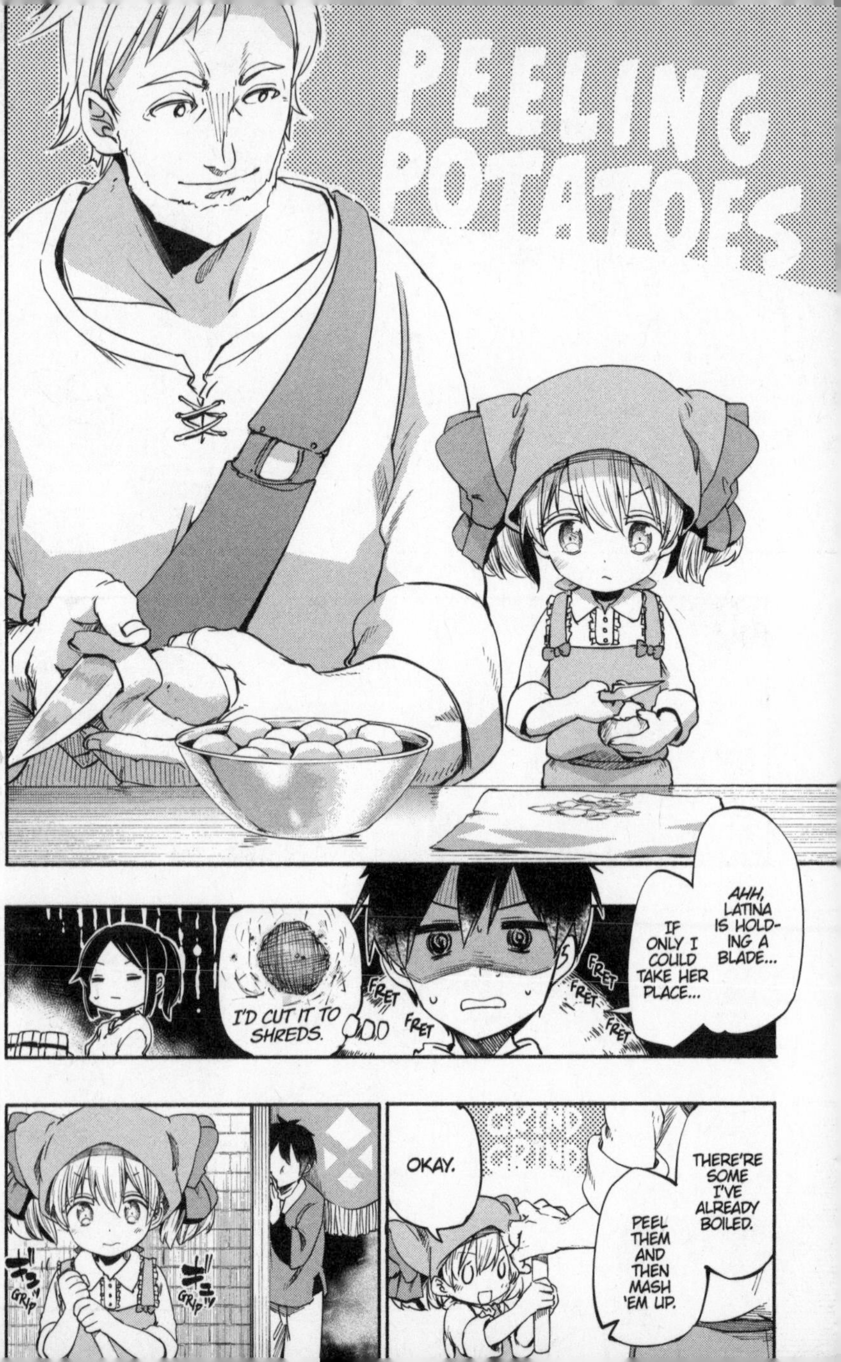
PEELING POTATOES
AHH, LATINA IS HOLDING A BLADE...
IF ONLY I COULD TAKE HER PLACE...
FRET FRET FRET FRET FRET
I'D CUT IT TO SHREDS.
GRIND GRIND
THERE'RE SOME I'VE ALREADY BOILED.
PEEL THEM AND THEN MASH 'EM UP.
OKAY.
GRIP GRIP

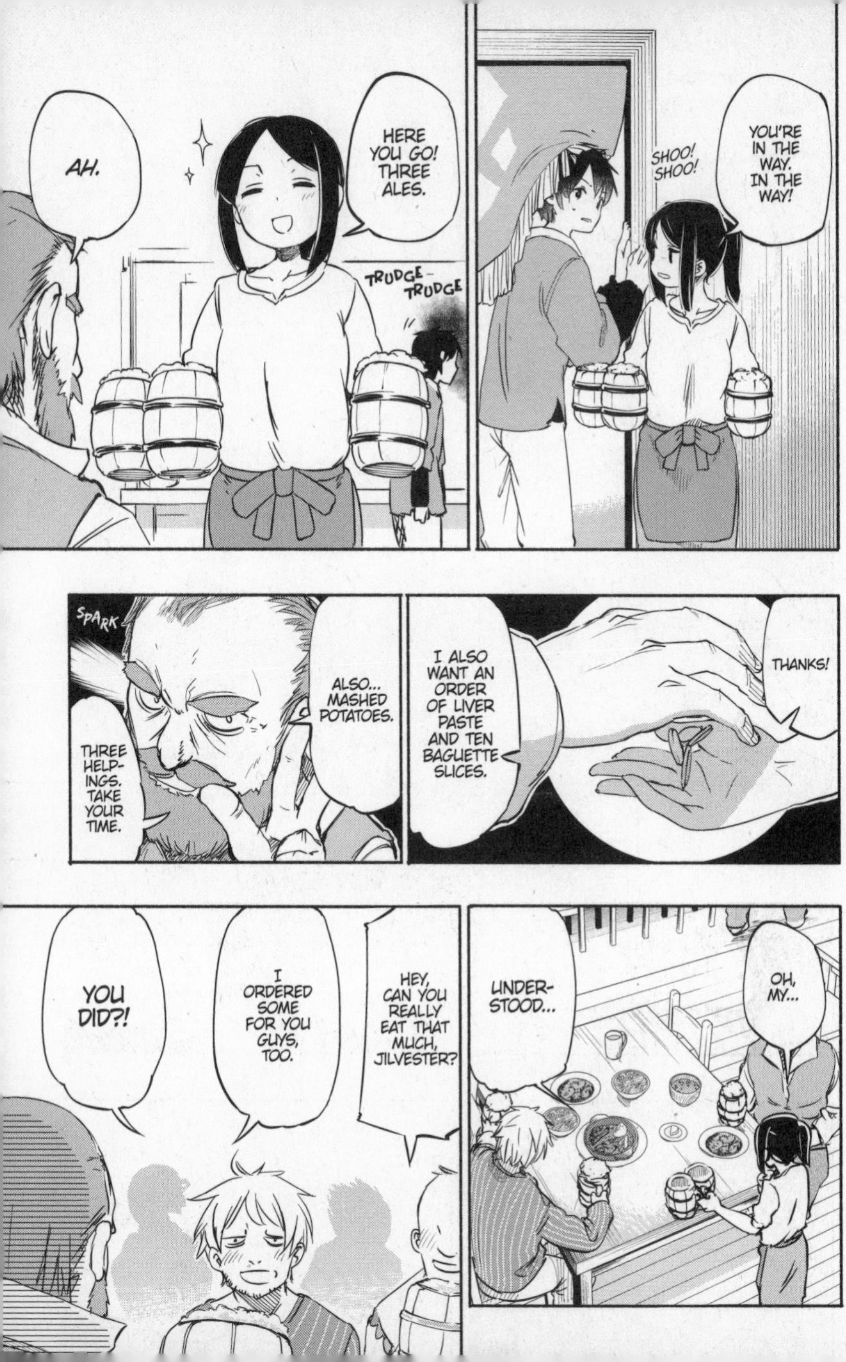
YOU'RE IN THE WAY. IN THE WAY!
SHOO! SHOO!
HERE YOU GO! THREE ALES.
AH.
TRUDGE-TRUDGE
THANKS!
I ALSO WANT AN ORDER OF LIVER PASTE AND TEN BAGUETTE SLICES.
ALSO... MASHED POTATOES.
SPARK
THREE HELP-INGS. TAKE YOUR TIME.
OH, MY...
UNDER-STOOD...
HEY, CAN YOU REALLY EAT THAT MUCH, JILVESTER?
I ORDERED SOME FOR YOU GUYS, TOO.
YOU DID?!

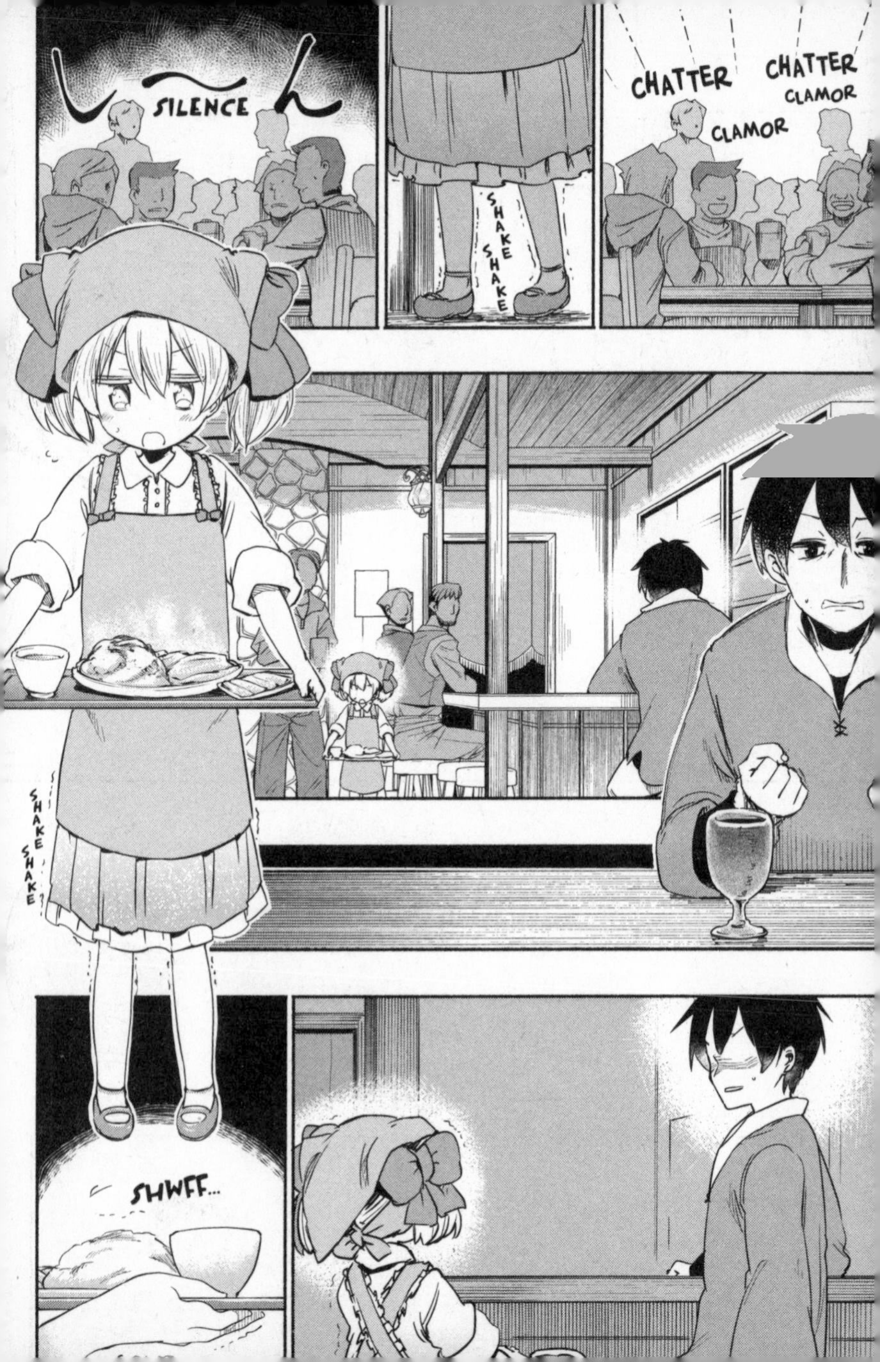
CHATTER
CHATTER
CLAMOR
CLAMOR
SHAKE SHAKE
しーん
SILENCE
SHAKE SHAKE
SHWFF...

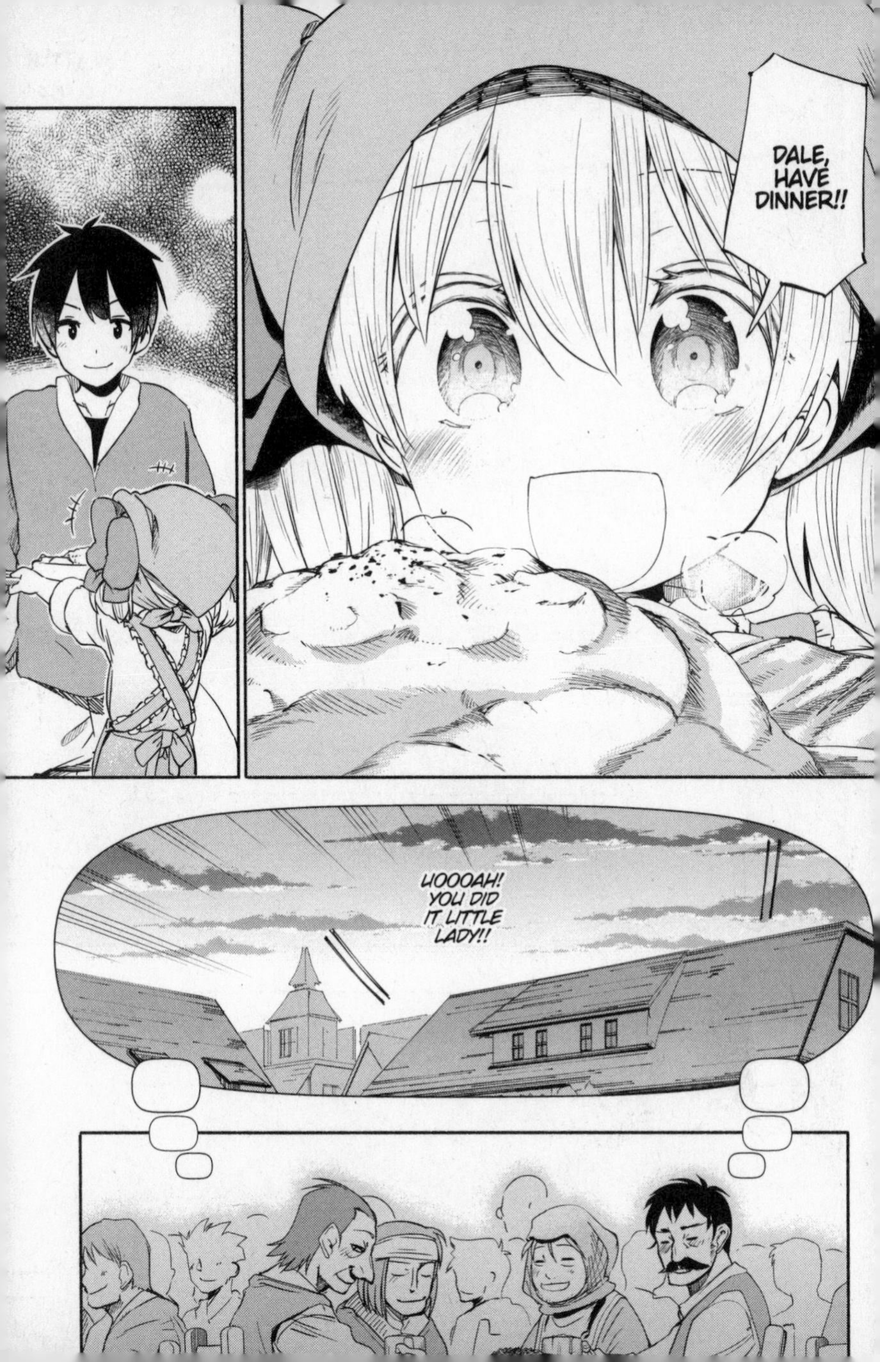
DALE, HAVE DINNER!!
UOOOAH! YOU DID IT LITTLE LADY!!

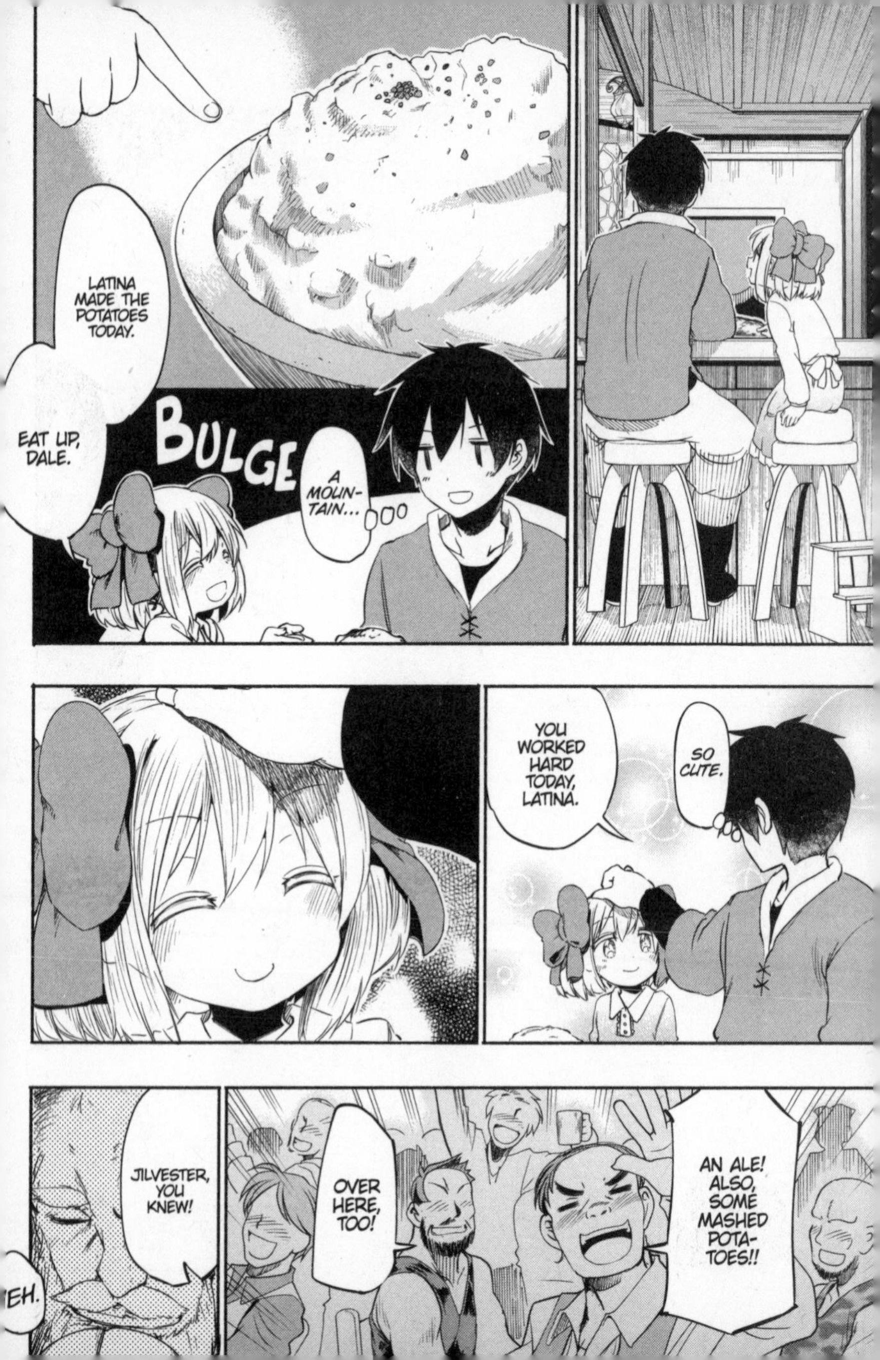
LATINA MADE THE POTATOES TODAY.
EAT UP, DALE.
A MOUN-TAIN...
BULGE
SO CUTE.
YOU WORKED HARD TODAY, LATINA.
AN ALE! ALSO, SOME MASHED POTA-TOES!!
OVER HERE, TOO!
JILVESTER, YOU KNEW!
EH.

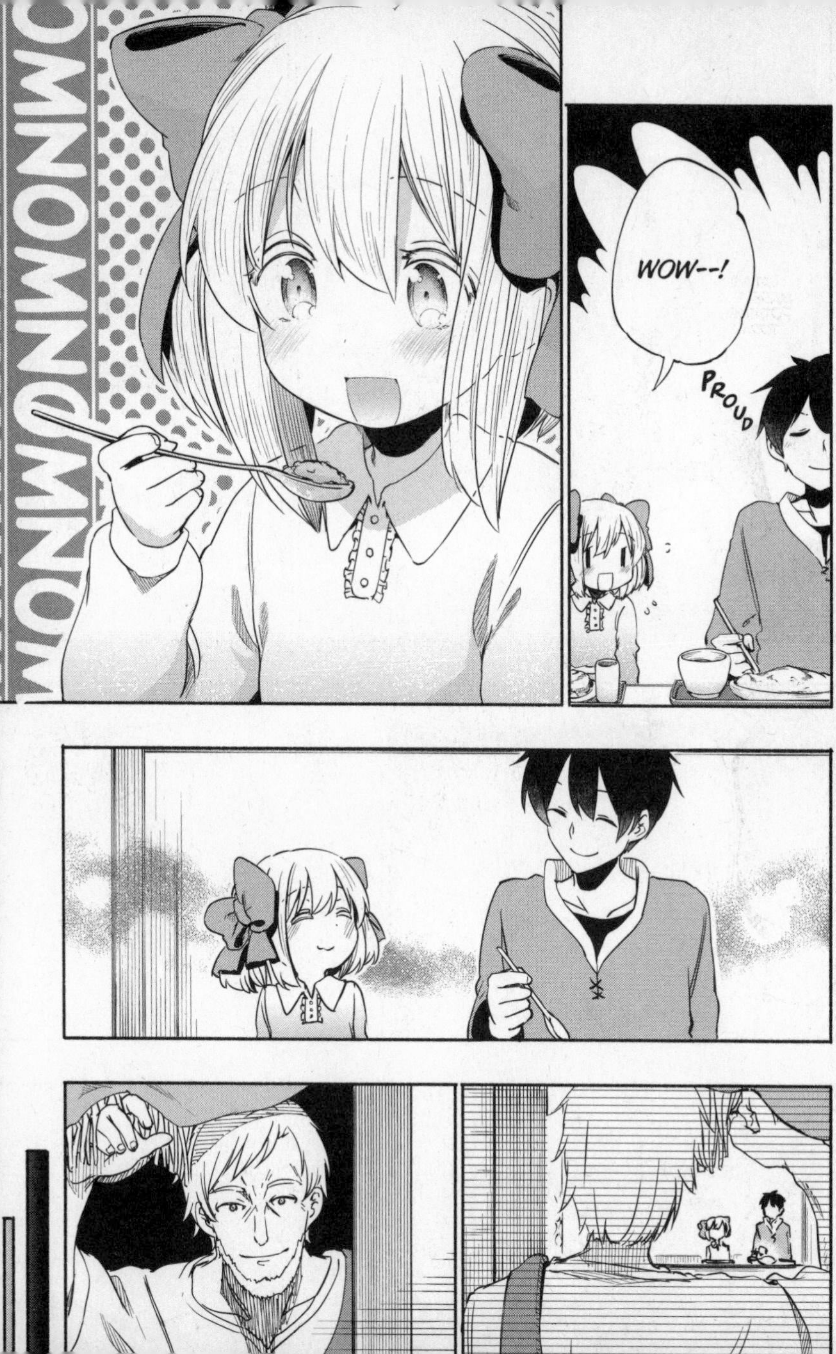
WOW--!
PROUD
MONMONMONMO

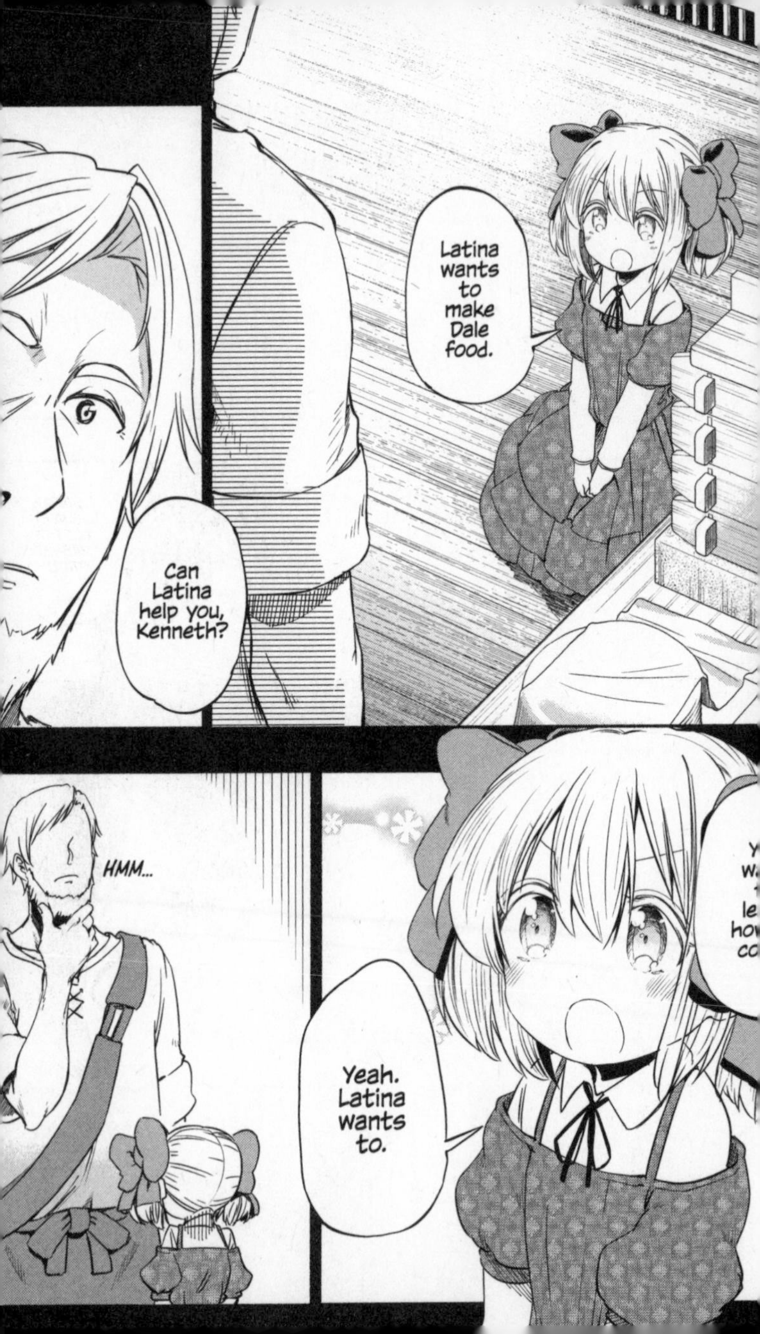
Latina wants to make Dale food.
Can Latina help you, Kenneth?
Yeah. Latina wants to.
HMM...

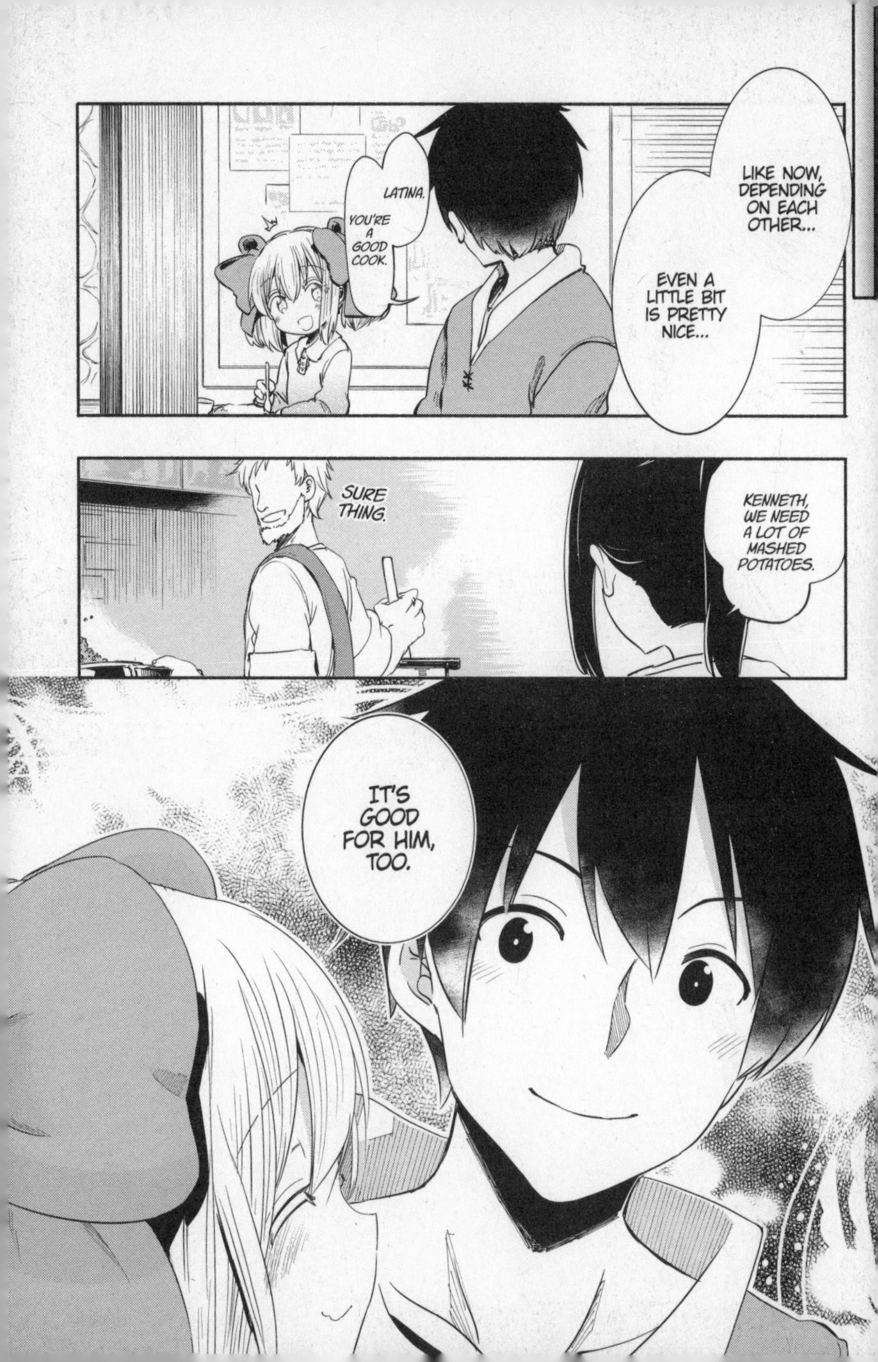
LIKE NOW, DEPENDING ON EACH OTHER...
EVEN A LITTLE BIT IS PRETTY NICE...
LATINA. YOU'RE A GOOD COOK.
KENNETH, WE NEED A LOT OF MASHED POTATOES.
SURE THING.
IT'S GOOD FOR HIM, TOO.

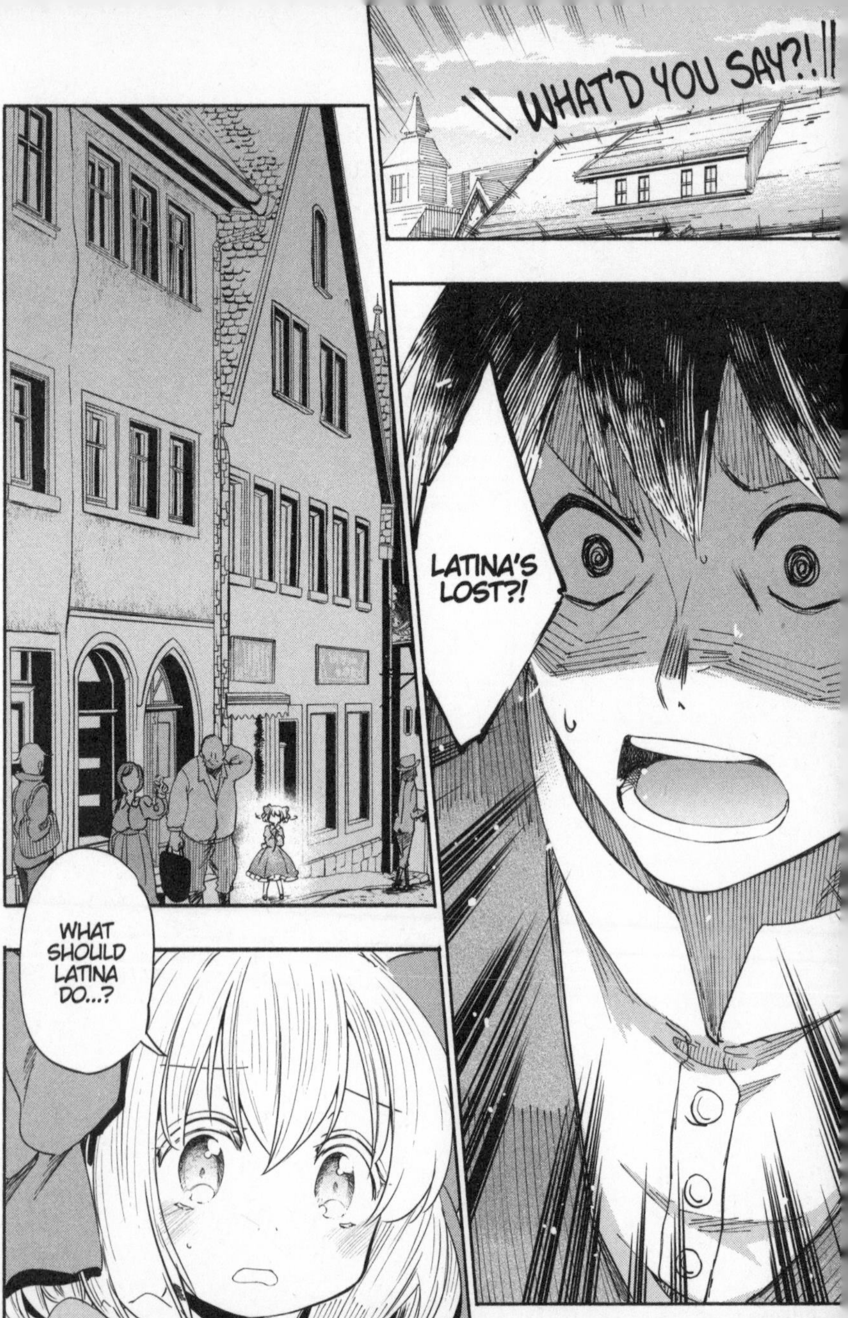
WHAT'D YOU SAY?!
LATINA'S LOST?!
WHAT SHOULD LATINA DO...?

IF It's
For My
Daughter
I'd Even Defeat
a Demon
Lord

If It's For My Daughter, I'd Even Defeat a Demon Lord.

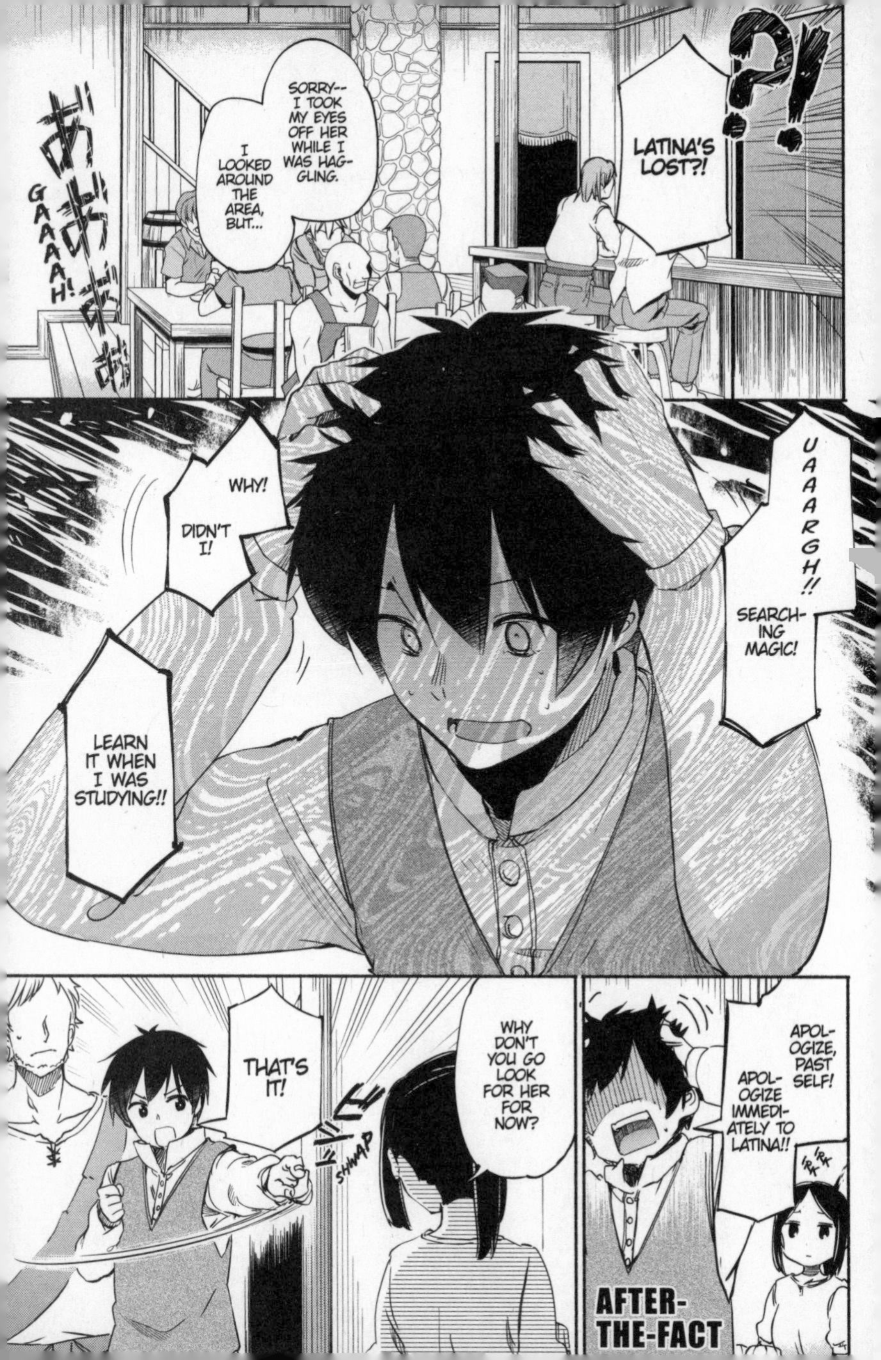
?!
LATINA'S LOST?!
SORRY-- I TOOK MY EYES OFF HER WHILE I WAS HAG-GLING.
I LOOKED AROUND THE AREA, BUT...
GAAAAH!
UAAAARGH!!
SEARCH-ING MAGIC!
WHY!
DIDN'T I!
LEARN IT WHEN I WAS STUDYING!!
APOL-OGIZE, PAST SELF!
APOL-OGIZE IMMEDI-ATELY TO LATINA!!
IRK IRK
AFTER-THE-FACT
WHY DON'T YOU GO LOOK FOR HER FOR NOW?
THAT'S IT!
SHWAP

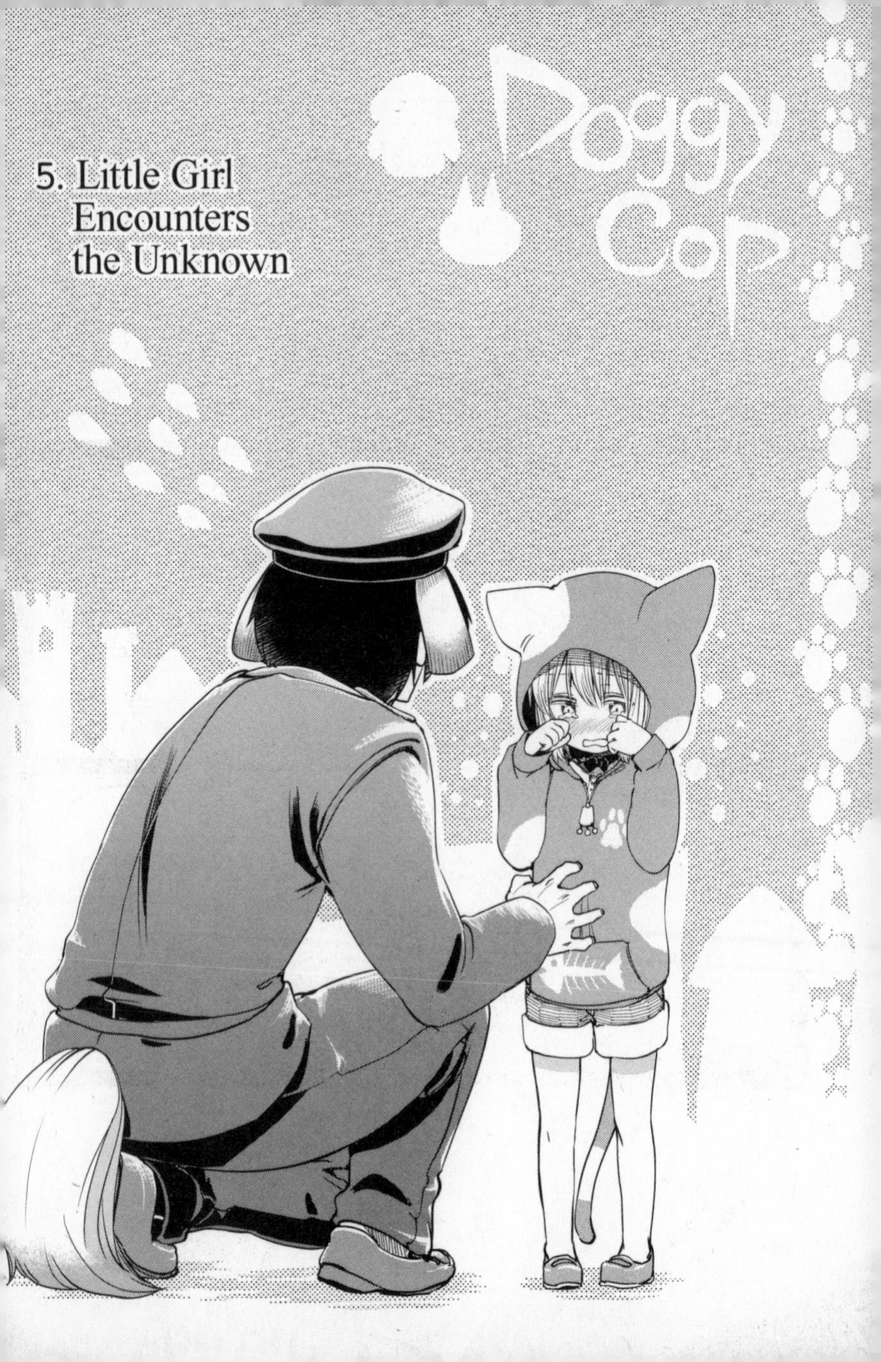
Doggy Cop
5. Little Girl Encounters the Unknown

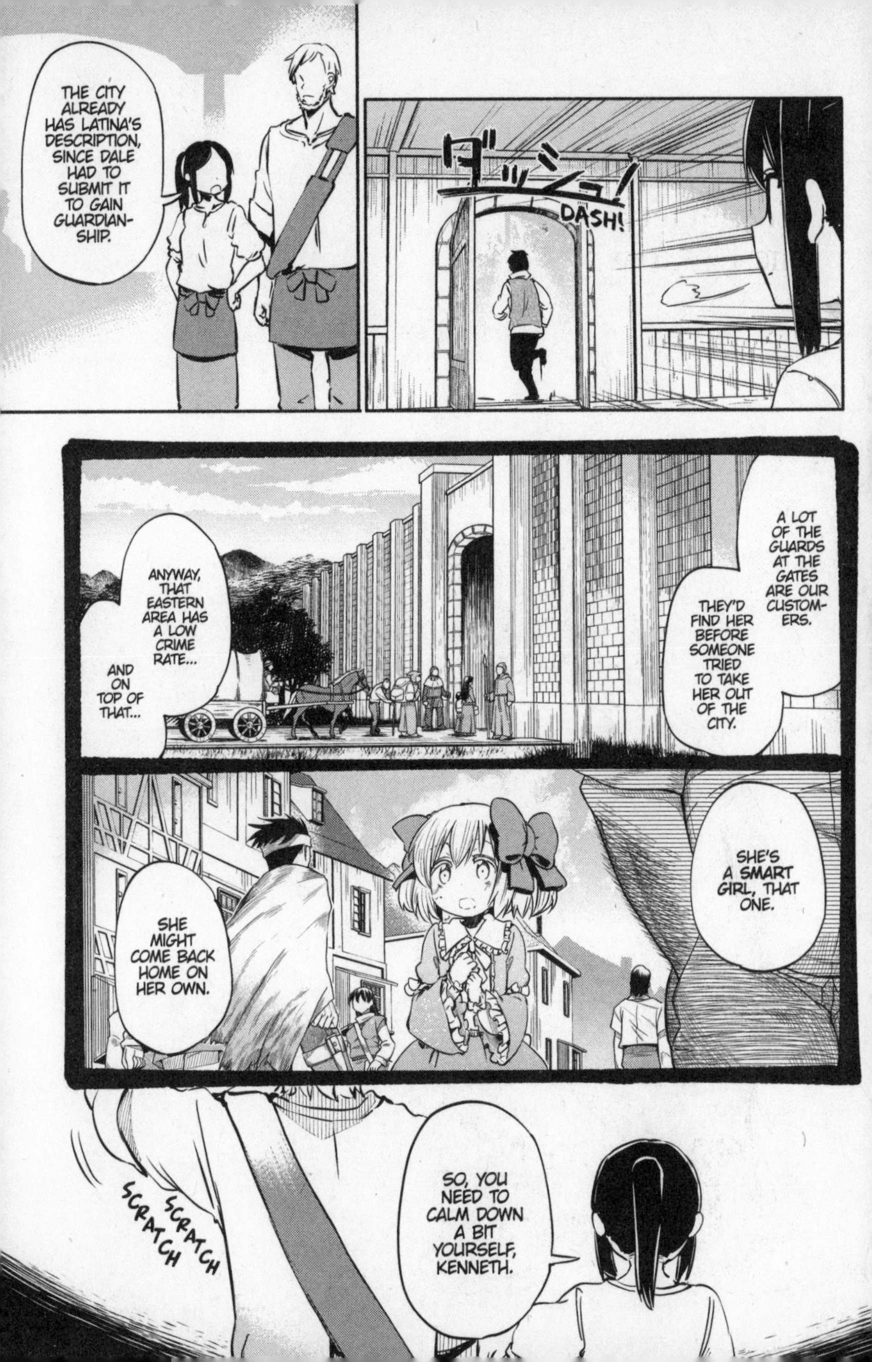
ダッシュ!
DASH!
THE CITY ALREADY HAS LATINA'S DESCRIPTION, SINCE DALE HAD TO SUBMIT IT TO GAIN GUARDIAN-SHIP.
A LOT OF THE GUARDS AT THE GATES ARE OUR CUSTOM-ERS.
THEY'D FIND HER BEFORE SOMEONE TRIED TO TAKE HER OUT OF THE CITY.
ANYWAY, THAT EASTERN AREA HAS A LOW CRIME RATE...
AND ON TOP OF THAT...
SHE'S A SMART GIRL, THAT ONE.
SHE MIGHT COME BACK HOME ON HER OWN.
SO, YOU NEED TO CALM DOWN A BIT YOURSELF, KENNETH.
SCRATCH SCRATCH

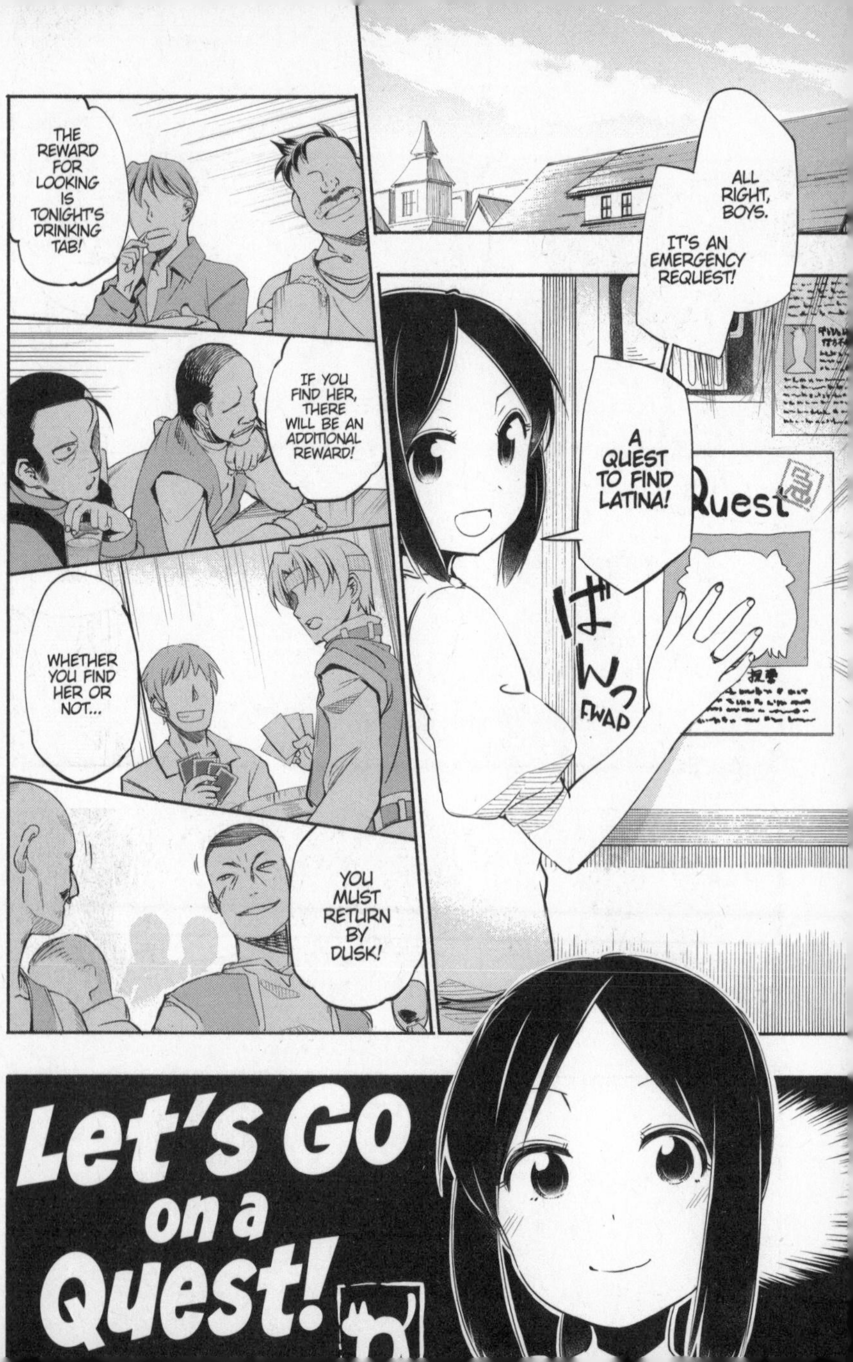
ALL RIGHT, BOYS.
IT'S AN EMERGENCY REQUEST!
A QUEST TO FIND LATINA!
Quest
ばんっ
FWAP
THE REWARD FOR LOOKING IS TONIGHT'S DRINKING TAB!
IF YOU FIND HER, THERE WILL BE AN ADDITIONAL REWARD!
WHETHER YOU FIND HER OR NOT...
YOU MUST RETURN BY DUSK!
Let's Go on a Quest!

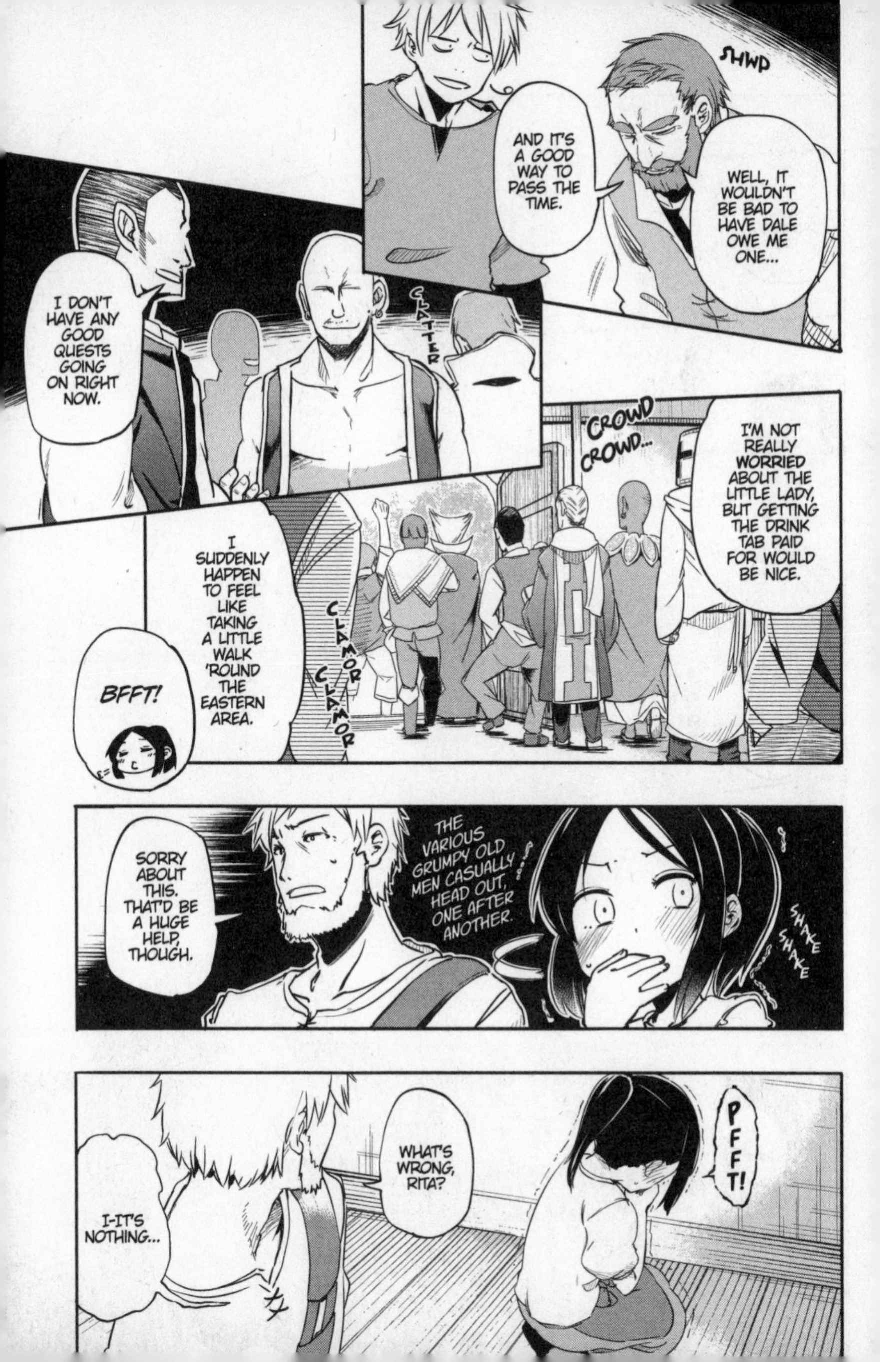
SHWD
WELL, IT WOULDN'T BE BAD TO HAVE DALE OWE ME ONE...
AND IT'S A GOOD WAY TO PASS THE TIME.
CLATTER
I DON'T HAVE ANY GOOD QUESTS GOING ON RIGHT NOW.
I'M NOT REALLY WORRIED ABOUT THE LITTLE LADY, BUT GETTING THE DRINK TAB PAID FOR WOULD BE NICE.
CROWD CROWD...
CLAMOR CLAMOR
I SUDDENLY HAPPEN TO FEEL LIKE TAKING A LITTLE WALK 'ROUND THE EASTERN AREA.
BFFT!
SHAKE SHAKE
THE VARIOUS GRUMPY OLD MEN CASUALLY HEAD OUT, ONE AFTER ANOTHER.
SORRY ABOUT THIS. THAT'D BE A HUGE HELP, THOUGH.
PFFT!
WHAT'S WRONG, RITA?
I-IT'S NOTHING...

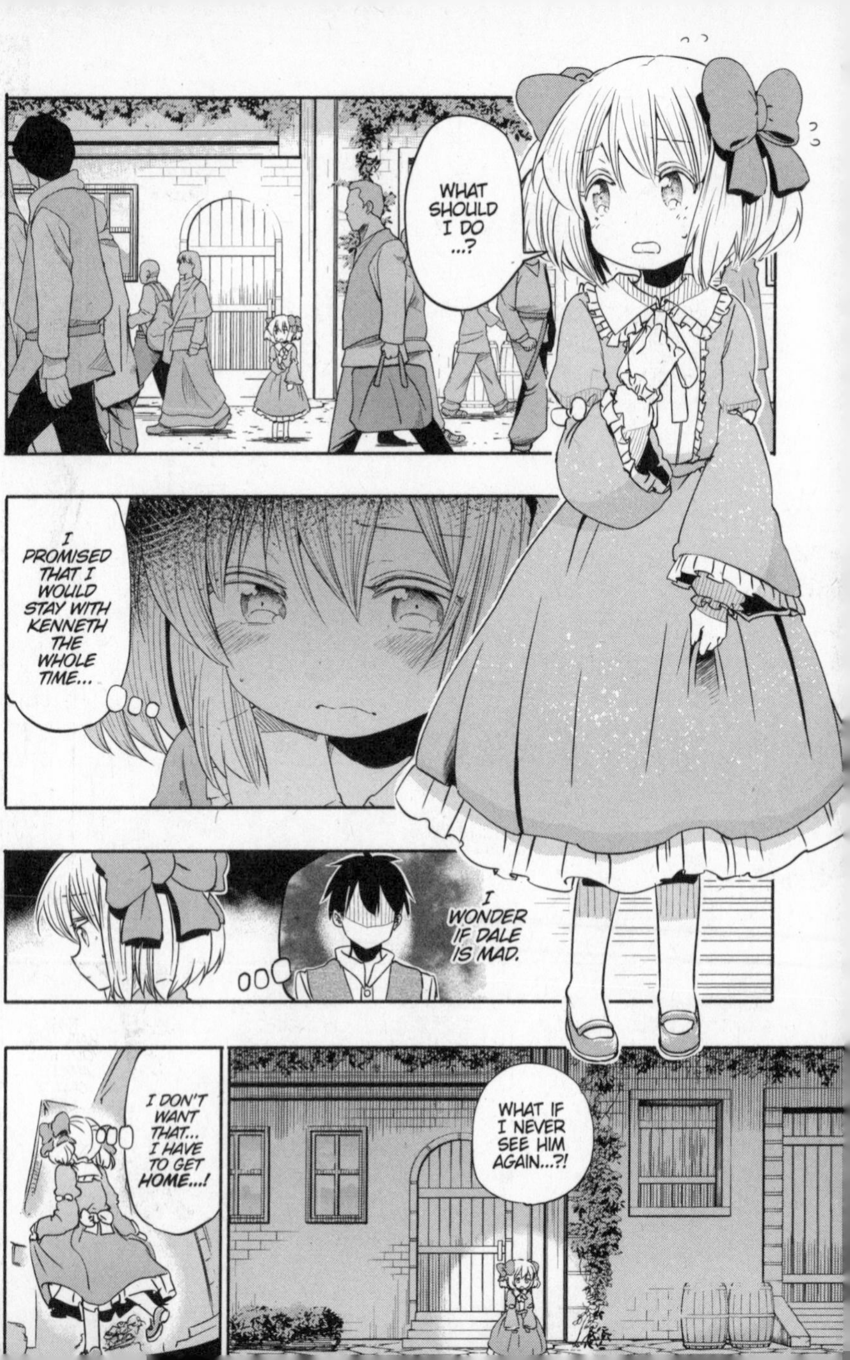
WHAT SHOULD I DO ...?
I PROMISED THAT I WOULD STAY WITH KENNETH THE WHOLE TIME...
I WONDER IF DALE IS MAD.
WHAT IF I NEVER SEE HIM AGAIN...?!
I DON'T WANT THAT... I HAVE TO GET HOME...!

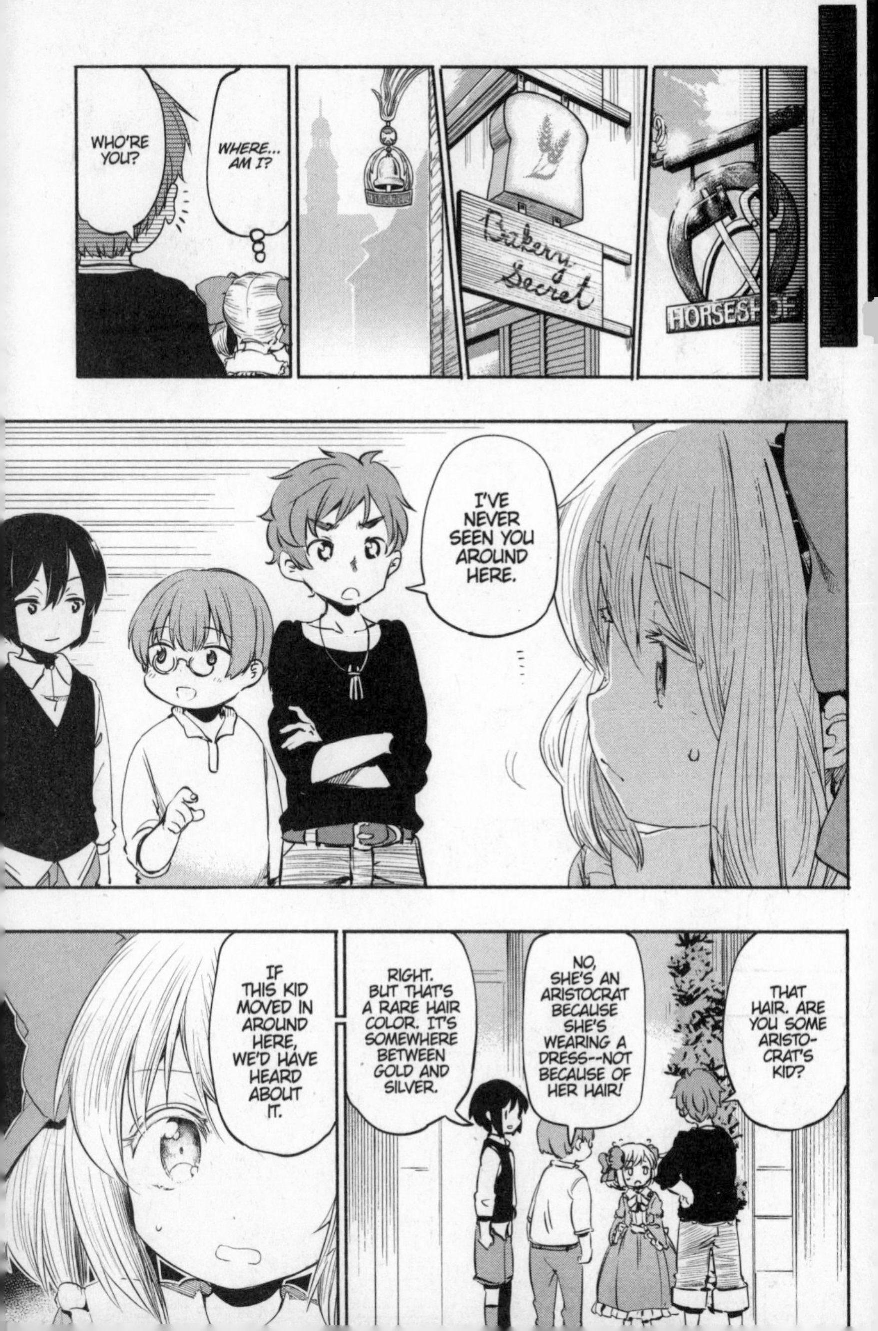
HORSESHO
Bakery Secret
WHERE... AM I?
WHO'RE YOU?
I'VE NEVER SEEN YOU AROUND HERE.
...
THAT HAIR. ARE YOU SOME ARISTOCRAT'S KID?
NO, SHE'S AN ARISTOCRAT BECAUSE SHE'S WEARING A DRESS--NOT BECAUSE OF HER HAIR!
RIGHT. BUT THAT'S A RARE HAIR COLOR. IT'S SOMEWHERE BETWEEN GOLD AND SILVER.
IF THIS KID MOVED IN AROUND HERE, WE'D HAVE HEARD ABOUT IT.

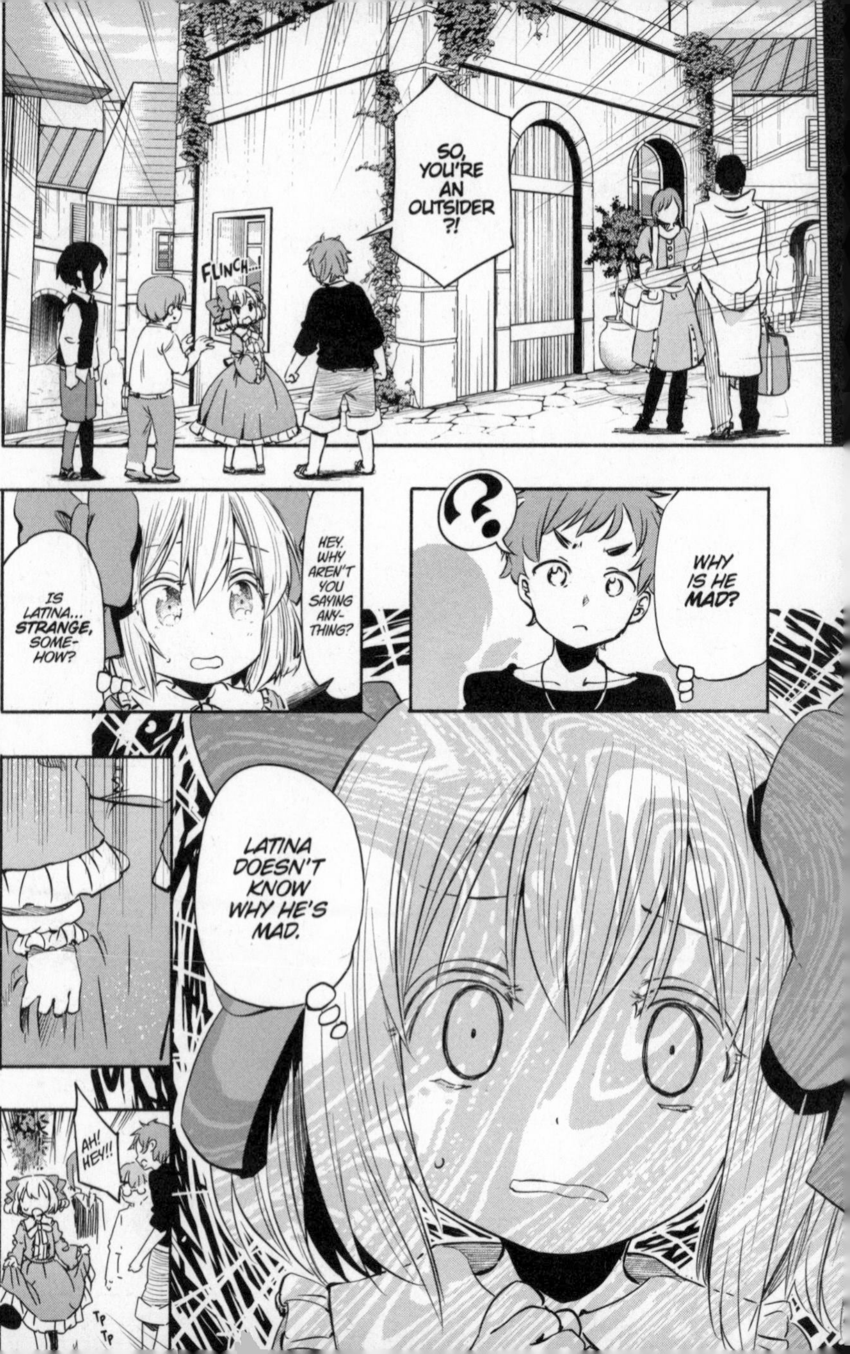
SO, YOU'RE AN OUTSIDER?!
FLINCH...!
WHY IS HE MAD?
HEY. WHY AREN'T YOU SAYING ANYTHING?
IS LATINA... STRANGE, SOMEHOW?
LATINA DOESN'T KNOW WHY HE'S MAD.
AH! HEY!!
TP TP

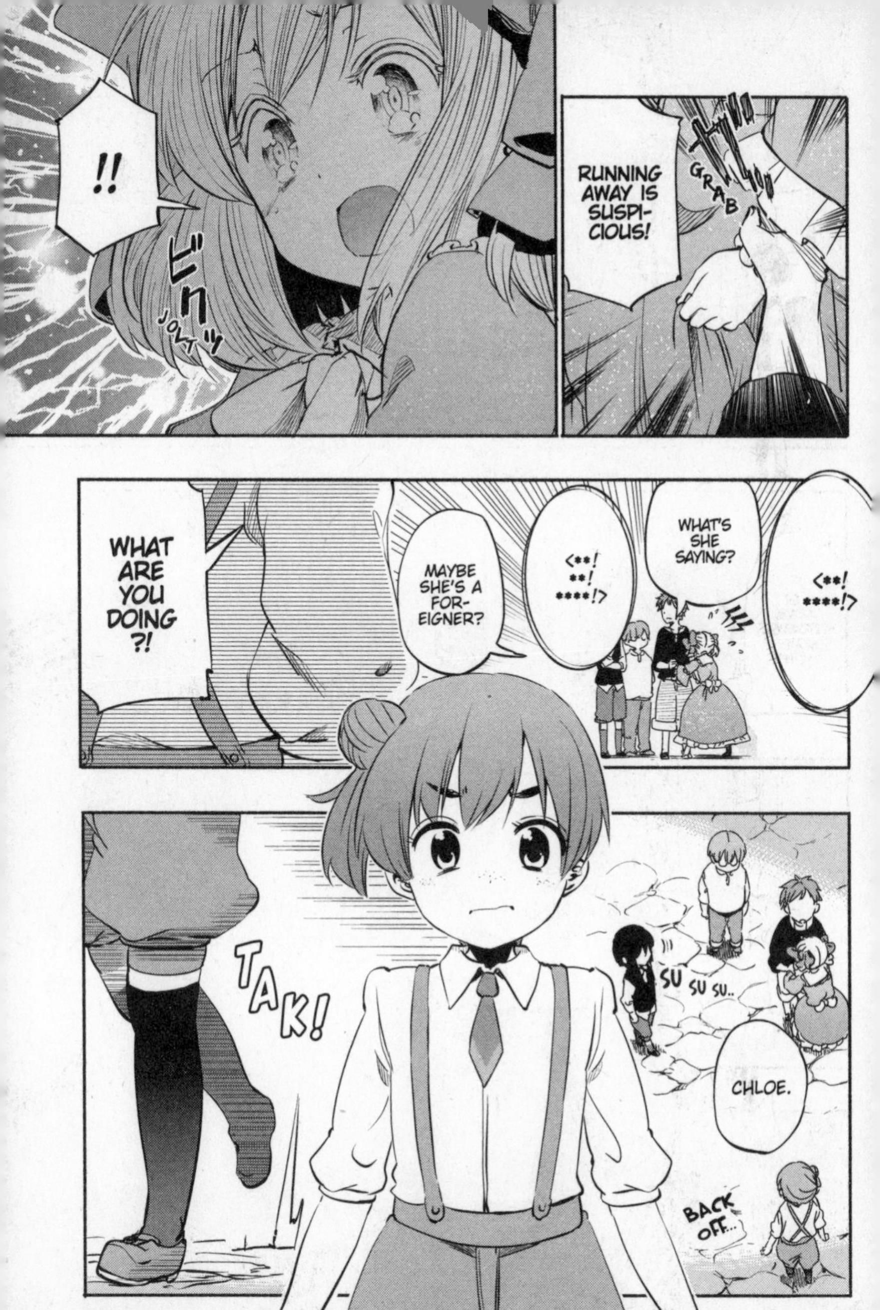
RUNNING AWAY IS SUSPICIOUS!
GRAB
!!
ビクッ
JOLT
<**! ****!>
WHAT'S SHE SAYING?
<**! **! ****!>
MAYBE SHE'S A FOR-EIGNER?
WHAT ARE YOU DOING?!
BACK OFF...
CHLOE.
SU SU SU..
TAK!

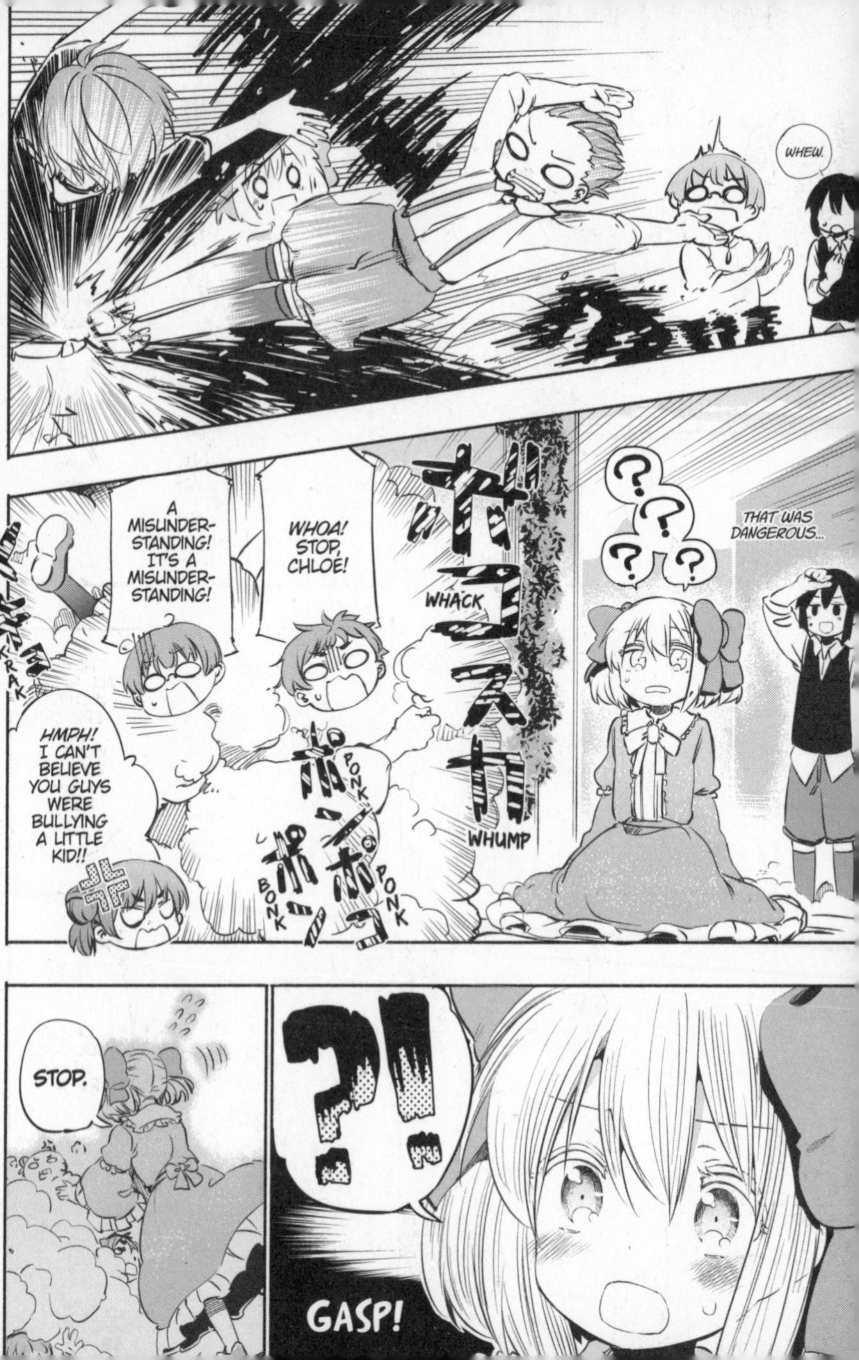
WHEW.
???
THAT WAS DANGEROUS...
WHACK
WHUMP
WHOA! STOP, CHLOE!
A MISUNDER-STANDING! IT'S A MISUNDER-STANDING!
PONK
PONK
BONK
KRAK
HMPH! I CAN'T BELIEVE YOU GUYS WERE BULLYING A LITTLE KID!!
?!
GASP!
STOP.

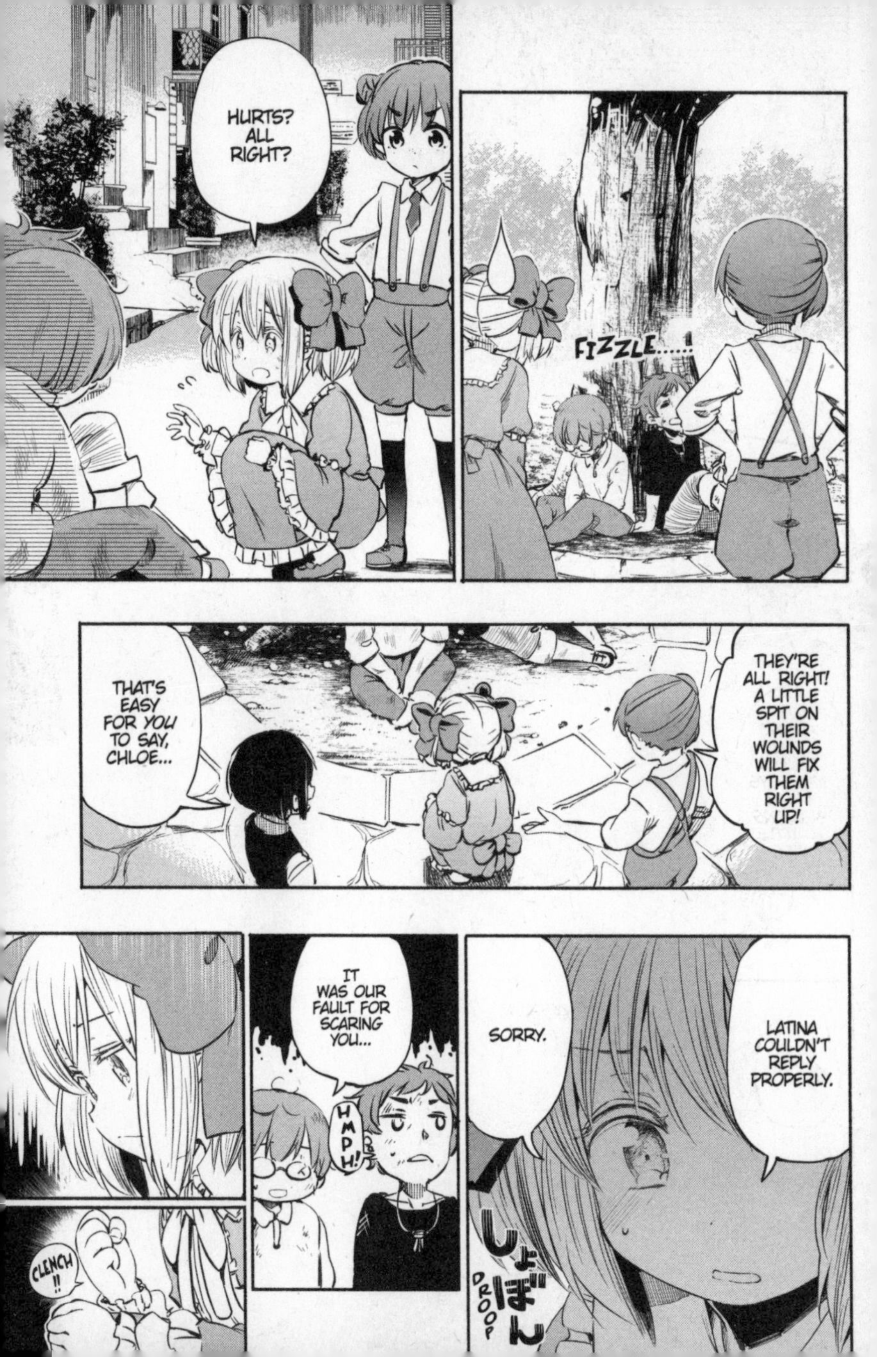
FIZZLE......
HURTS? ALL RIGHT?
THEY'RE ALL RIGHT! A LITTLE SPIT ON THEIR WOUNDS WILL FIX THEM RIGHT UP!
THAT'S EASY FOR YOU TO SAY, CHLOE...
LATINA COULDN'T REPLY PROPERLY.
SORRY.
しょぼん
DROOP
IT WAS OUR FAULT FOR SCARING YOU...
HMPH!
CLENCH!!

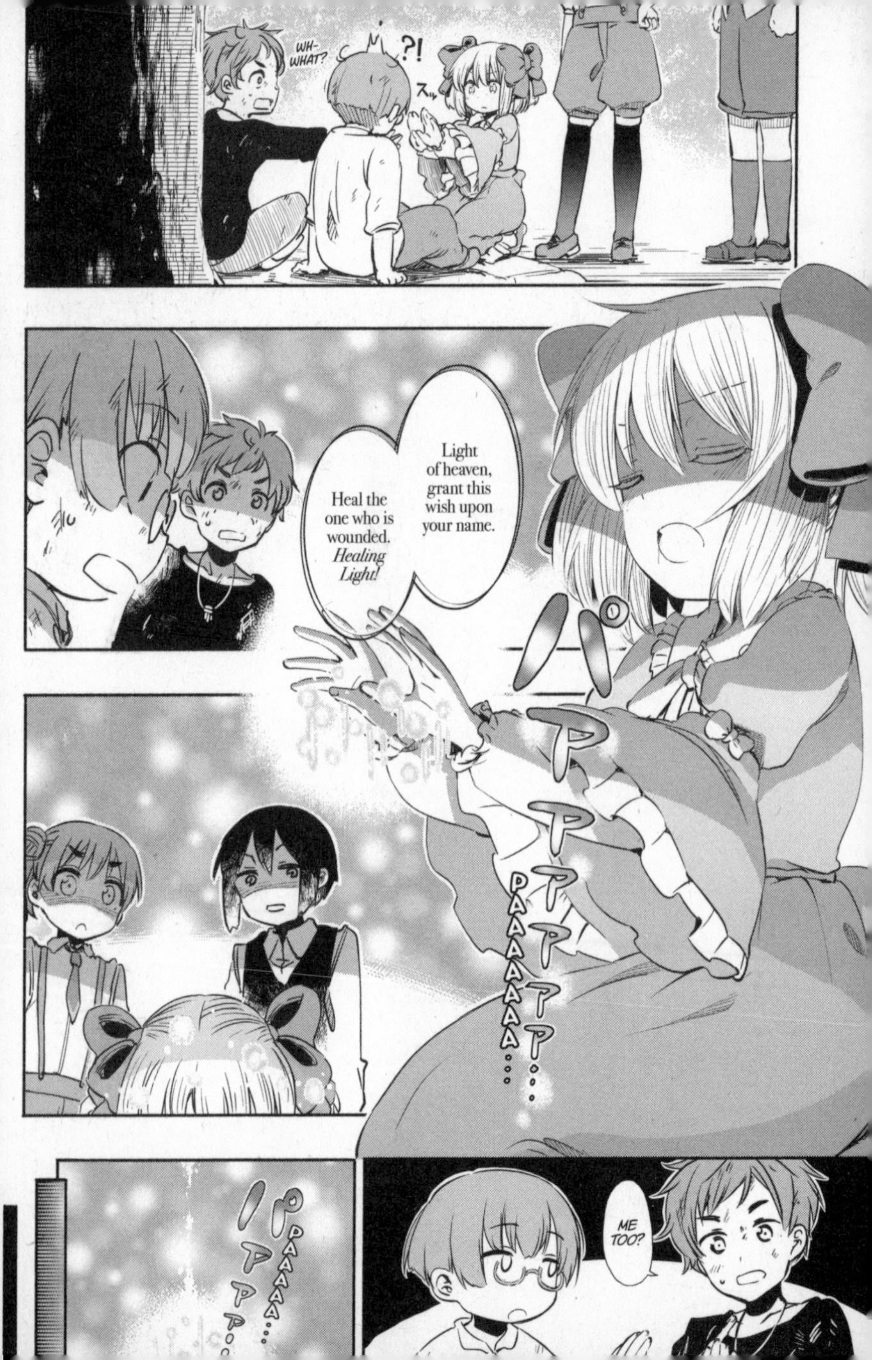
WH-WHAT?
?!
Light of heaven, grant this wish upon your name.
Heal the one who is wounded. *Healing Light!*
PAAAAAAAA...
ME TOO?
PAAAAA...

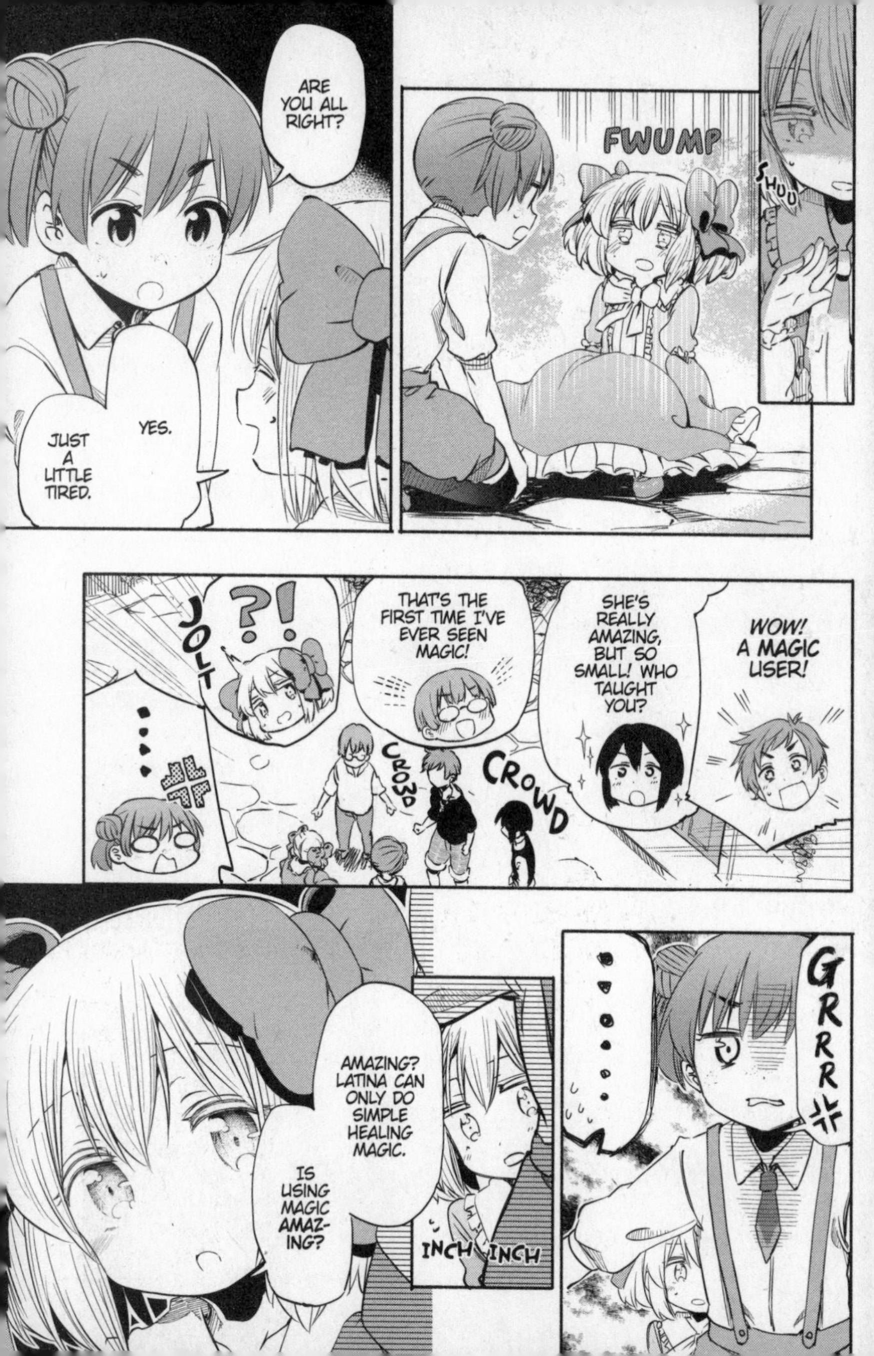
SHUU
FWUMP
ARE YOU ALL RIGHT?
YES.
JUST A LITTLE TIRED.
WOW! A MAGIC USER!
SHE'S REALLY AMAZING, BUT SO SMALL! WHO TAUGHT YOU?
THAT'S THE FIRST TIME I'VE EVER SEEN MAGIC!
CROWD
CROWD
?!
JOLT
...
GRRR
......
AMAZING? LATINA CAN ONLY DO SIMPLE HEALING MAGIC.
IS USING MAGIC AMAZ-ING?
INCH INCH

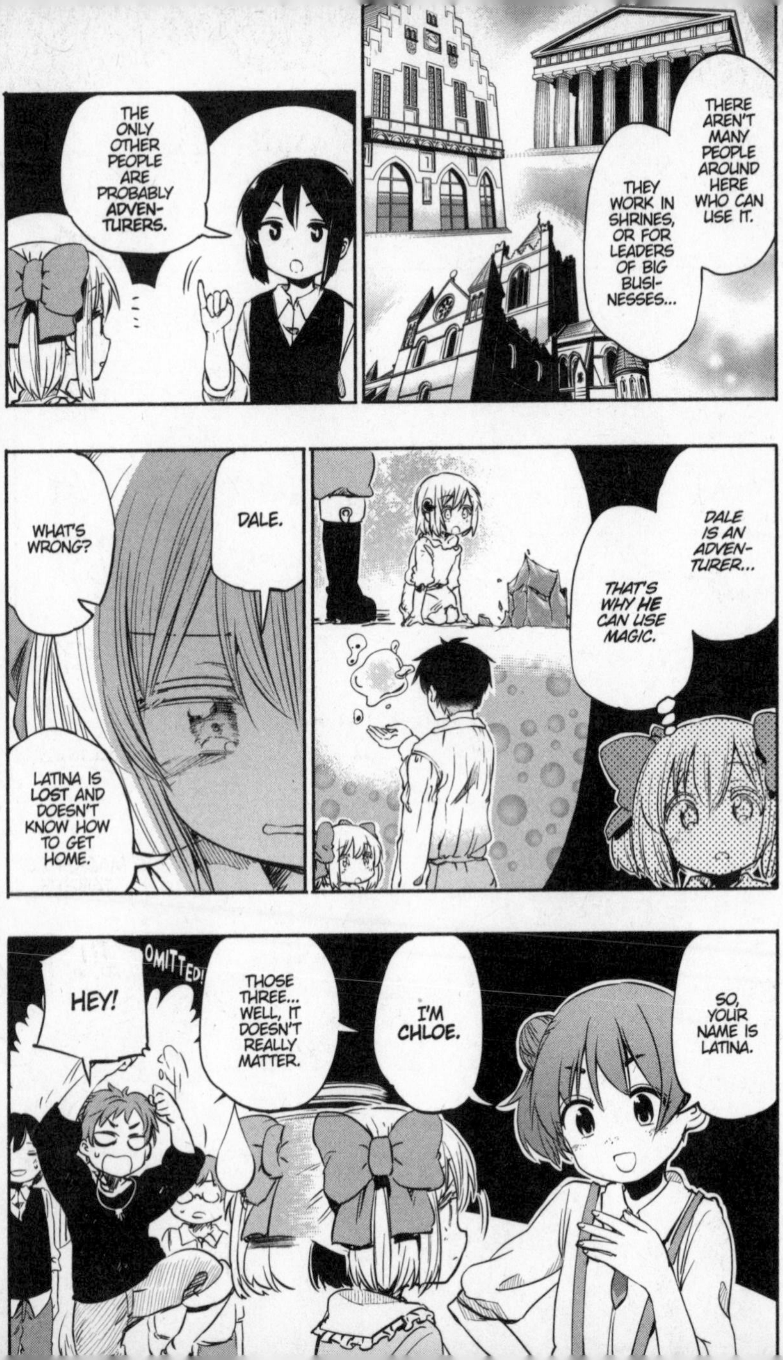
THERE AREN'T MANY PEOPLE AROUND HERE WHO CAN USE IT.
THEY WORK IN SHRINES, OR FOR LEADERS OF BIG BUSINESSES...
THE ONLY OTHER PEOPLE ARE PROBABLY ADVENTURERS.
DALE IS AN ADVENTURER...
THAT'S WHY HE CAN USE MAGIC.
DALE.
WHAT'S WRONG?
LATINA IS LOST AND DOESN'T KNOW HOW TO GET HOME.
SO, YOUR NAME IS LATINA.
I'M CHLOE.
THOSE THREE... WELL, IT DOESN'T REALLY MATTER.
OMITTED!
HEY!

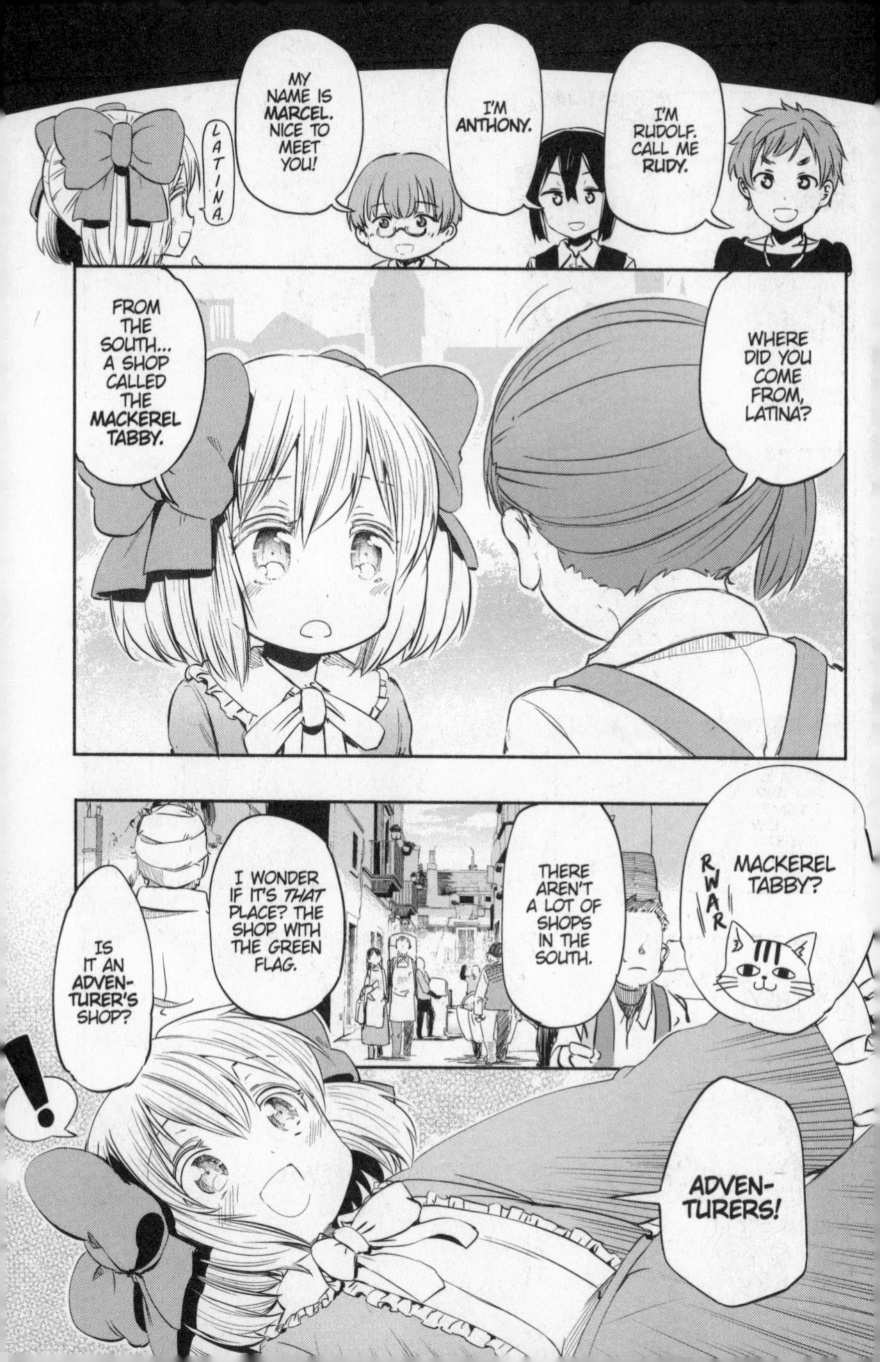
I'M RUDOLF. CALL ME RUDY.
I'M ANTHONY.
MY NAME IS MARCEL. NICE TO MEET YOU!
LATINA.
WHERE DID YOU COME FROM, LATINA?
FROM THE SOUTH... A SHOP CALLED THE MACKEREL TABBY.
MACKEREL TABBY?
RWAR
THERE AREN'T A LOT OF SHOPS IN THE SOUTH.
I WONDER IF IT'S *THAT* PLACE? THE SHOP WITH THE GREEN FLAG.
IS IT AN ADVENTURER'S SHOP?
!
ADVENTURERS!

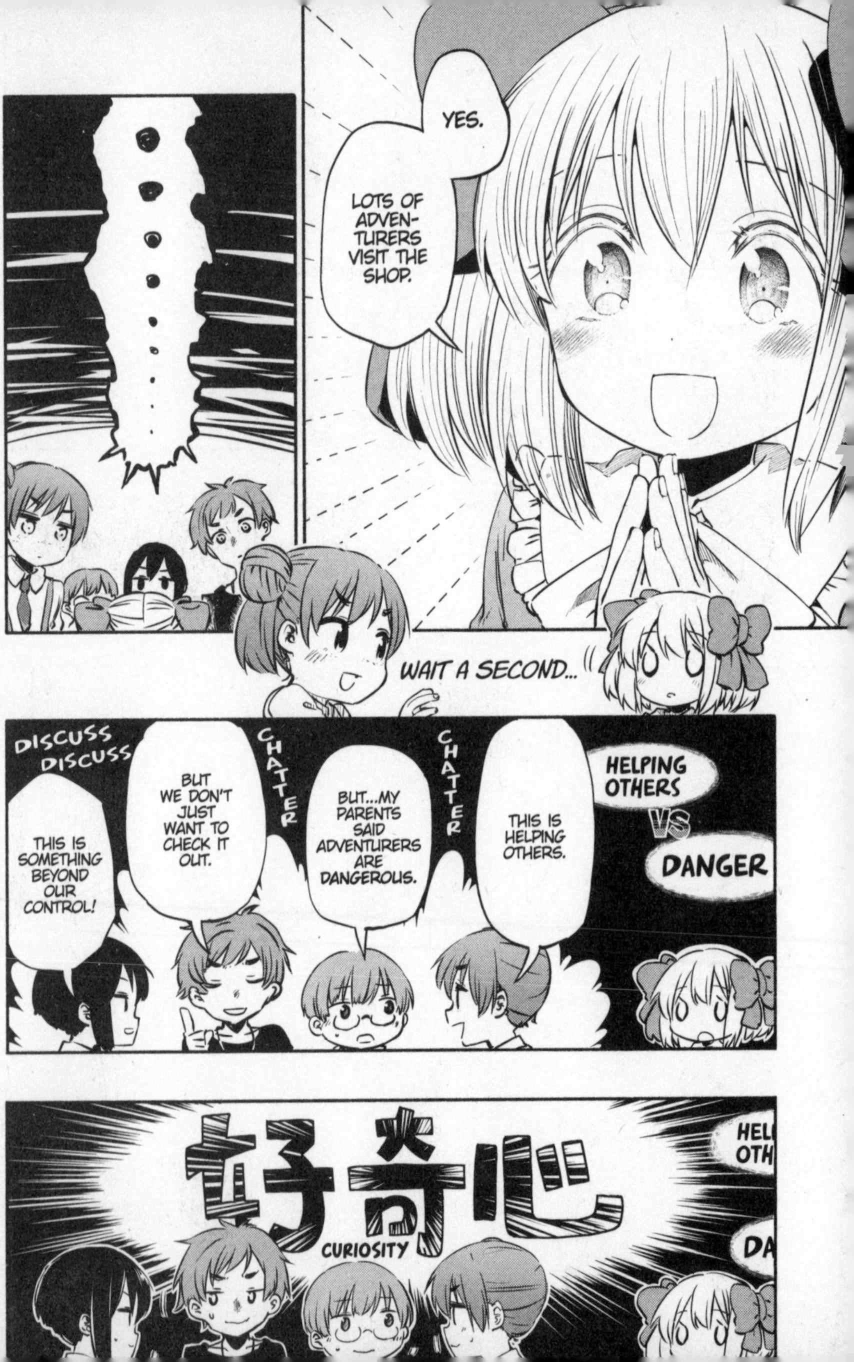
YES.
LOTS OF ADVEN-TURERS VISIT THE SHOP.
......
WAIT A SECOND...
HELPING OTHERS VS DANGER
THIS IS HELPING OTHERS.
CHATTER
BUT...MY PARENTS SAID ADVENTURERS ARE DANGEROUS.
CHATTER
BUT WE DON'T JUST WANT TO CHECK IT OUT.
DISCUSS DISCUSS
THIS IS SOMETHING BEYOND OUR CONTROL!
好奇心
CURIOSITY

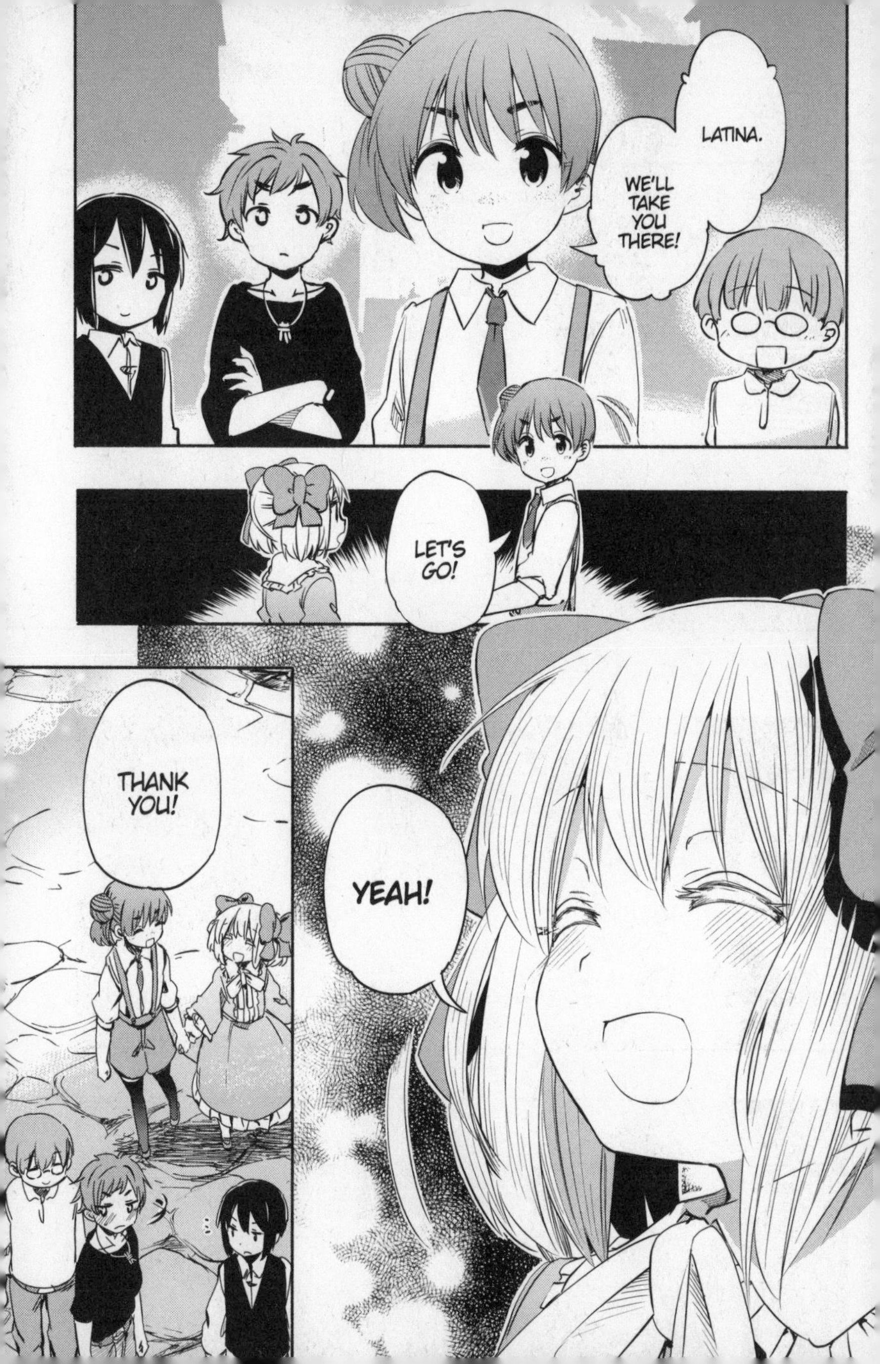

LATINA.
WE'LL TAKE YOU THERE!
LET'S GO!
YEAH!
THANK YOU!

If It's For My Daughter, I'd Even Defeat a Demon Lord.

6. Little Girl's "World" Expands a Little More

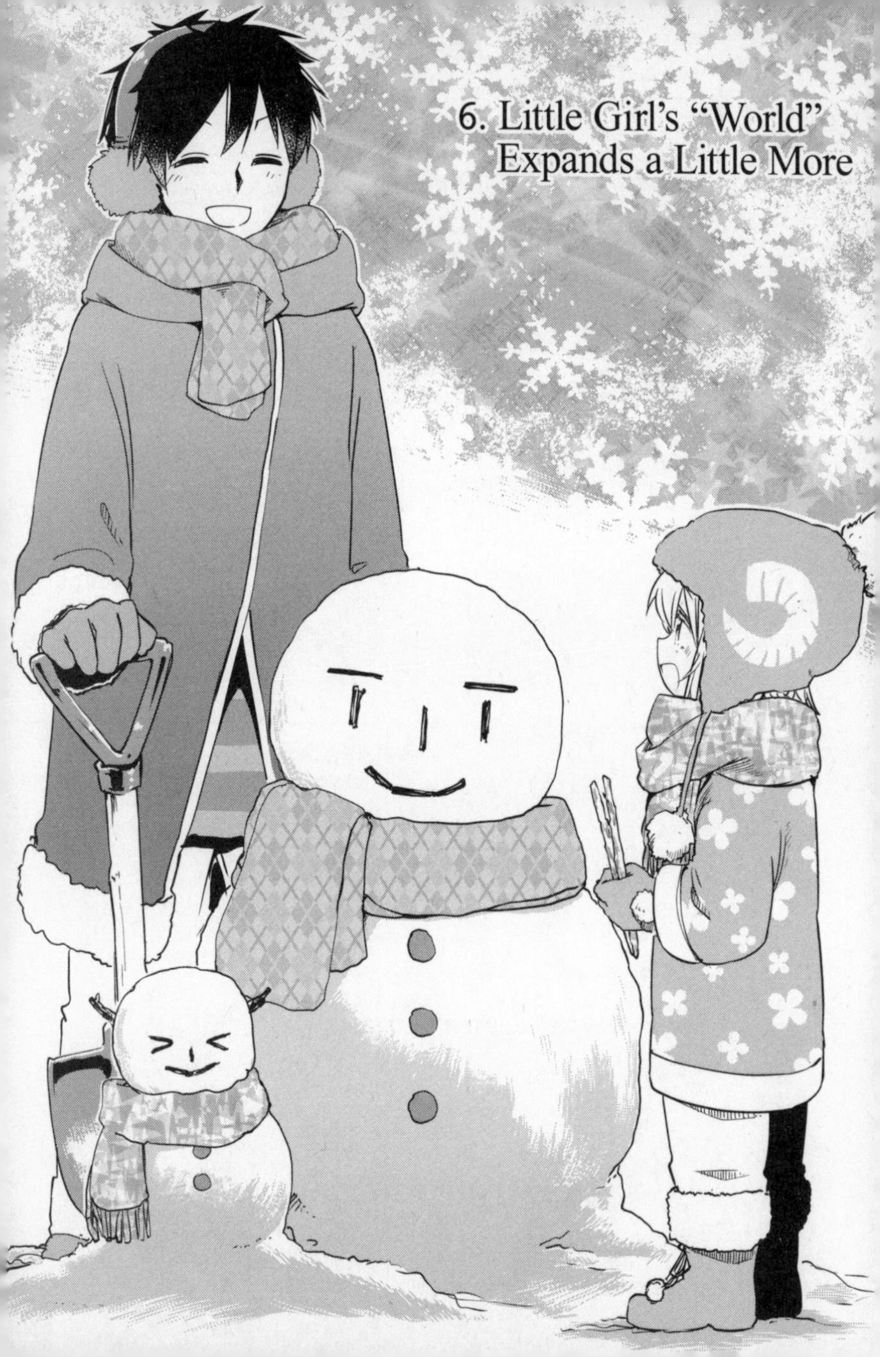

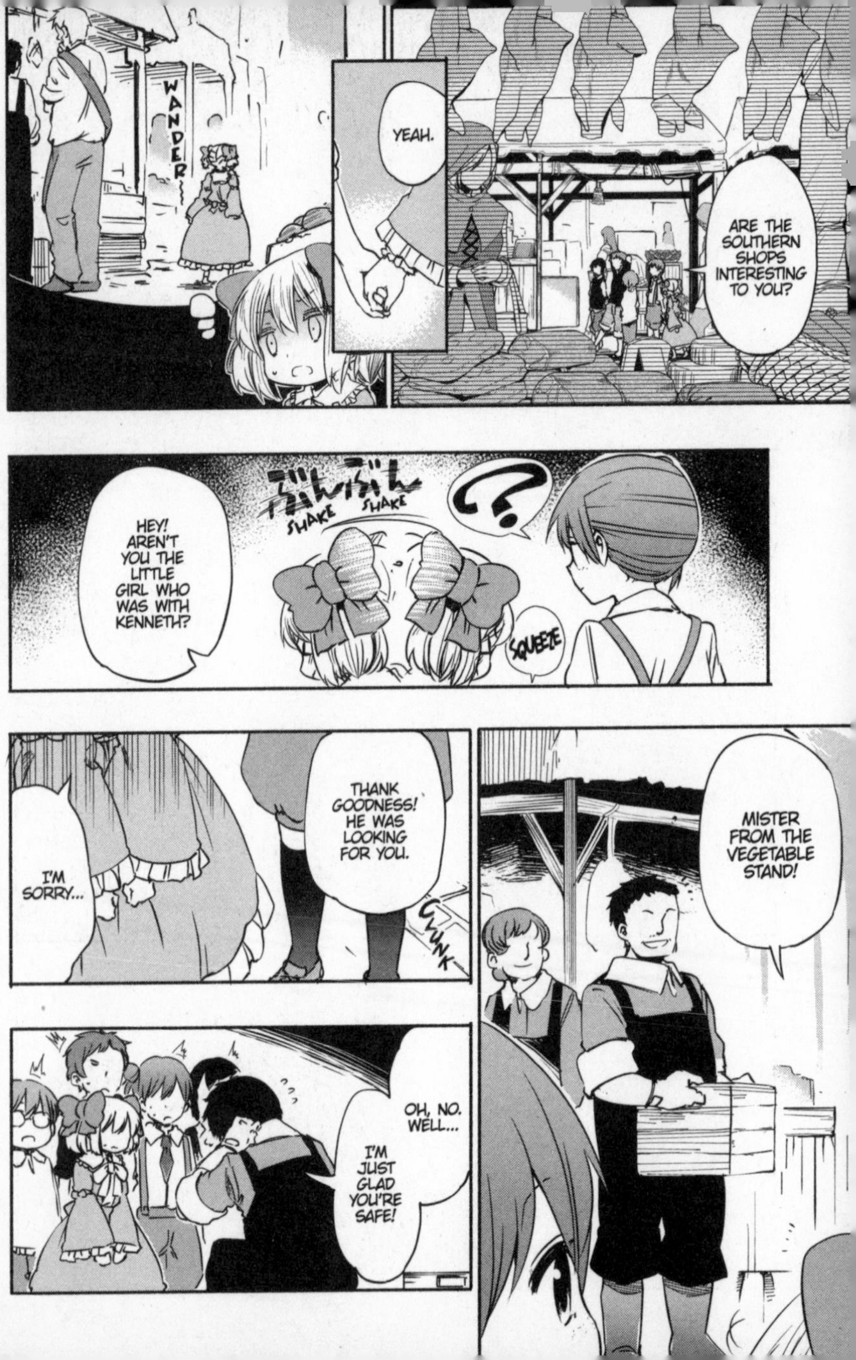
ARE THE SOUTHERN SHOPS INTERESTING TO YOU?
YEAH.
WANDER
SQUEEZE
SHAKE SHAKE
HEY! AREN'T YOU THE LITTLE GIRL WHO WAS WITH KENNETH?
MISTER FROM THE VEGETABLE STAND!
THANK GOODNESS! HE WAS LOOKING FOR YOU.
CLUNK
I'M SORRY...
OH, NO. WELL...
I'M JUST GLAD YOU'RE SAFE!

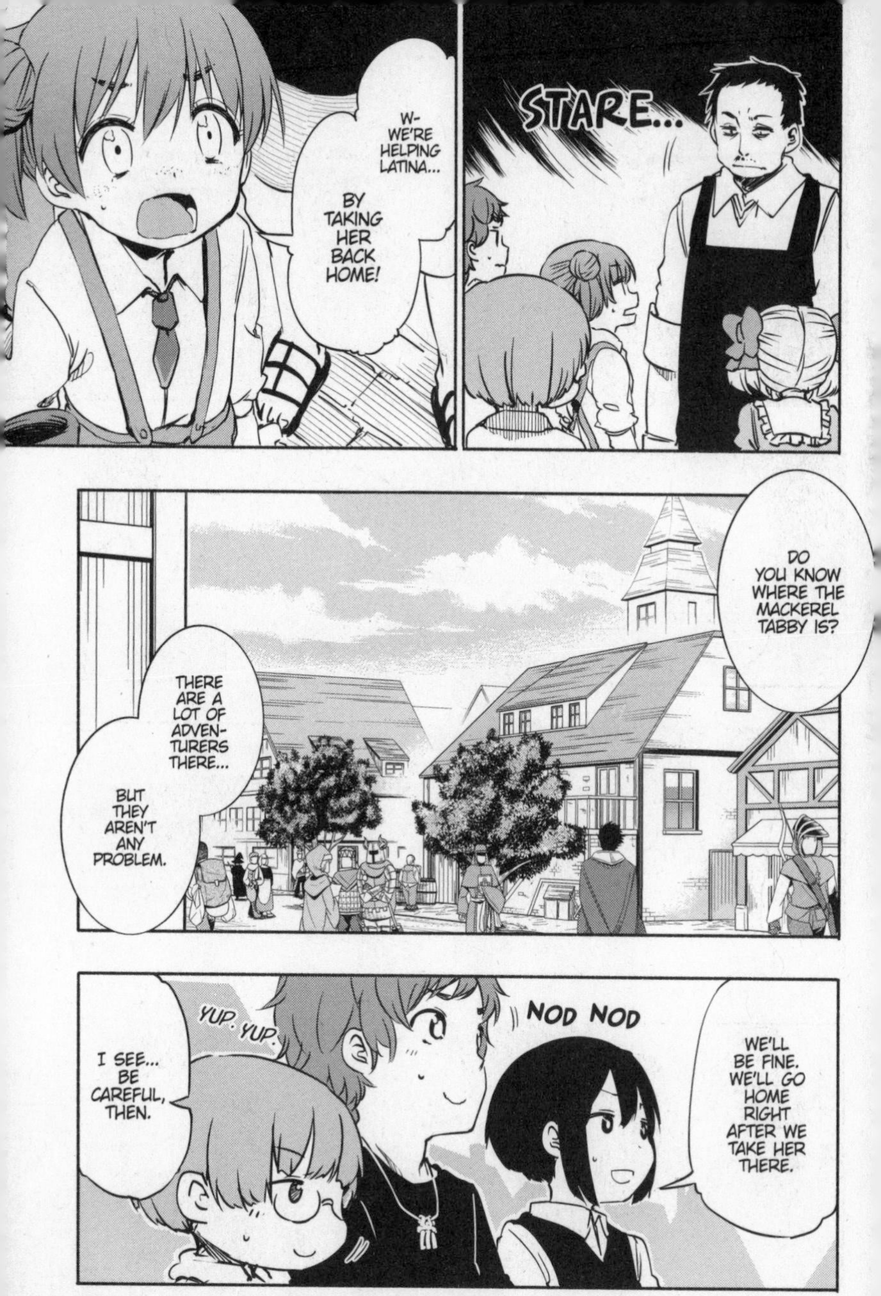
STARE...
W- WE'RE HELPING LATINA...
BY TAKING HER BACK HOME!
DO YOU KNOW WHERE THE MACKEREL TABBY IS?
THERE ARE A LOT OF ADVEN-TURERS THERE...
BUT THEY AREN'T ANY PROBLEM.
WE'LL BE FINE. WE'LL GO HOME RIGHT AFTER WE TAKE HER THERE.
NOD NOD
YUP. YUP.
I SEE... BE CAREFUL, THEN.

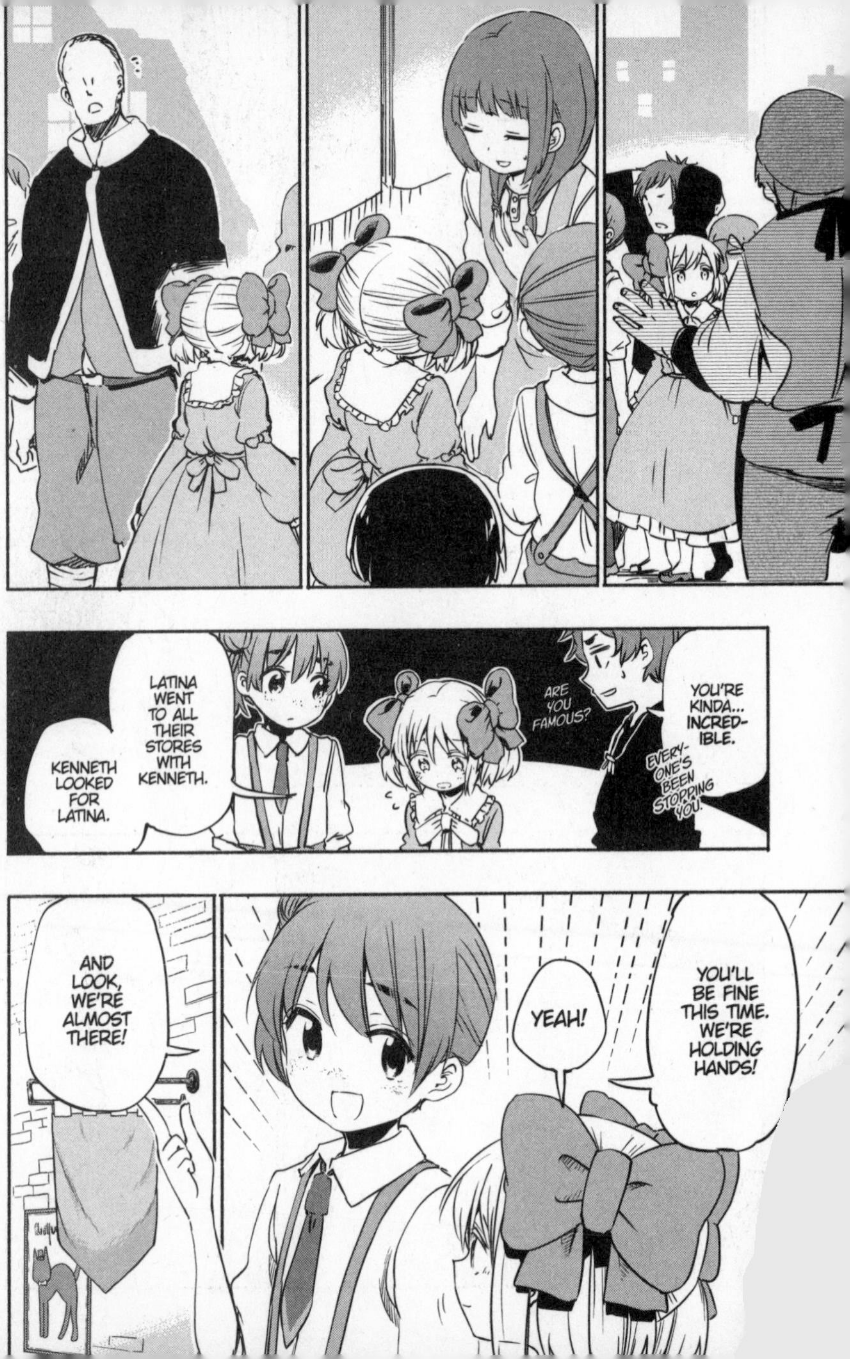
YOU'RE KINDA... INCREDIBLE.
EVERY-ONE'S BEEN STOPPING YOU.
ARE YOU FAMOUS?
LATINA WENT TO ALL THEIR STORES WITH KENNETH.
KENNETH LOOKED FOR LATINA.
YOU'LL BE FINE THIS TIME. WE'RE HOLDING HANDS!
YEAH!
AND LOOK, WE'RE ALMOST THERE!

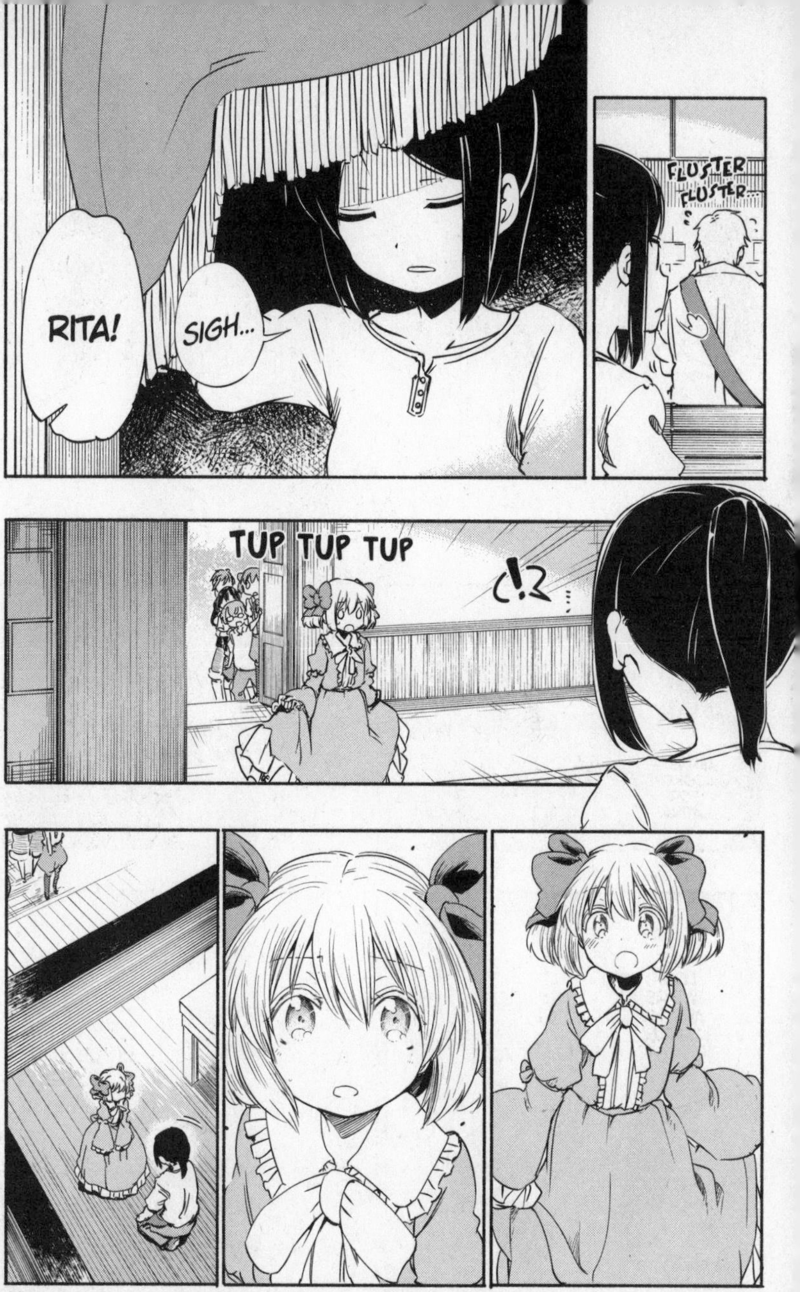

FLUSTER FLUSTER...
SIGH...
RITA!
TUP TUP TUP
!?

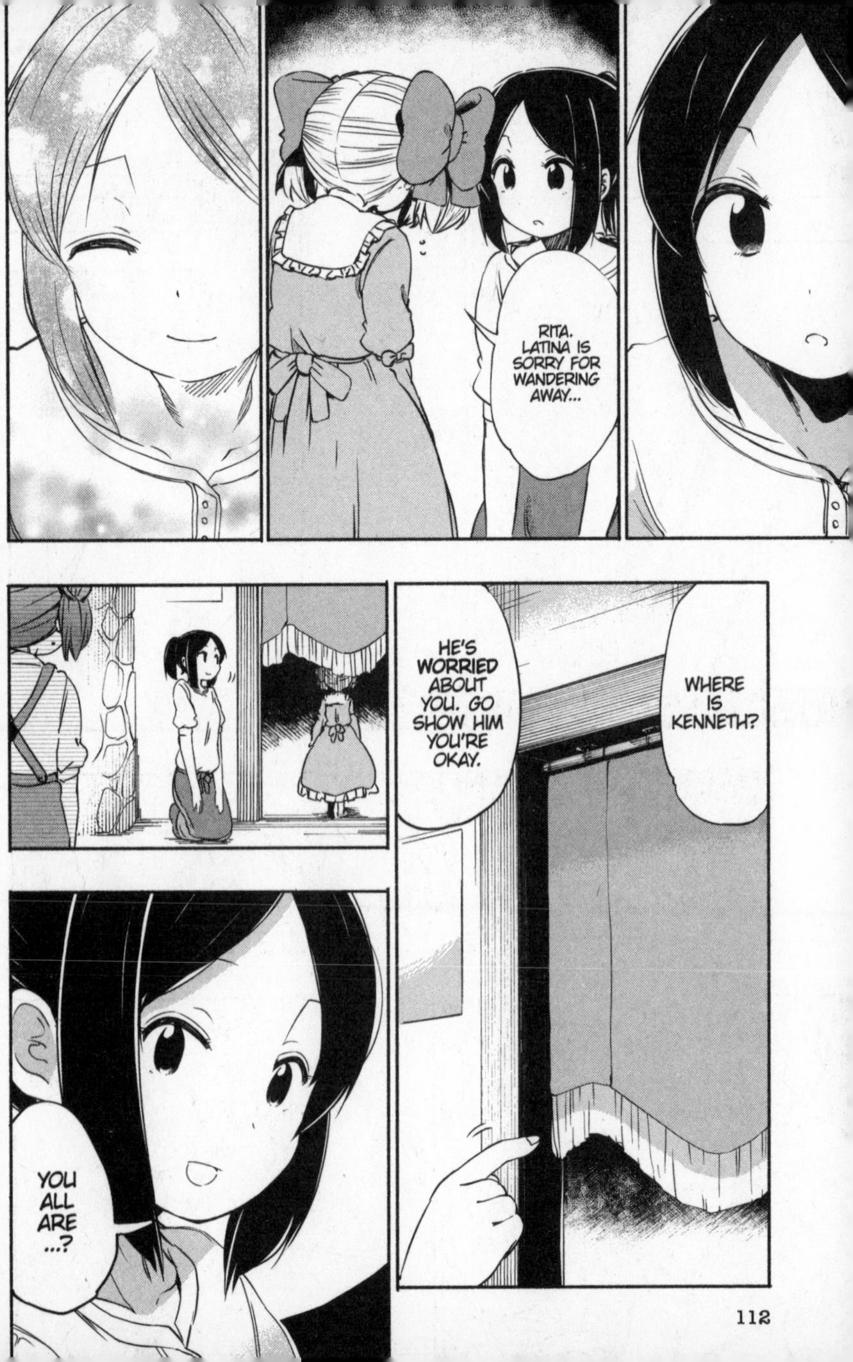
RITA. LATINA IS SORRY FOR WANDERING AWAY...
WHERE IS KENNETH?
HE'S WORRIED ABOUT YOU. GO SHOW HIM YOU'RE OKAY.
YOU ALL ARE ...?

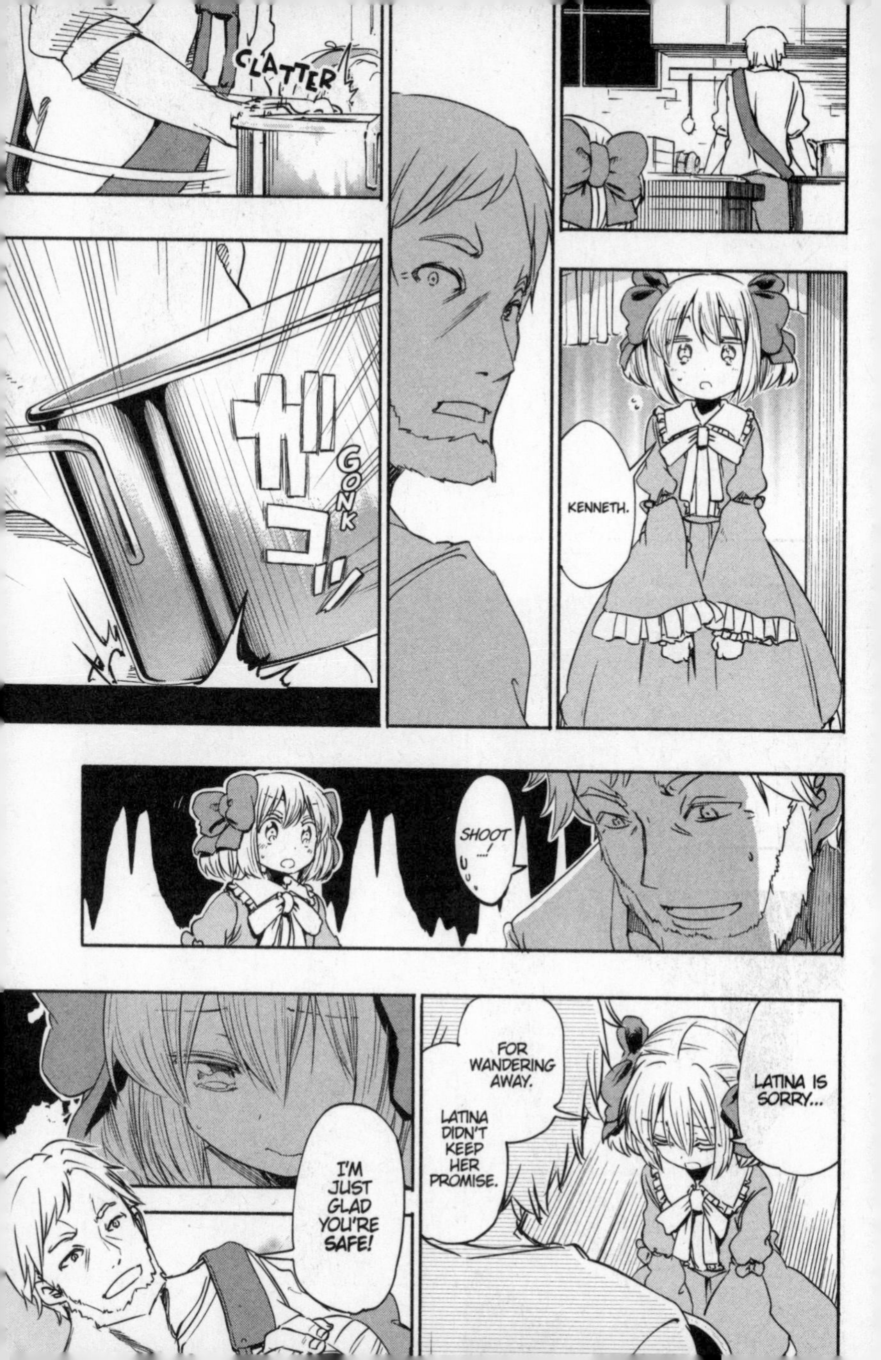
KENNETH.
CLATTER
GONK
SHOOT...!
LATINA IS SORRY...
FOR WANDERING AWAY.
LATINA DIDN'T KEEP HER PROMISE.
I'M JUST GLAD YOU'RE SAFE!

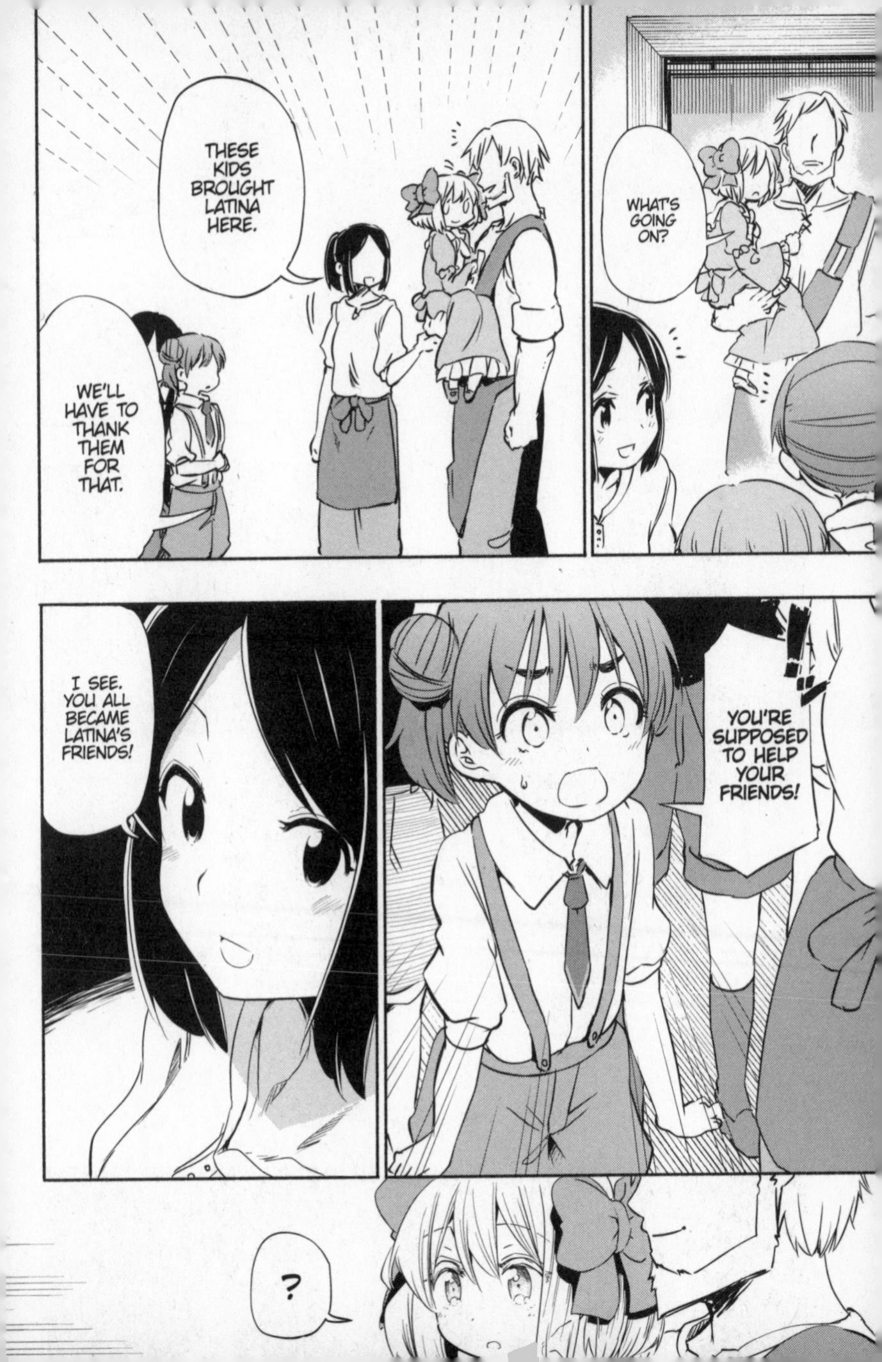
WHAT'S GOING ON?
THESE KIDS BROUGHT LATINA HERE.
WE'LL HAVE TO THANK THEM FOR THAT.
YOU'RE SUPPOSED TO HELP YOUR FRIENDS!
I SEE. YOU ALL BECAME LATINA'S FRIENDS!
?

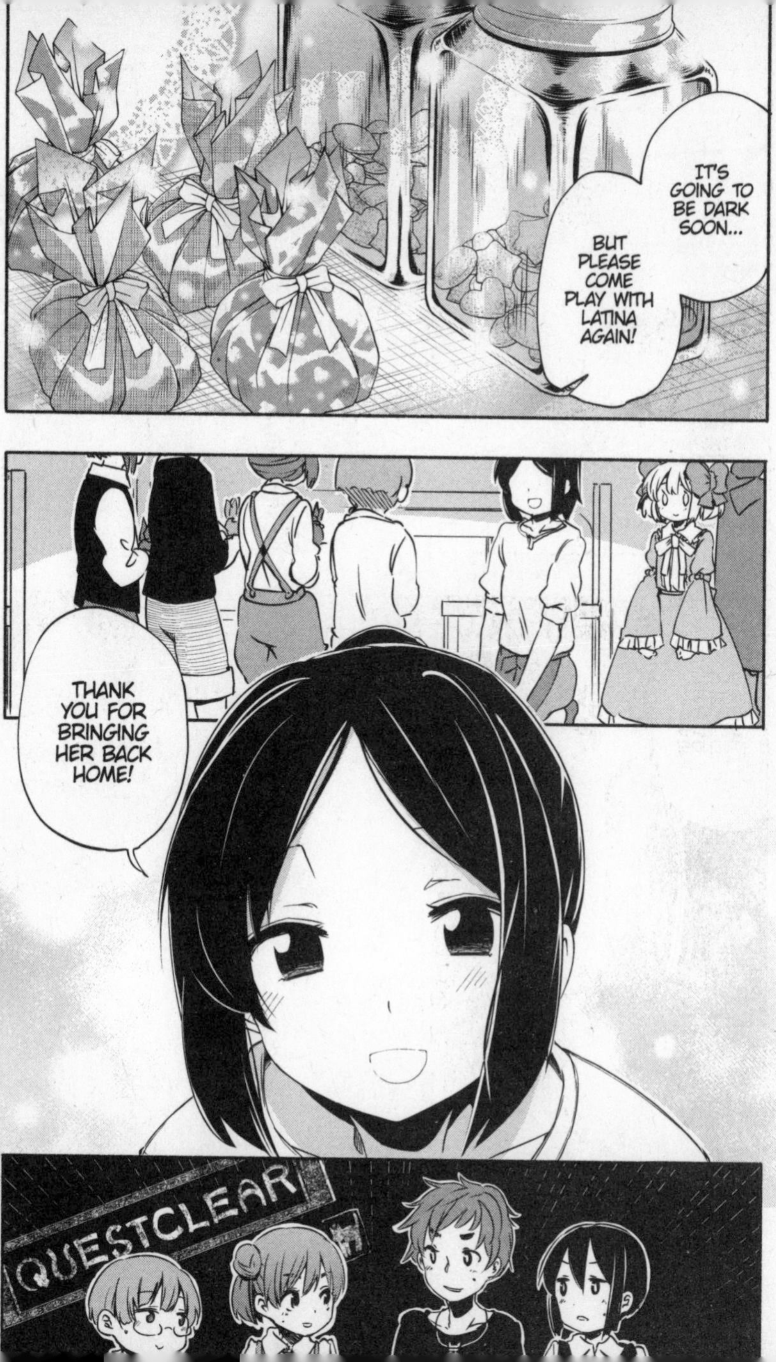
IT'S GOING TO BE DARK SOON...
BUT PLEASE COME PLAY WITH LATINA AGAIN!
THANK YOU FOR BRINGING HER BACK HOME!
QUESTCLEAR

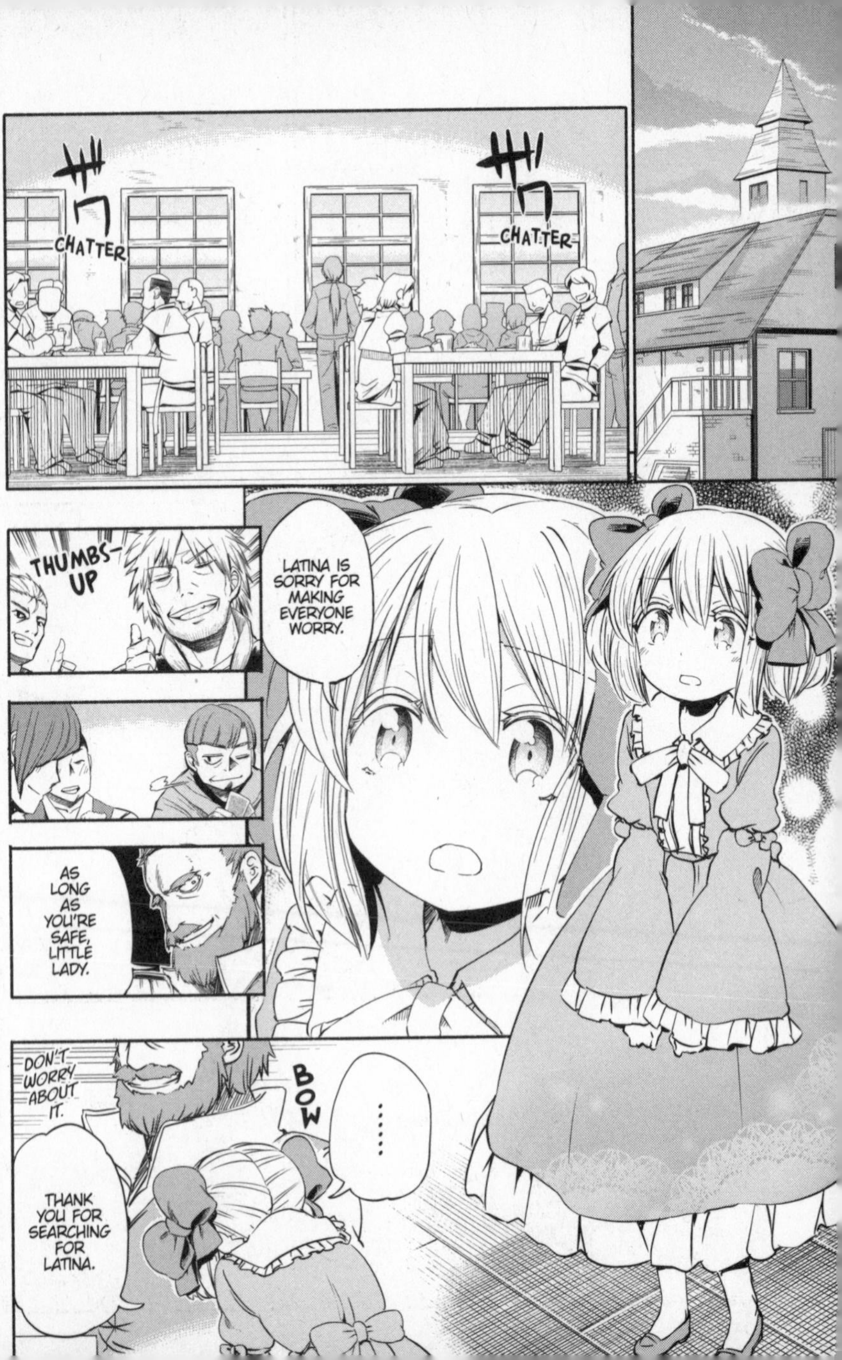
CHATTER
CHATTER
LATINA IS SORRY FOR MAKING EVERYONE WORRY.
THUMBS-UP
AS LONG AS YOU'RE SAFE, LITTLE LADY.
......
BOW
THANK YOU FOR SEARCHING FOR LATINA.
DON'T WORRY ABOUT IT.

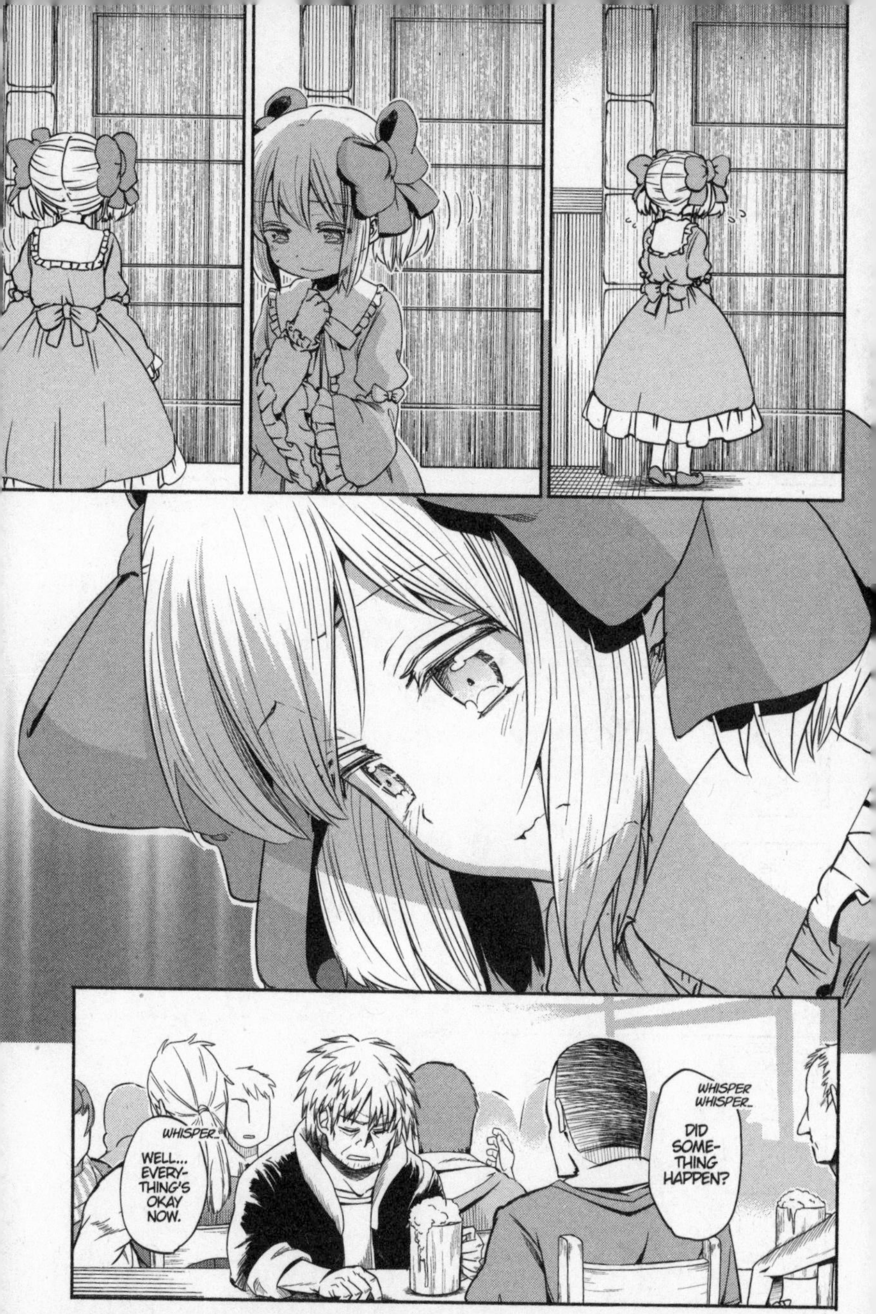
WHISPER WHISPER...
DID SOME-THING HAPPEN?
WHISPER...
WELL... EVERY-THING'S OKAY NOW.

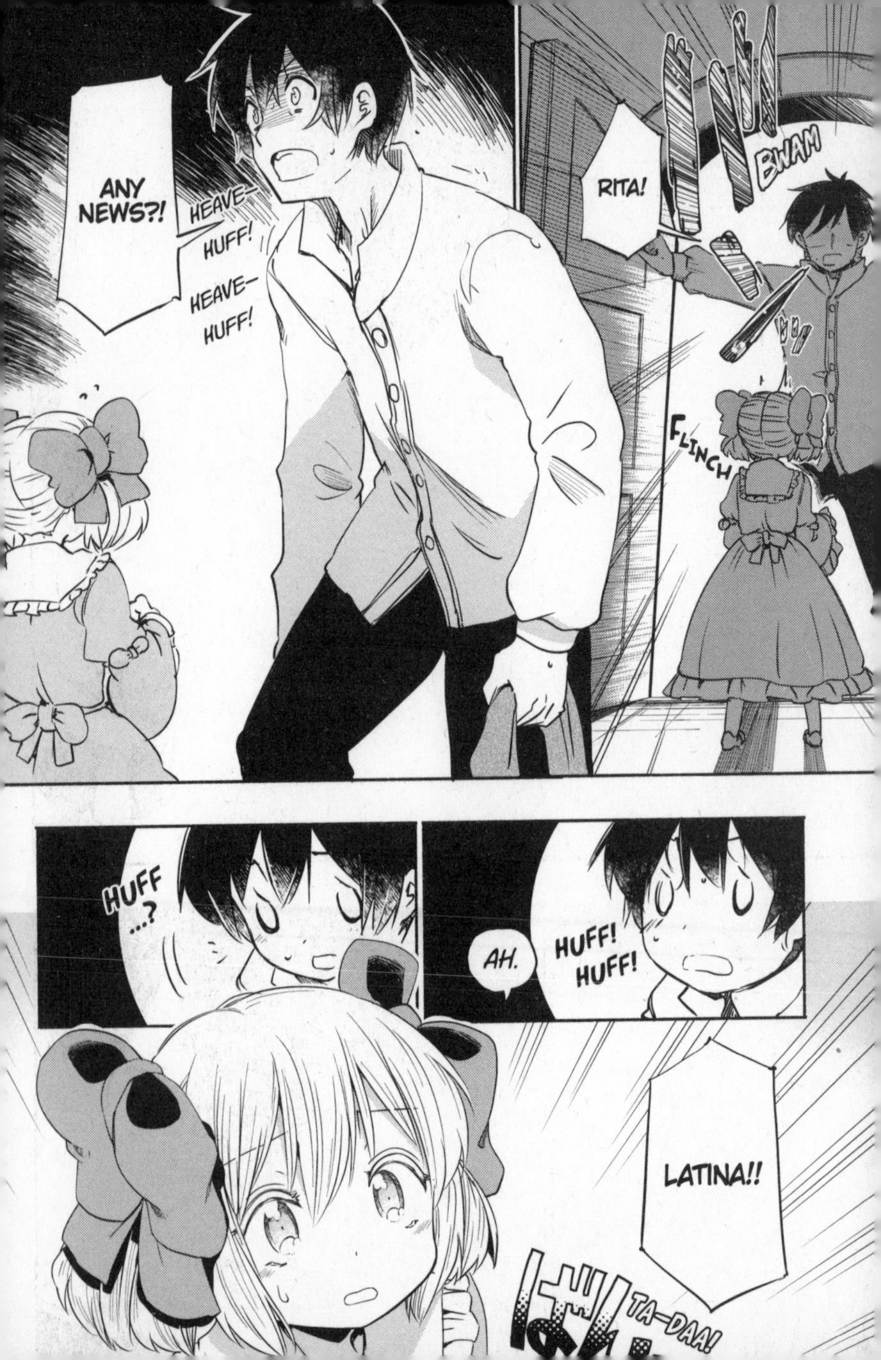
BWAM
RITA!
FLINCH
HEAVE-HUFF! HEAVE-HUFF!
ANY NEWS?!
AH.
HUFF! HUFF!
HUFF ...?
LATINA!!
TA-DAA!

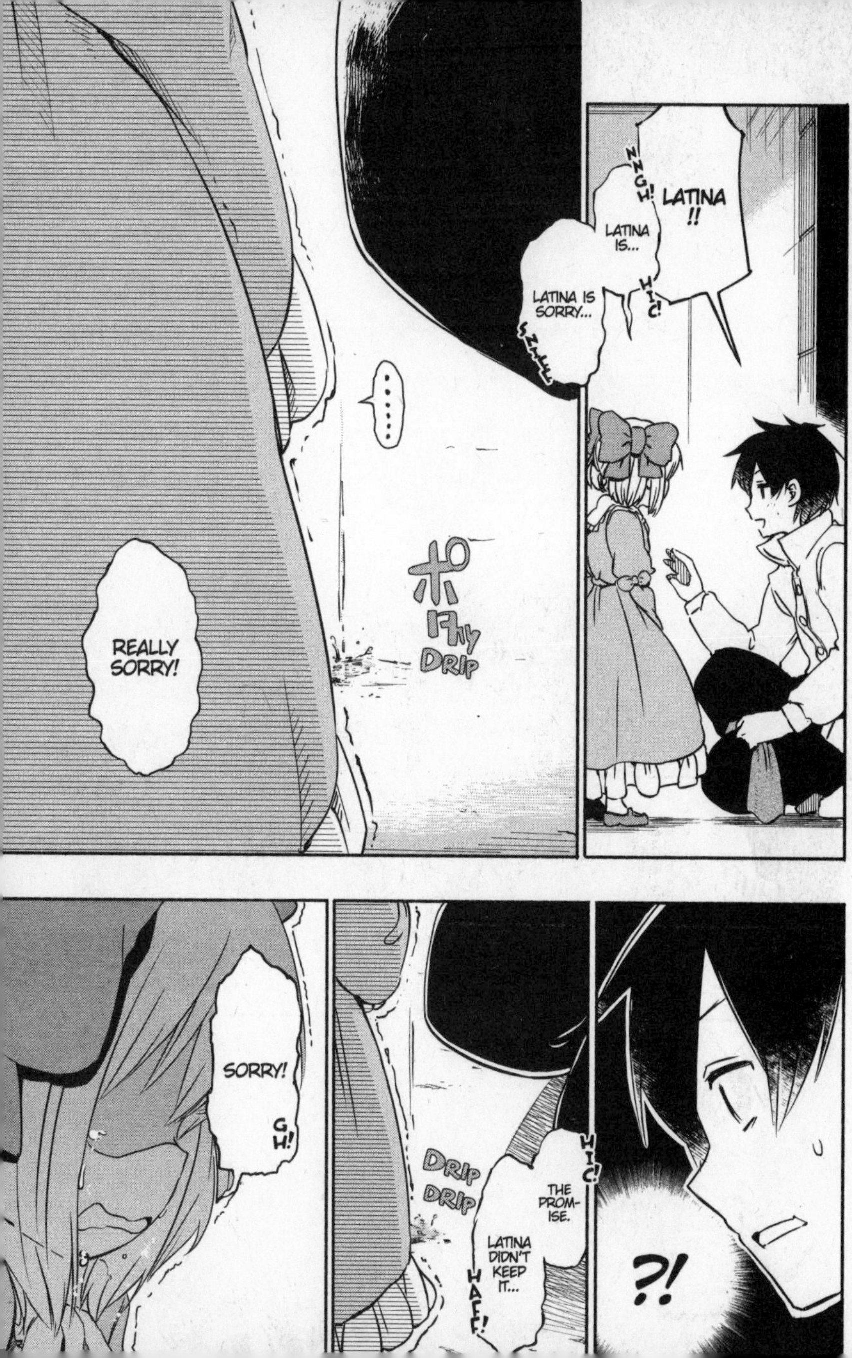
LATINA !!
NNGH!
LATINA IS...
HIC!
LATINA IS SORRY...
SNIFF
......
ポトッ DRIP
REALLY SORRY!
?!
HIC!
THE PROM-ISE.
LATINA DIDN'T KEEP IT...
HAFF!
DRIP DRIP
SORRY!
GH!

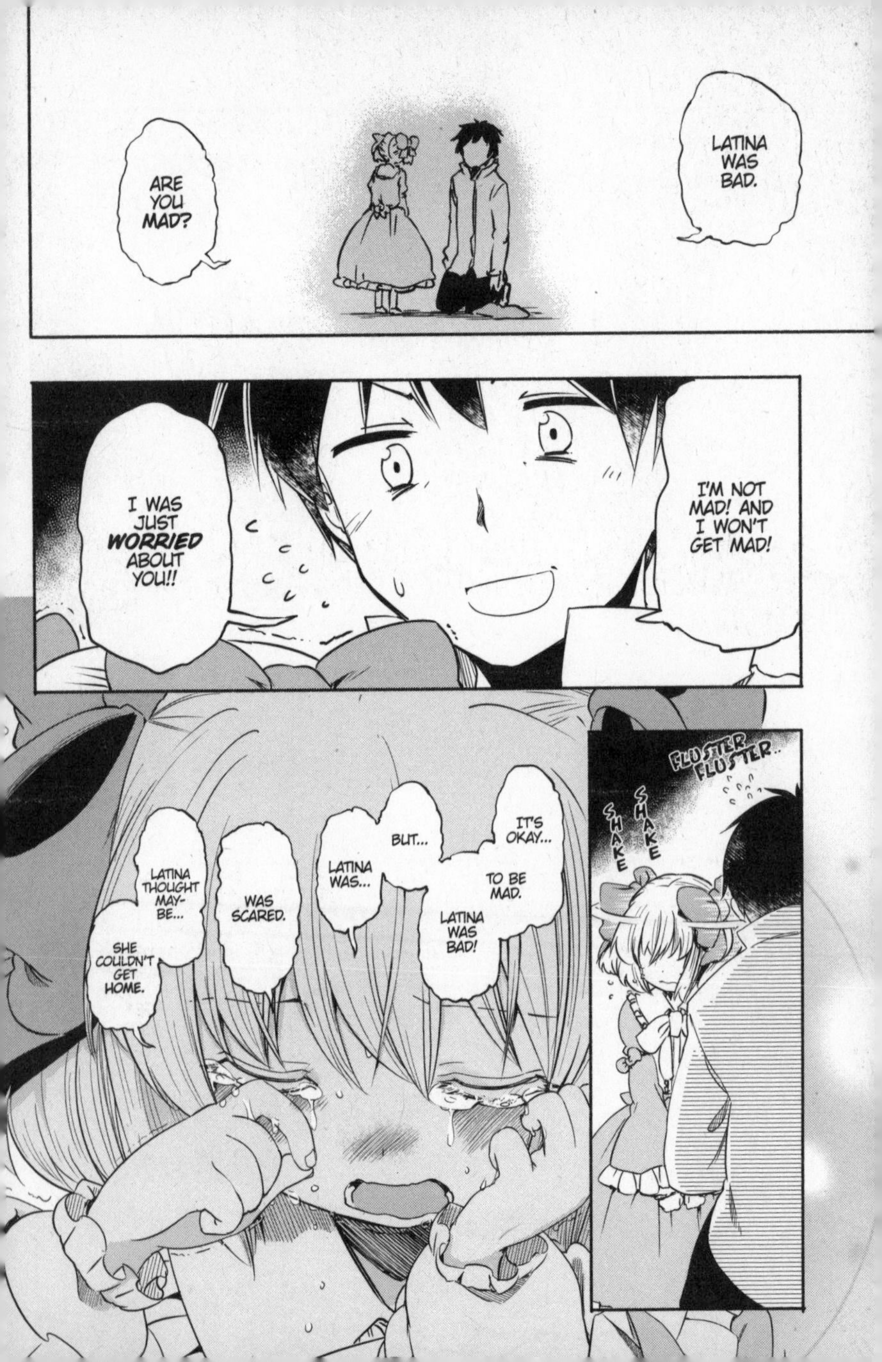
LATINA WAS BAD.
ARE YOU MAD?
I'M NOT MAD! AND I WON'T GET MAD!
I WAS JUST **WORRIED** ABOUT YOU!!
FLUSTER FLUSTER..
SHAKE SHAKE
IT'S OKAY... TO BE MAD. LATINA WAS BAD!
BUT... LATINA WAS...
WAS SCARED.
LATINA THOUGHT MAY-BE... SHE COULDN'T GET HOME.

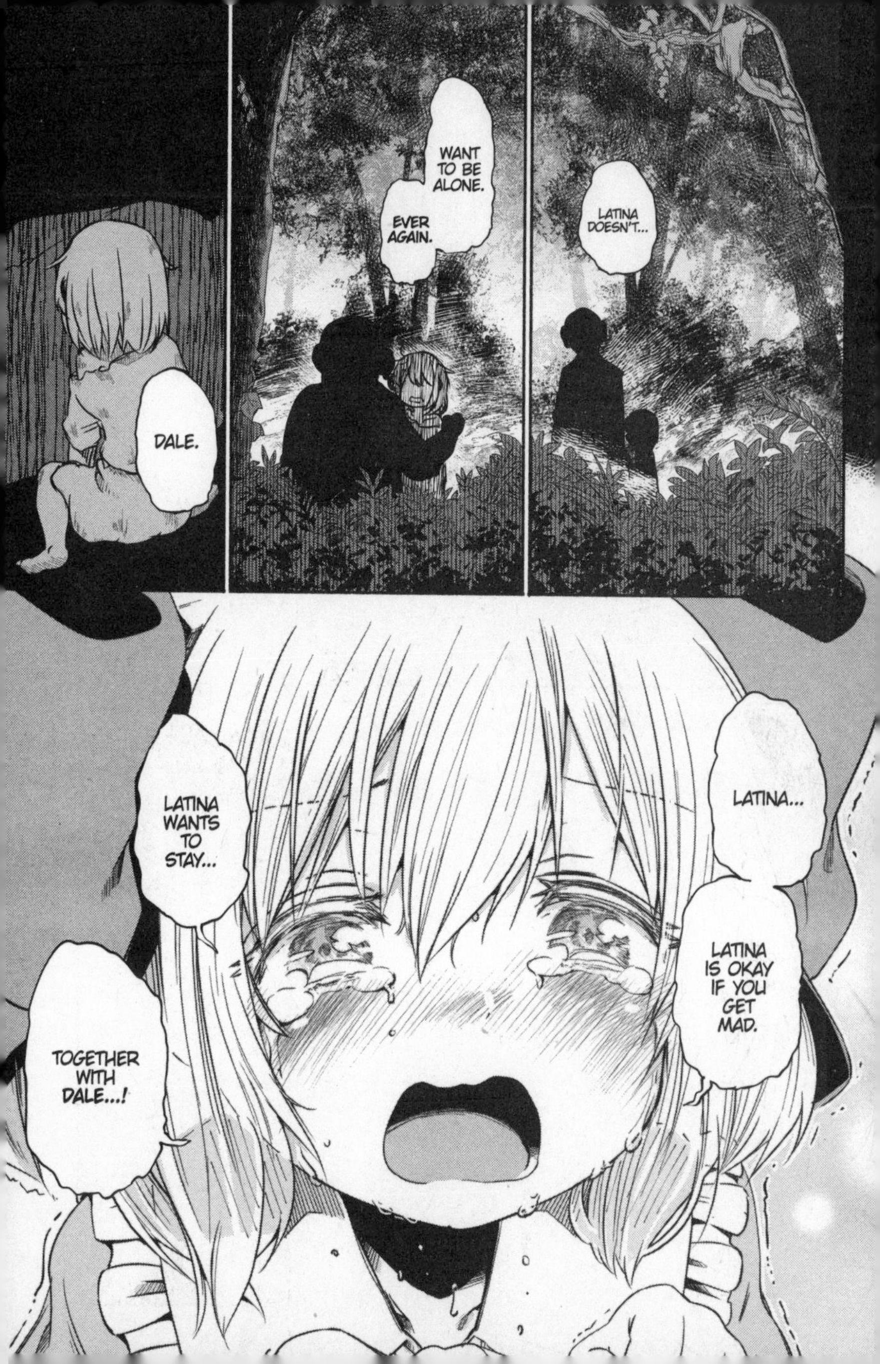
LATINA DOESN'T...
WANT TO BE ALONE.
EVER AGAIN.
DALE.
LATINA...
LATINA IS OKAY IF YOU GET MAD.
LATINA WANTS TO STAY...
TOGETHER WITH DALE...!

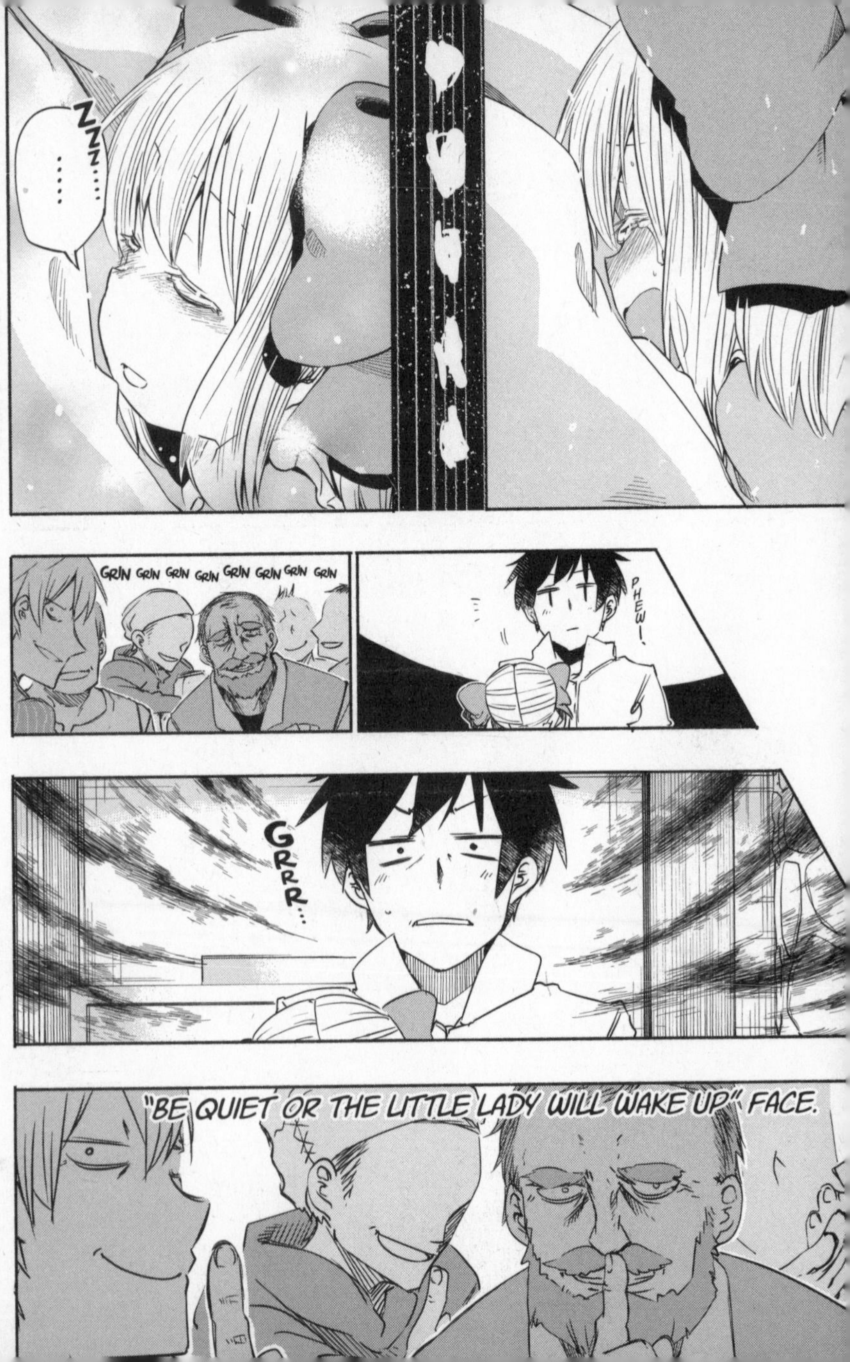
ZZZ....
......
PHEW!
GRIN GRIN GRIN GRIN GRIN GRIN GRIN GRIN
GRRR...
"BE QUIET OR THE LITTLE LADY WILL WAKE UP" FACE.

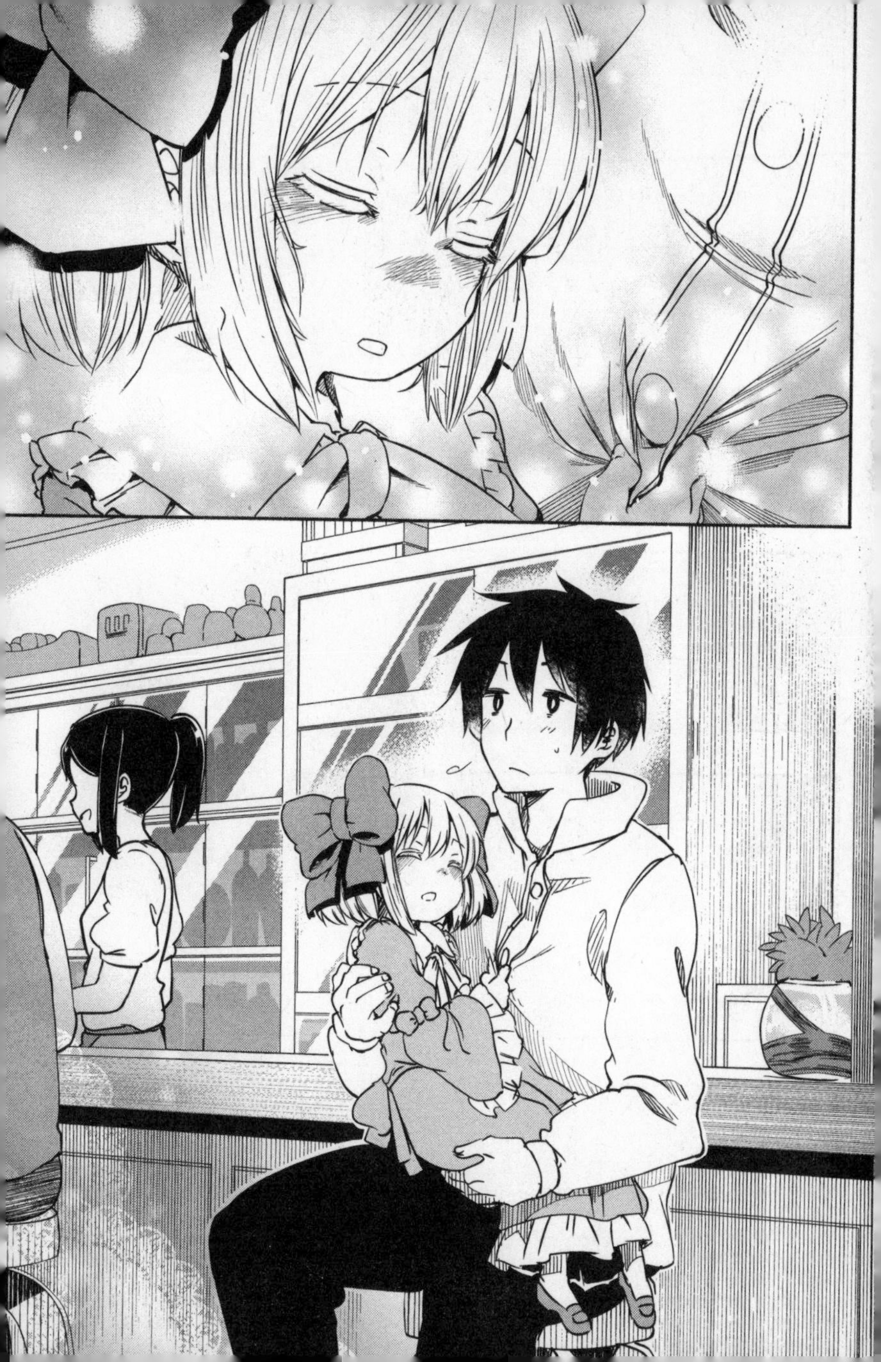

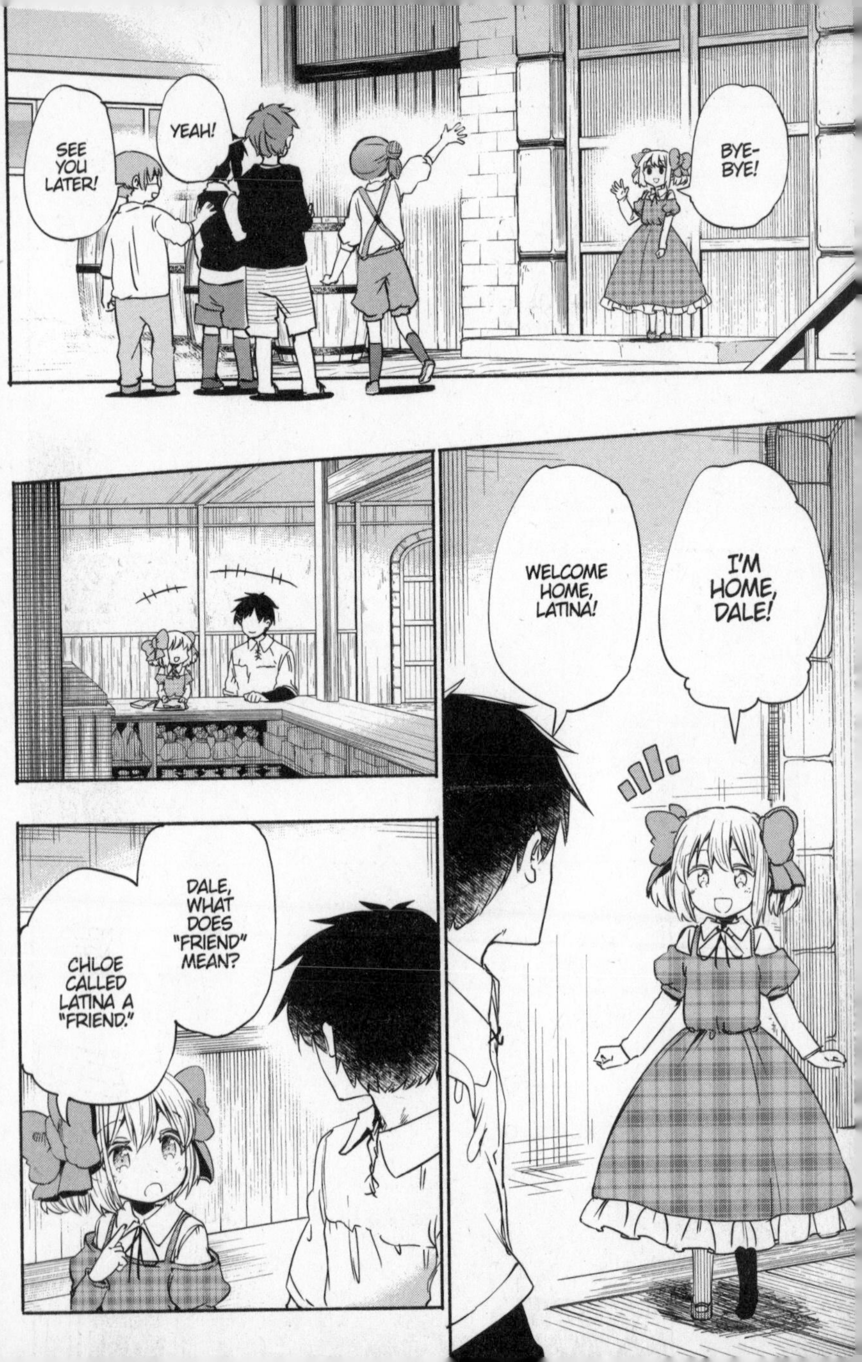
BYE-BYE!
YEAH!
SEE YOU LATER!
I'M HOME, DALE!
WELCOME HOME, LATINA!
DALE, WHAT DOES "FRIEND" MEAN?
CHLOE CALLED LATINA A "FRIEND."

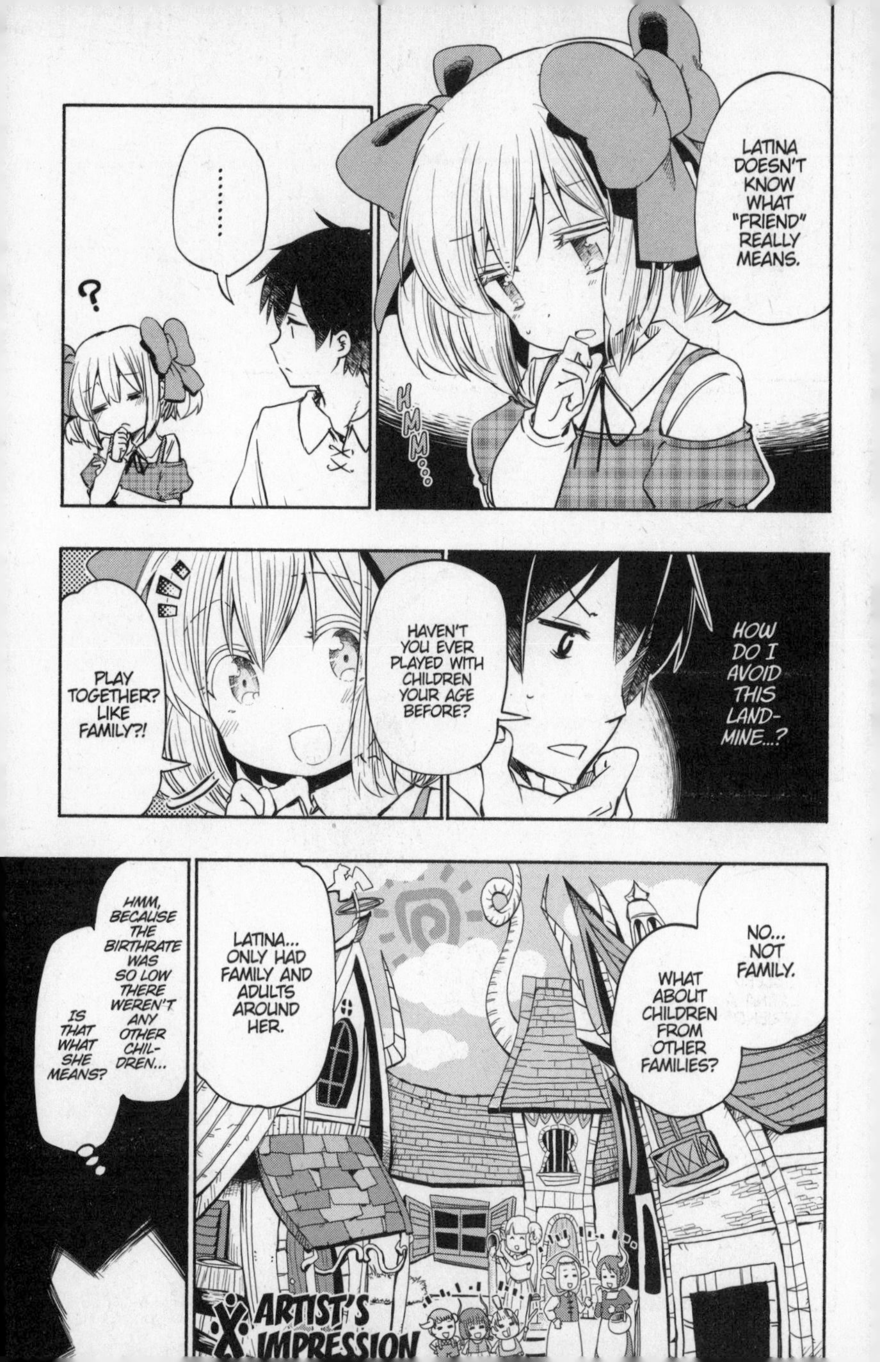
LATINA DOESN'T KNOW WHAT "FRIEND" REALLY MEANS.
HMM...
......
?
HOW DO I AVOID THIS LAND-MINE...?
HAVEN'T YOU EVER PLAYED WITH CHILDREN YOUR AGE BEFORE?
!!
PLAY TOGETHER? LIKE FAMILY?!
NO... NOT FAMILY.
WHAT ABOUT CHILDREN FROM OTHER FAMILIES?
LATINA... ONLY HAD FAMILY AND ADULTS AROUND HER.
ARTIST'S IMPRESSION
HMM, BECAUSE THE BIRTHRATE WAS SO LOW THERE WEREN'T ANY OTHER CHIL-DREN...
IS THAT WHAT SHE MEANS?

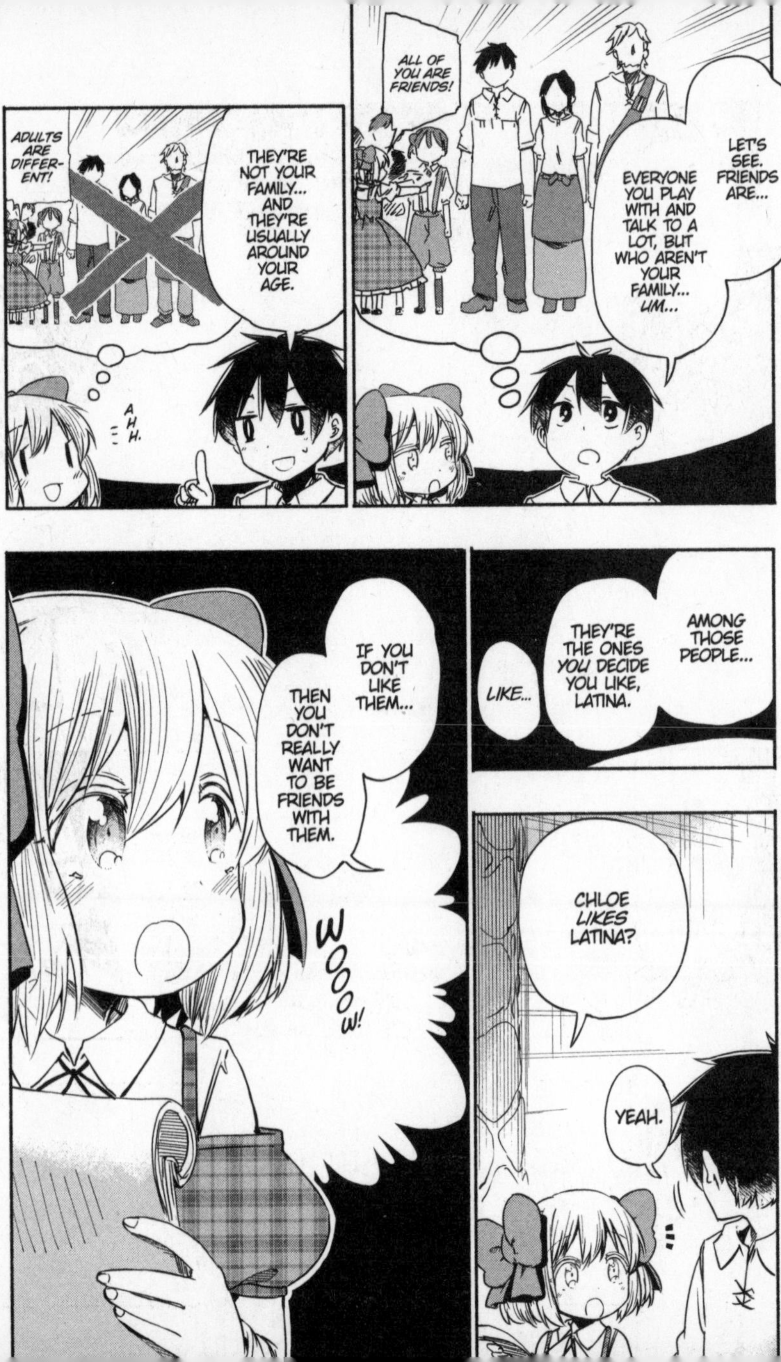
LET'S SEE. FRIENDS ARE...
EVERYONE YOU PLAY WITH AND TALK TO A LOT, BUT WHO AREN'T YOUR FAMILY... UM...
ALL OF YOU ARE FRIENDS!
THEY'RE NOT YOUR FAMILY... AND THEY'RE USUALLY AROUND YOUR AGE.
ADULTS ARE DIFFER-ENT!
AHH.
AMONG THOSE PEOPLE...
THEY'RE THE ONES YOU DECIDE YOU LIKE, LATINA.
LIKE...
CHLOE LIKES LATINA?
YEAH.
IF YOU DON'T LIKE THEM...
THEN YOU DON'T REALLY WANT TO BE FRIENDS WITH THEM.
WOOOOW!

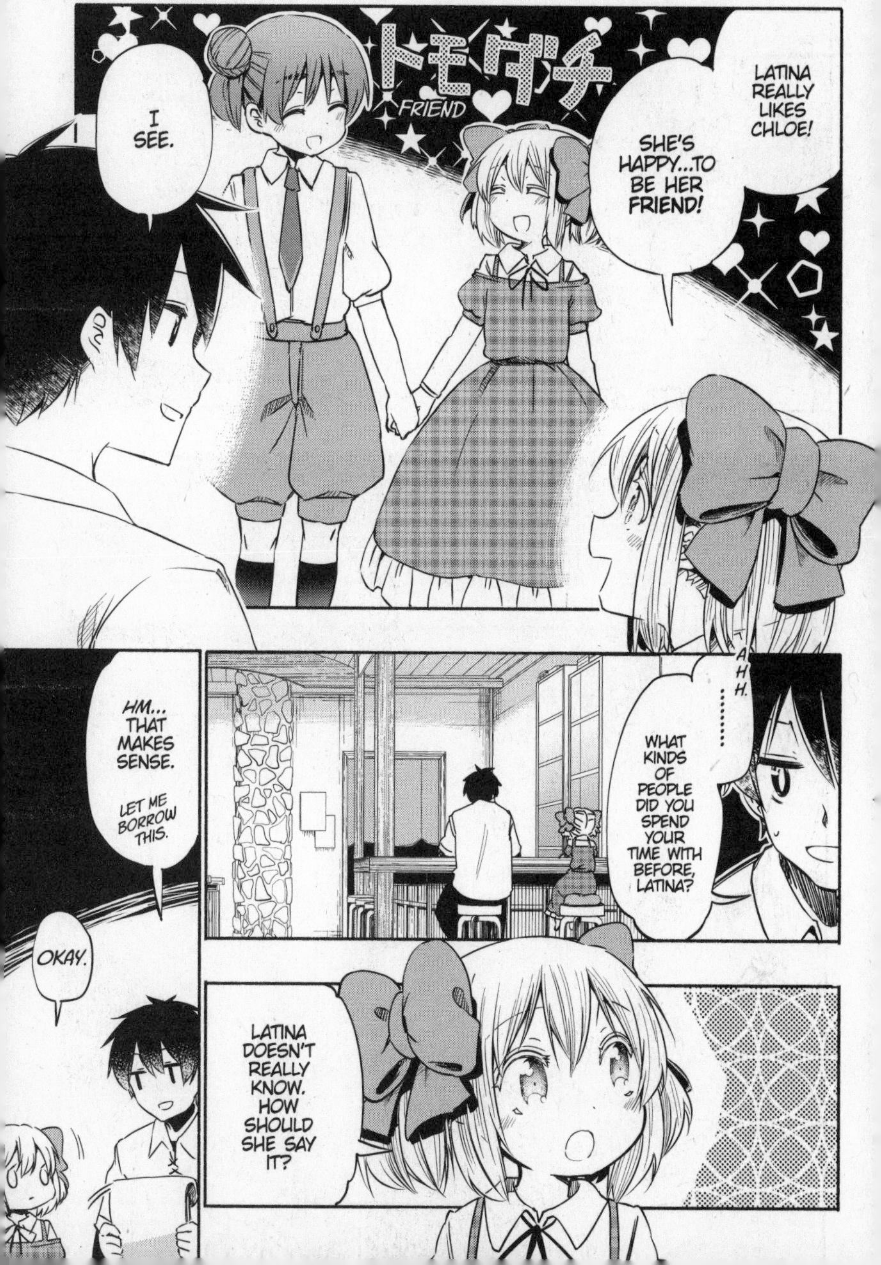
LATINA REALLY LIKES CHLOE!
SHE'S HAPPY...TO BE HER FRIEND!
トモダチ
FRIEND
I SEE.
AHH.
......
WHAT KINDS OF PEOPLE DID YOU SPEND YOUR TIME WITH BEFORE, LATINA?
LATINA DOESN'T REALLY KNOW. HOW SHOULD SHE SAY IT?
HM... THAT MAKES SENSE.
LET ME BORROW THIS.
OKAY.

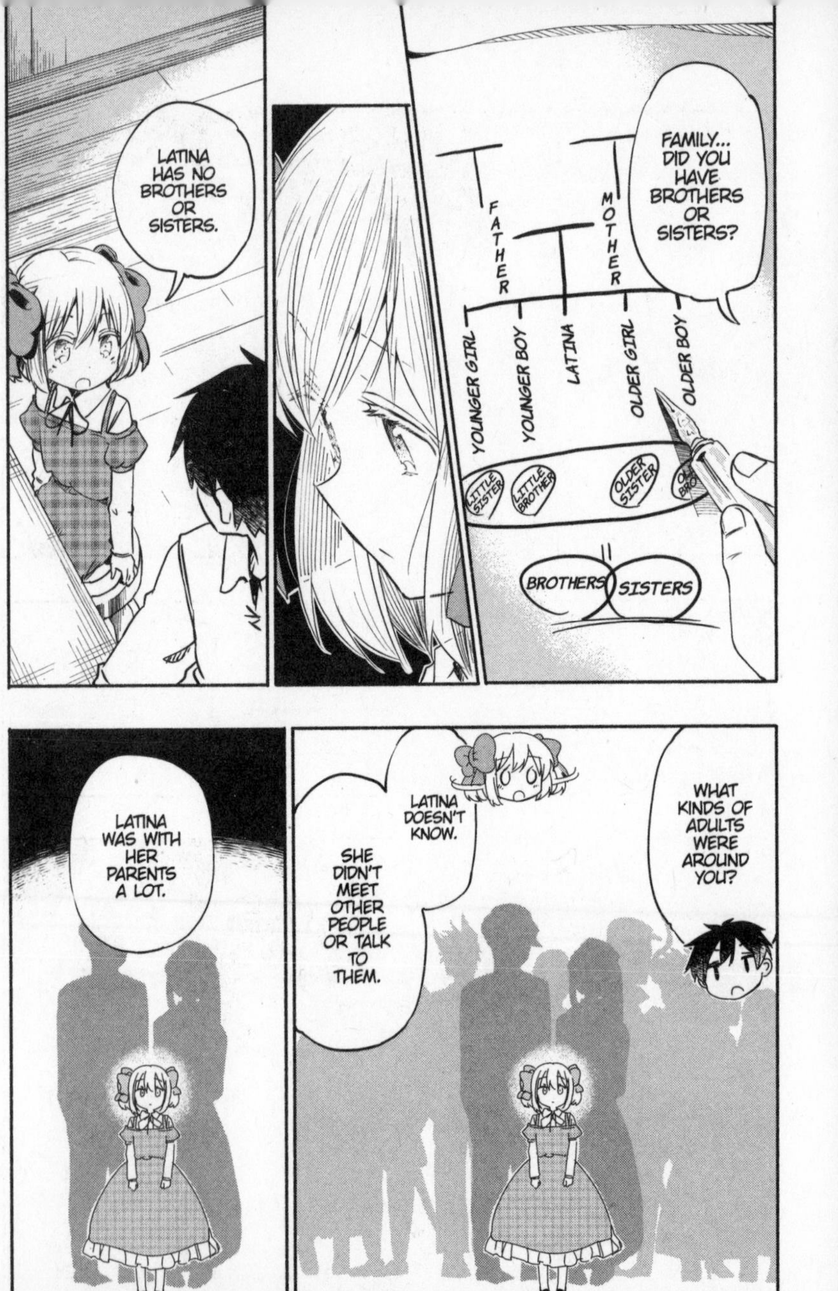
FAMILY... DID YOU HAVE BROTHERS OR SISTERS?
FATHER
MOTHER
OLDER BOY
OLDER GIRL
LATINA
YOUNGER BOY
YOUNGER GIRL
OLDER SISTER
LITTLE BROTHER
LITTLE SISTER
BROTHERS
SISTERS
LATINA HAS NO BROTHERS OR SISTERS.
WHAT KINDS OF ADULTS WERE AROUND YOU?
LATINA DOESN'T KNOW.
SHE DIDN'T MEET OTHER PEOPLE OR TALK TO THEM.
LATINA WAS WITH HER PARENTS A LOT.

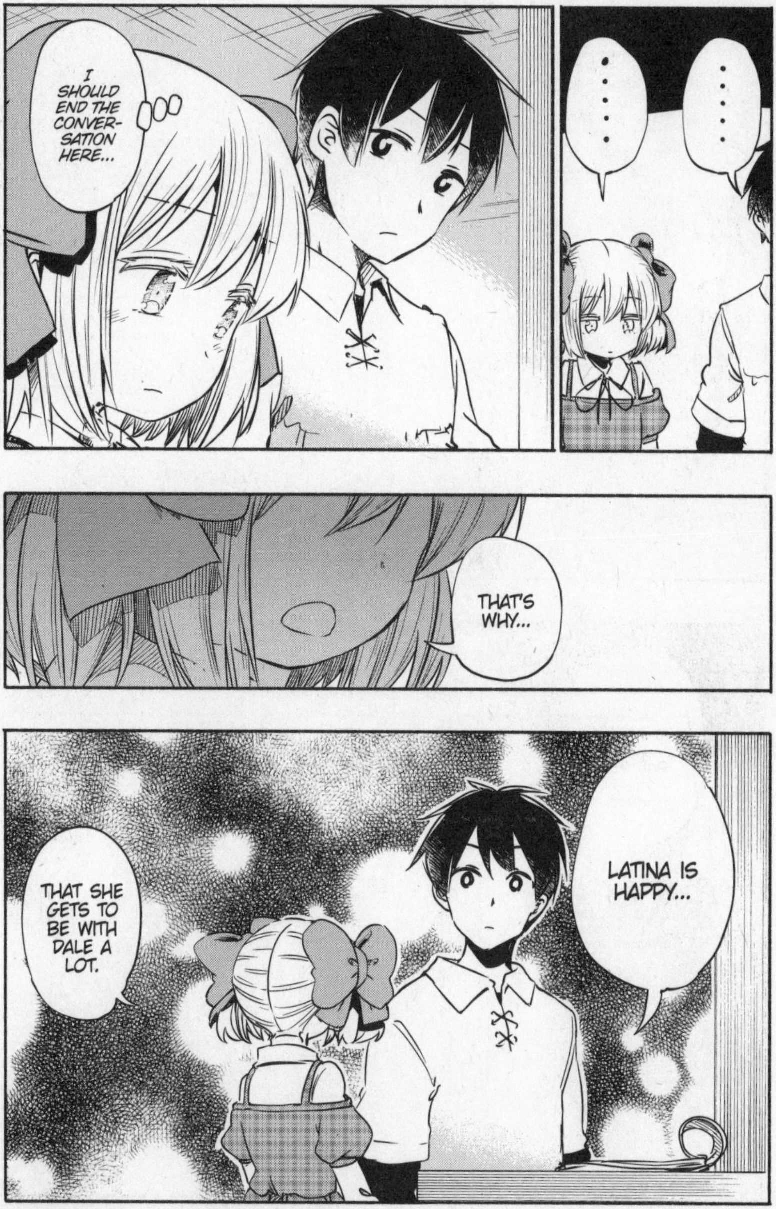
.....
.....
I SHOULD END THE CONVERSATION HERE...
THAT'S WHY...
LATINA IS HAPPY...
THAT SHE GETS TO BE WITH DALE A LOT.

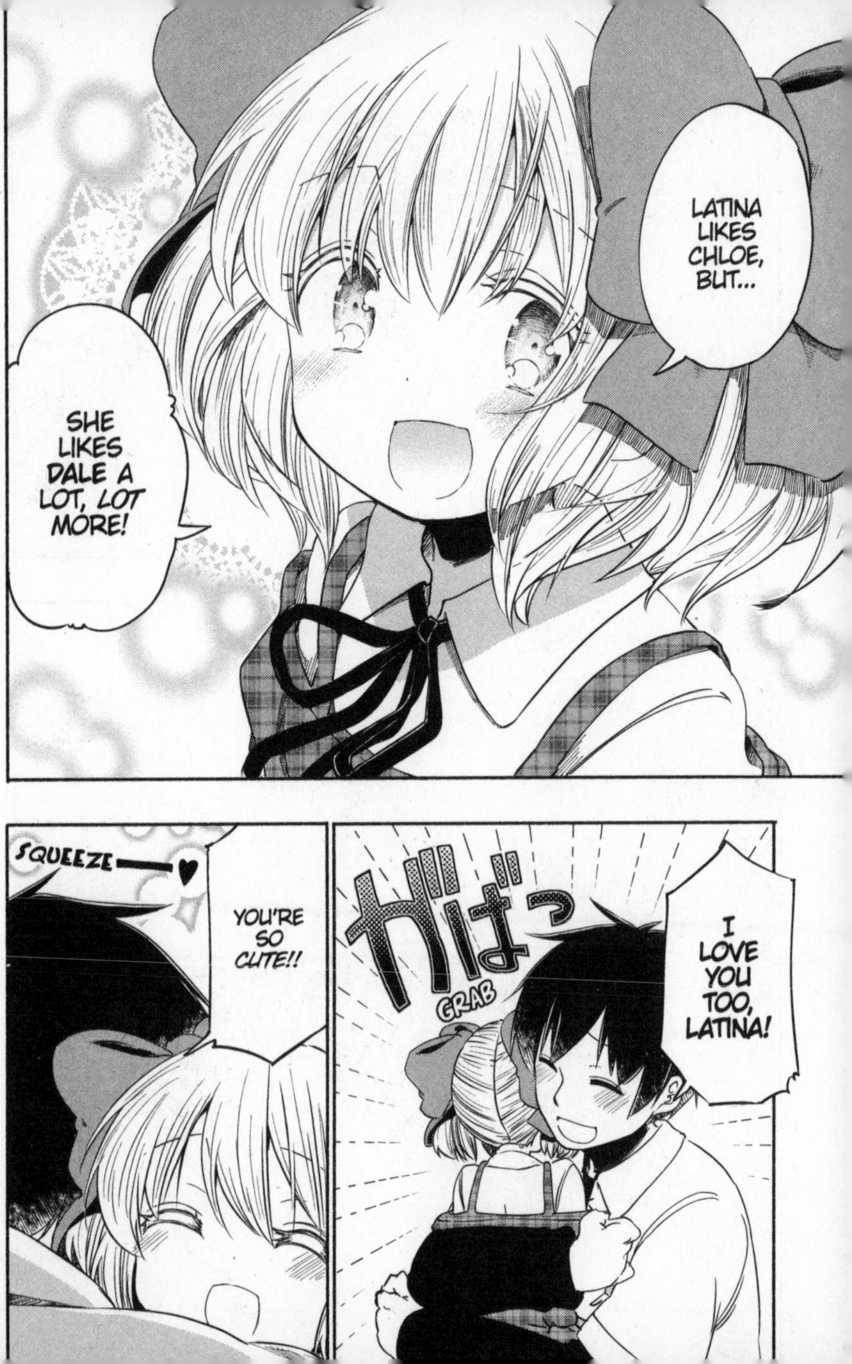
LATINA LIKES CHLOE, BUT...
SHE LIKES DALE A LOT, *LOT* MORE!
I LOVE YOU TOO, LATINA!
がばっ
GRAB
YOU'RE SO CUTE!!
SQUEEZE——♥

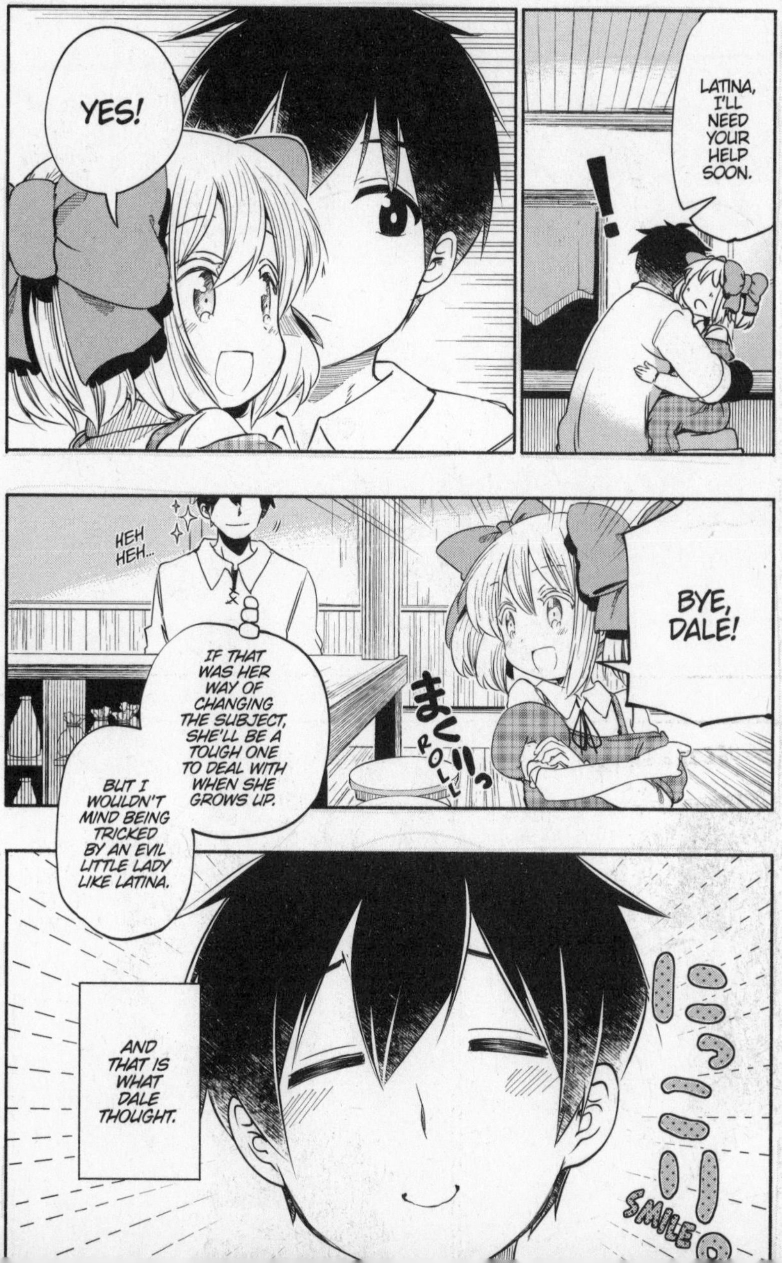
LATINA, I'LL NEED YOUR HELP SOON.
!
YES!
BYE, DALE!
まくりっ
ROLL
HEH HEH...
IF THAT WAS HER WAY OF CHANGING THE SUBJECT, SHE'LL BE A TOUGH ONE TO DEAL WITH WHEN SHE GROWS UP.
BUT I WOULDN'T MIND BEING TRICKED BY AN EVIL LITTLE LADY LIKE LATINA.
AND THAT IS WHAT DALE THOUGHT.
SMILE

If It's For My Daughter I'd Even Defeat a Demon Lord

If It's For My Daughter, I'd Even Defeat a Demon Lord

SHORT STORY

CHIROLU

Little Girl Helps New Adventurers a Bit

The city of Kreutz, in the Kingdom of Laband, is so prosperous that it is often called the second capital city. This city, which lies in a vital area between the port and the royal capital, is a gathering place for rowdy adventurers who fight the magical beasts that live in the southern region.

Kreutz's financial growth was greatly boosted by the influx of foreign merchants flocking to the city. It used these funds to post bounties, protecting themselves from the threat of magical beasts. Even now, travelers continue to be the framework of this city. This fact merged with the views of Laband Kingdom's primary deity of discipline, the Red Deity, to create a new culture unique to the city.

A city like Kreutz never failed to attract people with get-rich-quick schemes or hopes to turn their lives around.

"Whoa...!"

"Incredible..."

The two young men looking up in amazement at the grand walls that protected the city were just such people.

"It's even bigger than the people back in the village said it would be..."

"There's a line over there. Just like we heard. Let's go!"

The two men were sons of farmers from a nearby region. For the past few decades, the reign of the King had been stable in Laband, especially the area around the royal capital. The watchful eyes of the kingdom ensured that the nearby domains didn't put the citizens under a heavy tax burden. However, the number of sons who could inherit land from their parents was limited. Families had many children in order to gain more manpower for the fields, but second and third sons had difficulty finding marriage prospects.

In an effort to escape that reality, the two young men had left their homes and traveled to Kreutz to become adventurers.

Kreutz, just like its name, was a city in the form of a misshapen cross.

The residence of the feudal lord was in its center and different sections of the city spread from there to the east, west, south, and north. To enter Kreutz, a traveler had to enter through one of the gates stationed in each direction. The two young men were currently at the eastern gate, the gate that was closest to their hometown.

They were lined up with various peddlers and people with loaded carts. It was easy to tell that most of them were merchants. It seemed like the guards were checking the identities of everyone who wanted passage. However, the guards let many people through without even a glance at the paperwork, perhaps because they recognized those seeking entry.

"Hey."

The guard called out to the two men as soon as they

reached the front of the line, making both of them jump. Each hastily pulled out coins for passage—as they had been instructed to do by a merchant passing through their village—and presented them to the guard.

The guard looked them over quickly and gave a big sigh. A worn-out long sword in need of maintenance and a large staff in only a slightly-less-sorry state were better than nothing at all. He knew immediately from their clothes that they were from farming families. They wore the basic equipment of any new adventurer.

"If you plan on finding work in this city, look for a shop with a green flag in the south quadrant. Don't accept sweet-sounding deals unless you want to be conned."

The guard gave them a word of advice because he had seen what happened to many people who "wanted to be an adventurer" since taking this job. Only a small handful of people attained success. He didn't want to let these young men step onto the wrong path.

After watching them head toward the south as he had directed, he mumbled to himself, "That little girl is at that shop... They'll treat you right." Then, he turned back to face the line of people.

The stalls that lined the streets sold things the two men had never seen before, and it was more crowded than the annual festival that was held in their village. As they walked through the eastern quadrant, known as the business district, and entered the southern quadrant, they felt a sudden change of atmosphere.

The young men came to a stop, startled by the people walking around armed with swords and wearing weathered armor. However, none of the normal citizens batted an eye at the sight. Little did the young men know, but the southern quadrant was considered the most significant area of Kreutz. It was both the housing district for commoners and an area that provided various amenities for travelers.

There were high-class inns to accommodate travelers of rank, with rooms that had special magical locks, as well as cheap lodgings where one could share a room with a complete stranger. There were restaurants and bars, too--both ones a girl could go to without any worry, and others where powdered females drew men in. This quadrant was filled with many mysterious, new things, even more than the eastern quadrant.

The young men's curiosity shifted into anxiety, and they huddled together as they looked for the shop in question.

"Green flag..."

They found themselves in front of a bar facing the main road.

Hanging from the entrance was a sign that had a strangely dressed mackerel tabby made of wrought iron on it, and a green flag embroidered with a winged horse.

"<Dancing Mackerel Tabby>...?"

As they spoke, the two of them peeked into the shop and then quickly took a few steps back in fear.

"Wh-wh-wha..."

"No way... We have to go into a place like this...?"

The bar was full of the faces of men who obviously specialized in violent acts. Even though it was the middle of the day, many were drinking and playing cards. Even meeting their eyes when the two had quickly glanced in had been enough to send a chill down their spines. It felt like they might be scowled to death.

Suddenly, the idea of finding work in a field frequented by

people with faces like those inside—people often considered to be rogues—sounded a lot less appealing. Even so, they couldn't just stand in front of the entrance forever. They began to feel like the passersby were mocking their hesitation. And so, as subtly as they could, the two men quietly entered.

Everyone's eyes immediately focused on them, making their hearts stop.

"Uh, wh-wh...?"

"U-um..."

They looked like beginners, and the people of the "Mackerel Tabby" did not show them kind expressions. If they couldn't withstand a harsh glare, they certainly weren't ready to handle being adventurers.

"Hah?"

"Heek!"

"We're very sorry!"

Boys who trembled at mere looks were dismissed out of hand. Kids such as the ones who'd just walk in needed to be discouraged before they got ideas—it would be best if they just went back home. With a simple look, the regulars made their intentions clear and their stares grew colder.

Suddenly, the young men heard an innocent, young voice.

"Welcome."

The tense atmosphere of the room changed in an instant.

"You are a new customer. Welcome."

It took the two young men a moment to find the source of the voice. They lowered their gaze down toward the floor and realized that a little girl was looking up at them. Her platinum hair was tied up in pigtails with a ribbon on each side, her bright gray eyes shone, and she had the sweetest face they had ever seen. The moment their eyes met hers, she smiled and their shoulders relaxed.

"Are you adventurer customers? Did you come to ask for work?" She tilted her head to one side, speaking with unsteady words.

"Little lady, you can tell that it's their first time?" asked an elderly man. He bore such a startling face that the two men gasped. The young girl turned and toddled over to the table where he was sitting.

"Latina remembers every customer she meets," she said.

"Even if it's just once?"

"Yeah," the little girl said. "Even once, Latina would probably know. But Latina doesn't know the customers that are here when she isn't here."

"Well, amazing as you are, little lady, I suppose even you couldn't know that."

The men burst into laughter, lightening the mood. It was such a change for the two young men; they felt like it had actually become a little easier to breathe.

The little girl returned to the two travelers and smiled sweetly. "Latina can explain the Mackerel Tabby to you."

She had watched the landlady of the shop, Rita, explain the process to newcomers many times and had remembered everything. While the two young men didn't know that, they instinctively knew that this little girl was their ally in this place. They nodded earnestly. The little girl smiled happily and puffed her chest with pride.

Her skirt fluttered as she made a half turn and made her way to the bulletin board near the entrance of the shop. She pointed at it with a small finger. "Um, the jobs from the people in the city are posted here."

"From the people of the city...?"

"When the people of the city have a problem, they come to us to ask for help."

The two men looked at the bulletin board and saw that there were all sorts of requests, from finding a lost item to being a bodyguard, from here to the next town over. Most of the jobs for adventurers were duller than expected. There were many requests for package carriers.

"The temple of the Green Deity posts their notices here, too."

Among the flyers on the bulletin board were ones with the seal of the Green Deity. Latina pointed them out and stopped. After some thought, her face brightened, and she continued her explanation.

"The temple puts up wanted posters and warns us about dangerous things. They put a stamp on it."

The Seven-Colored Gods were the deities, the seven pillars of the world, and each held the name of a color. The Temple of the Green Deity, the god of information and safe travel, collected and stored all sorts of information. Like the Dancing Mackerel Tabby, shops that hung a flag with the seal of the Green Deity were officially sanctioned information posts.

"That's amazing, little lady. You remembered all that?"

It seemed the old men in the bar had listened to her determined explanation more earnestly than the two newcomers.

She smiled happily at the compliment. "Did Latina do a good job?"

A group at one table clapped heartily at her performance. "Yeah. Good job. Good job!" They were like old men doting on their granddaughter. Indeed, even if they had grandchildren of their own, it would be hard to imagine that they could possibly be cuter than this little girl.

"Mr. Jil."

"Hm? What is it, little lady?"

"Latina doesn't know everything. So, will you teach them for her? Please?"

"Ah...ahh..."

The old man the little girl called "Mr. Jil" scratched his head a bit and made a troubled face. The adventurer Jilvester Delius was not only well known in this country, but in many of the neighboring ones, as well. Though he was practically in retirement, he was still respected, and other adventurers often asked him for advice.

The little girl had no idea what he had done in the past. However, she knew that he was someone she could ask for help when she "wasn't sure what to do." The old man, for his part, wanted to live up to the expectations of their little poster child.

Indeed, all the older men there wanted to show their good side in front of this little girl. If they did that, the little girl would always look up to them with innocent admiration and say "wow" with complete honesty. It was a reward more valuable than anything else.

"Guess it can't be helped..."

Jilvester turned to glare at the young men, a severe expression on his face. The two stood up straight.

"If you really want to become adventurers...I'll introduce you to someone who can take care of you. You guys sure you're serious about this?"

"Yes!"

"Please!"

As Latina watched them respond instinctively, she smiled with a happy heart as her platinum hair swayed gently.

* * *

"Hey, Kenneth."

Dale removed his trademark coat made of magical beast hide and hung it on a chair as he spoke to Kenneth, the landlord of the Dancing Mackerel Tabby—and a man who was like a big brother to him.

"What is it?"

"Hasn't the number of young adventurers in here increased lately?"

Dale himself wasn't much older than the "youngsters" and "beginners," but he had accomplished a great deal since leaving his homeland at the age of fifteen. His experience had far surpassed these "youngsters" of whom he spoke.

"It's true, they have increased."

Some people entered the shop to confirm a client's information on the bulletin board and then left. Others, after collecting their small earnings, bought the cheapest menu item in the bar, which was known for its affordable prices, in celebration. Among these people, Kenneth had begun to see the younger generation pop up here and there.

The shop had many regulars who were veteran adventurers. Because of that, the bar itself gave off a unique atmosphere that made it difficult for beginners to stay for long. That was how it had "always been" in this place.

"Well, beginners should use legitimate places like us because of the safety we provide. It isn't a bad change."

"I suppose you're right about that."

Many pubs without the flag of Akudaru, the Green Deity, tried to give adventurers work. However, those jobs were far more likely to be of an illegitimate nature. Naïve adventurers from the country quickly found themselves caught up with criminals and veered from the honest path.

Since they knew that all too well, Dale and Kenneth didn't feel like the change was a bad one.

"Dale!"

As soon as he heard her voice, Dale's face went pathetically slack. He turned quickly and gave the little girl a hug with open arms.

"Welcome home, Latina! Did you go play with your friends?"

"Yep! Also, welcome home from work!"

"Yeah. I'm home, too!"

Dale paid no heed to his surroundings as he squeezed her with an expression of pure happiness, but Kenneth didn't miss it. A young adventurer bowed his head slightly toward her as the others watched her with warm expressions.

I bet she's up to something we aren't aware of, Kenneth thought to himself, knowing that—whatever she was doing—it was surely a good thing. He had no doubt that her place as their poster child would only continue to grow.

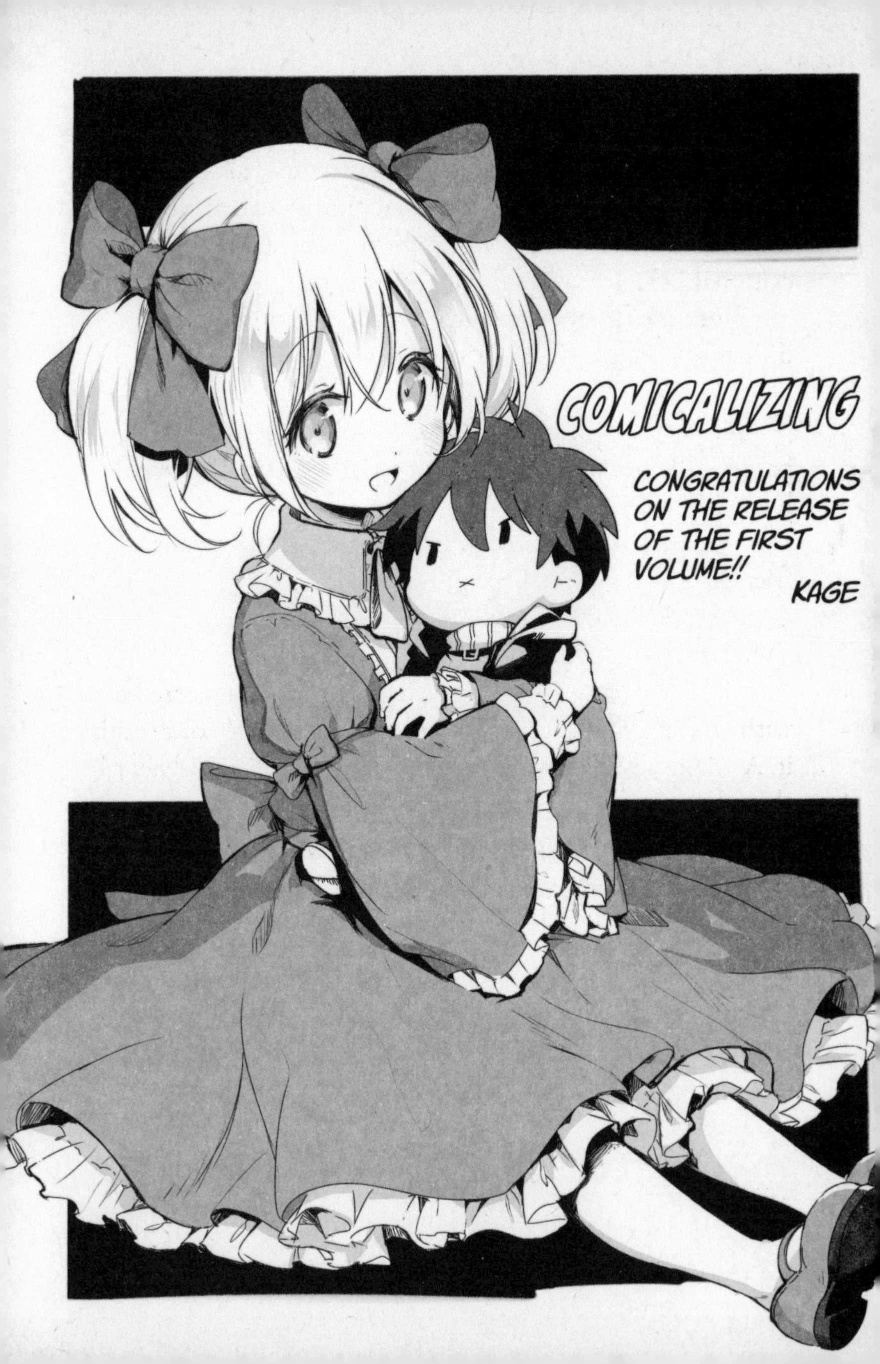
COMICALIZING
CONGRATULATIONS ON THE RELEASE OF THE FIRST VOLUME!!
KAGE

Afterword

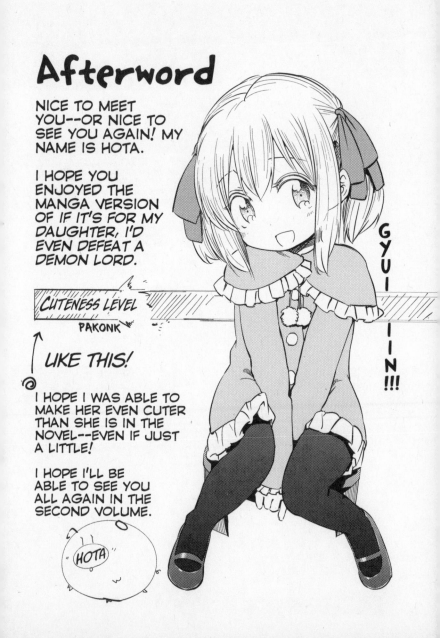

NICE TO MEET YOU--OR NICE TO SEE YOU AGAIN! MY NAME IS HOTA.

I HOPE YOU ENJOYED THE MANGA VERSION OF IF IT'S FOR MY DAUGHTER, I'D EVEN DEFEAT A DEMON LORD.

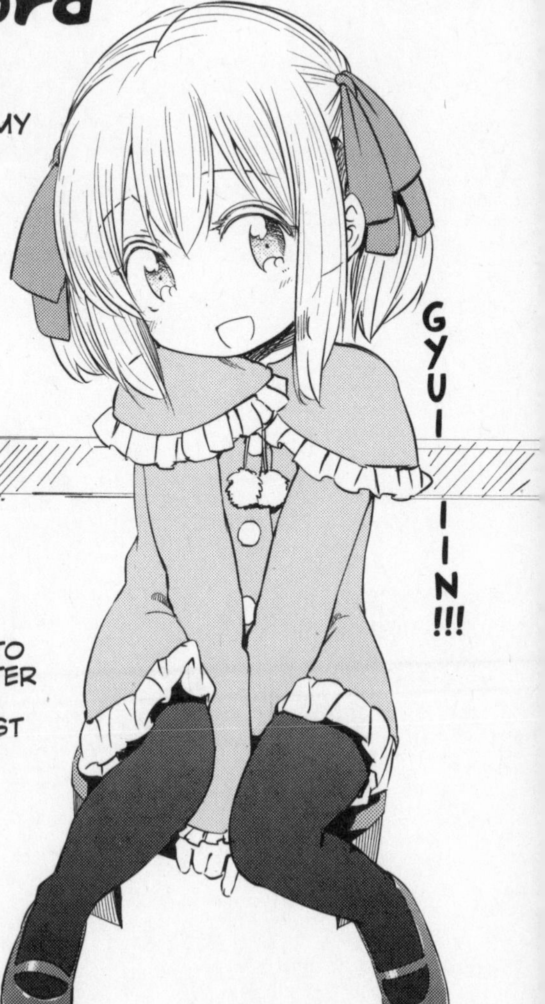
GYUIIIIN!!!
CUTENESS LEVEL
PAKONK

LIKE THIS!

I HOPE I WAS ABLE TO MAKE HER EVEN CUTER THAN SHE IS IN THE NOVEL--EVEN IF JUST A LITTLE!

I HOPE I'LL BE ABLE TO SEE YOU ALL AGAIN IN THE SECOND VOLUME.

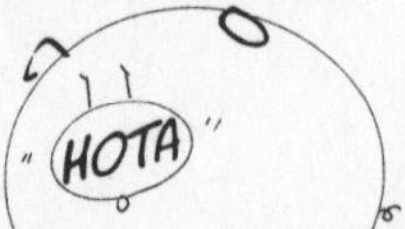
HOTA

IF It's
For My
Daughter
I'd Even Defeat
a Demon
Lord

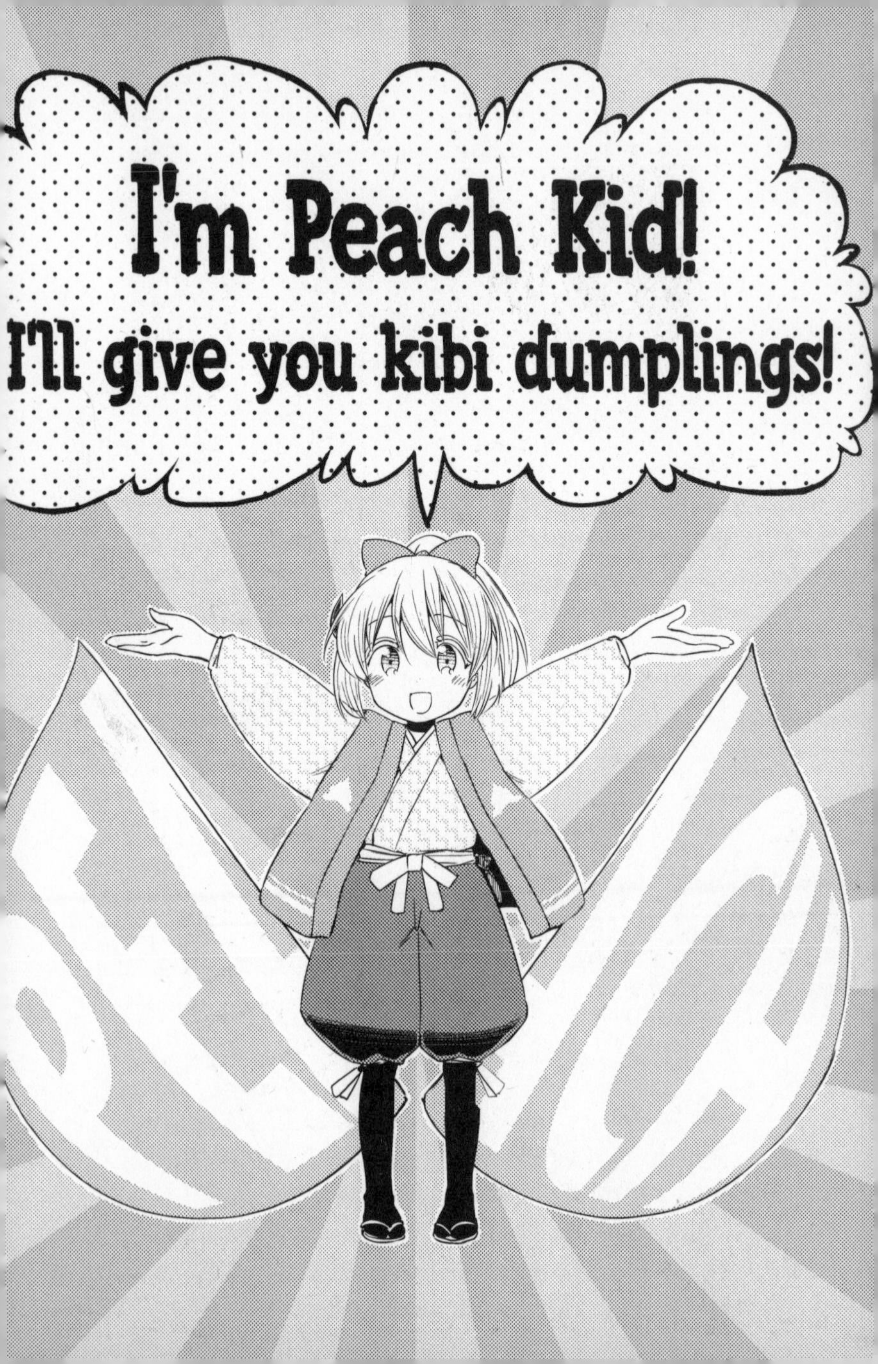
I'm Peach Kid! I'll give you kibi dumplings!

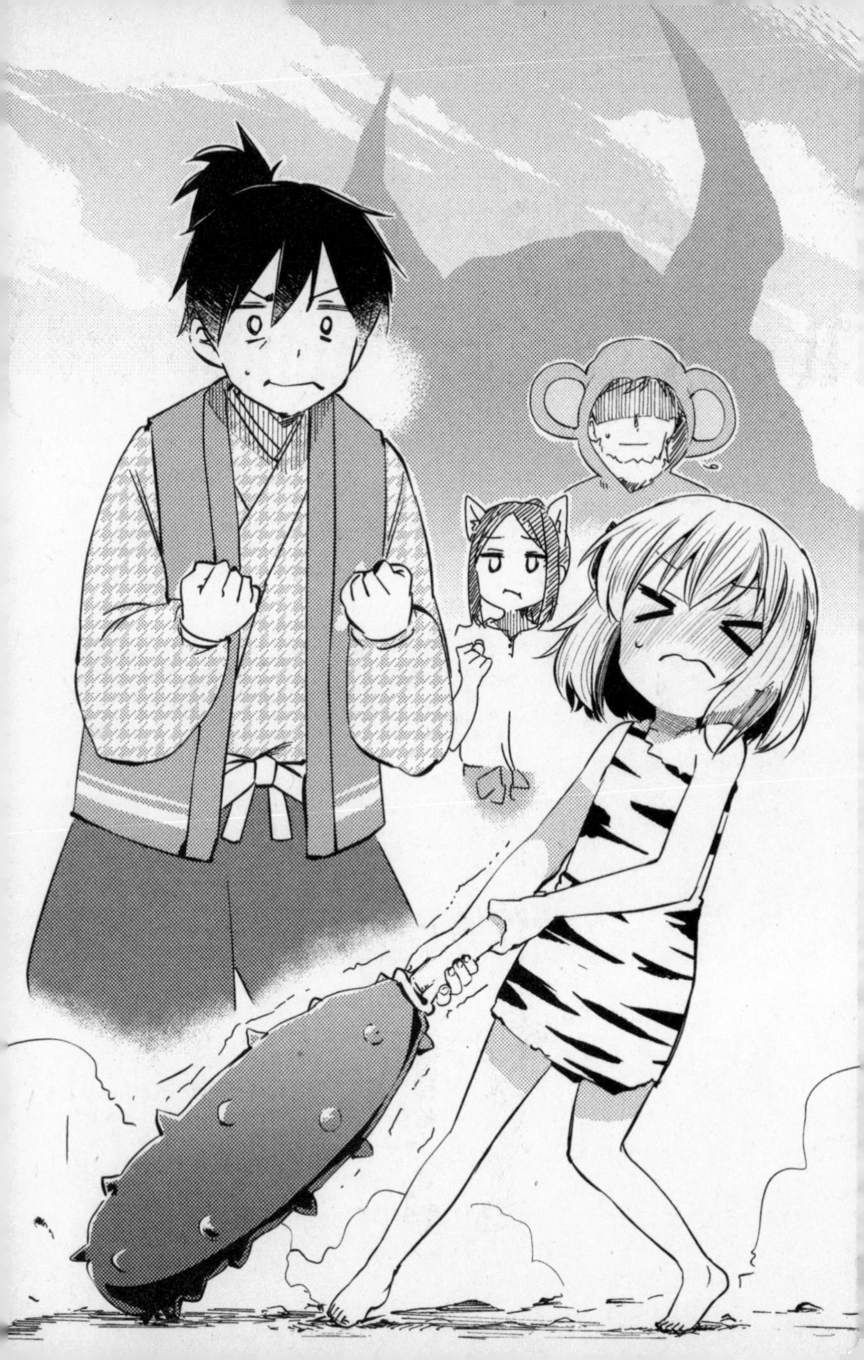

SEVEN SEAS ENTERTAINMENT PRESENTS

IF It's For My Daughter I'd Even Defeat a Demon Lord

vol.1

story by **CHIROLU**   art by **HOTA**   character design by **KEI·TRUFFLE**

TRANSLATION
Angela Liu

ADAPTATION
Julia Kinsman

LETTERING
Ochie Caraan

COVER DESIGN
KC Fabellon

PROOFREADER
Kurestin Armada
Janet Houck

EDITOR
Jenn Grunigen

PRODUCTION ASSISTANT
CK Russell

PRODUCTION MANAGER
Lissa Pattillo

EDITOR-IN-CHIEF
Adam Arnold

PUBLISHER
Jason DeAngelis

UCHINOKO NO TAMENARABA, ORE HA MOSHIKASHITARA MAOU MO
TAOSERU KAMOSHIRENAI VOL. 1
©Hota. 2017
©CHIROLU 2017
First published in Japan in 2017 by KADOKAWA CORPORATION, Tokyo.
English translation rights arranged with KADOKAWA CORPORATION, Tokyo.

Seven Seas books may be purchased in bulk for promotional, educational, or
business use. Please contact your local bookseller or the Macmillan Corporate
and Premium Sales Department at 1-800-221-7945, extension 5442, or by
e-mail at MacmillanSpecialMarkets@macmillan.com.

Seven Seas and the Seven Seas logo are trademarks of
Seven Seas Entertainment, LLC. All rights reserved.

ISBN: 978-1-626927-96-4

Printed in Canada

First Printing: May 2018

10 9 8 7 6 5 4 3 2 1

FOLLOW US ONLINE: *www.sevenseasentertainment.com*

READING DIRECTIONS

This book reads from *right to left*, Japanese style.
If this is your first time reading manga, you start
reading from the top right panel on each page and
take it from there. If you get lost, just follow the
numbered diagram here. It may seem backwards at
first, but you'll get the hang of it! Have fun!!

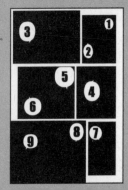

"D" is for Demon Girl

While on a job, Dale—a young but accomplished adventurer—comes across a little demon girl all alone in the forest. Dale can't bear to leave her there to die, so instead, he takes her home! Demon or not, Latina is beyond adorable, and it is not long before he finds himself head over heels with being her guardian. Can Dale handle the trials and tribulations of childcare and being an adventurer?

TEEN

$12.99 USA
($15.99 CAN)

ISBN 978-1-626927-96-4

51299>

9 781626 927964

Seven Seas Entertainment, LLC.
www.sevenseasentertainment.com
Distributed by Macmillan